The Ultimate FE Lecturer's Handbook

Other Titles in the Essential FE Toolkit Series

Books for Lecturers

Teaching the FE Curriculum – Mark Weyers

e-Learning in FE – John Whalley, Theresa Welch and Lee Williamson

FE Lecturer's Survival Guide – Angela Steward

FE Lecturer's Guide to Diversity and Inclusion – Anne-Marie Wright, Sue Colquhoun, Sina Abdi-Jama, Jane Speare and Tracey Partridge

How to Manage Stress in FE – Elizabeth Hartney

Guide to Teaching 14–19 – James Ogunleye

A to Z of Teaching in FE – Angela Steward

Getting the Buggers Motivated in FE – Sue Wallace

Books for Managers

Everything you need to know about FE policy – Yvonne Hillier

Middle Management in FE – Ann Briggs

Managing Higher Education in Colleges – Gareth Parry, Anne Thompson and Penny Blackie

Survival Guide for College Managers and Leaders – David Collins

Guide to Leadership and Governance in FE – Adrian Perry

Guide to Financial Management in FE – Julian Gravatt

Guide to Race Equality in FE – Beulah Ainley

Ultimate FE Leadership and Management Handbook – Jill Jameson and Ian McNay

A to Z for Every Manager in FE – Susan Wallace and Jonathan Gravells

Guide to VET – Christopher Winch and Terry Hyland

The Ultimate FE Lecturer's Handbook

Ros Clow and Trevor Dawn

continuum

Continuum International Publishing Group

The Tower Building   80 Maiden Lane, Suite 704
11 York Road   New York
London SE1 7NX   NY 10038

British Library Cataloguing-in-Publication Data
A catalogue record for this book is available from the British Library.

ISBN: 0 8264 9025 5 (paperback)

Library of Congress Cataloging-in-Publication Data
A catalog record for this book is available from the Library of Congress.

Typeset by YHT Ltd, London
Printed and bound in Great Britain by Ashford Colour Press, Gosport, Hampshire

Contents

Series Foreword   vi
Series Intoduction   xi
Acknowledgements   xiii
Lists of Figures and Tables   xv
Introduction   1

Part One: Teaching and learning   5
1   Gaining learner interest and sustaining it   7
2   Using small groups in the classroom   31
3   The academic teacher   50
4   Using role-play   70

Part Two: Working with learners   89
5   Learner characteristics   91
6   Tutorials: working with the individual learner   107
7   Managing behaviour   142
8   Teaching gifted and talented learners on vocational courses   161

Part Three: Working as teachers   179
9   Work smarter not harder   181
10   Team teaching   190

Part Four: Putting it into practice   203
11   Teaching strategies   205

Conclusion   236
Bibliography   239
Index   249

Series Foreword

THE ESSENTIAL FE TOOLKIT SERIES

Jill Jameson
Series Editor

In the autumn of 1974, a young woman newly arrived from Africa landed in Devon to embark on a new life in England. Having travelled halfway round the world, she still longed for sunny Zimbabwe. Not sure what career to follow, she took a part-time job teaching EFL to Finnish students. Enjoying this, she studied thereafter for a PGCE at the University of Nottingham in Ted Wragg's Education Department. After teaching in secondary schools, she returned to university in Cambridge, and, having graduated, took a job in ILEA in 1984 in adult education. She loved it: there was something about adult education that woke her up, made her feel fully alive, newly aware of all the lifelong learning journeys being followed by so many students and staff around her. The adult community centre she worked in was a joyful place for diverse multi-ethnic communities. Everyone was cared for, including 90 year olds in wheelchairs, toddlers in the crèche, ESOL refugees, city accountants in business suits and university level graphic design students. In her eyes, the centre was an educational ideal, a remarkable place in which, gradually, everyone was helped to learn to be who they wanted to be. This was the Chequer Centre, Finsbury, EC1, the 'red house', as her daughter saw it, toddling in from the crèche. And so began the story of a long interest in further education that was to last for many years . . . why, if they did such good work for so many, were FE centres so under-funded and unrecognized, so under-appreciated?

It is with delight that, 32 years after the above story began, I write the Foreword to *The Essential FE Toolkit*, Continuum's new series of 24 books on further education (FE) for teachers and college leaders. The idea behind the *Toolkit* is to provide a comprehensive guide to FE in a series of compact, readable books. The suite of 24 individual books are gathered together to provide the practitioner with an overall FE toolkit in specialist, fact-filled volumes designed to be easily accessible, written by experts with significant knowledge and experience in their individual fields. All of the authors have in-depth understanding of further education. But – '*Why is further education important? Why does it merit a whole series to be written about it?*' you may ask.

At the Association of Colleges Annual Conference in 2005, in a humorous speech to college principals, John Brennan said that, whereas in 1995 further education was a 'political backwater', by 2005 FE had become 'mainstream'. John recalled that, since 1995, there had been '36 separate government or government-sponsored reports or white papers specifically devoted to the post-16 sector'. In our recent regional research report (2006) for the Learning and Skills Development Agency, my co-author Yvonne Hillier and I noted that it was no longer 'raining policy' in FE, as we had described earlier (Hillier and Jameson 2003): there is now a torrent of new initiatives. We thought, in 2003, that an umbrella would suffice to protect you. We'd now recommend buying a boat to navigate these choppy waters, as it looks as if John Brennan's 'mainstream' FE, combined with a tidal wave of government policies, will soon lead to a flood of new interest in the sector, rather than end anytime soon.

There are good reasons for all this government attention on further education. In 2004/5, student numbers in LSC council-funded further education increased to 4.2m, total college income was around £6.1 billion, and the average college had an annual turnover of £15m. Further education has rapidly increased in national significance regarding the need for ever greater achievements in UK education and skills training for millions of learners, providing qualifications and workforce training to feed a UK national economy hungrily in competition with other OECD nations. The 120 recommendations of the Foster Review (2005) therefore in the main encourage colleges to focus their work on vocational skills, social inclusion and achieving academic progress. This series is here to consider all three of these areas and more.

The series is written for teaching practitioners, leaders and managers in the 572 FE/LSC-funded institutions in the UK, including FE colleges, adult education and sixth-form institutions, prison education departments, training and workforce development units, local education authorities and community agencies. The series is also written for PGCE/Cert Ed/City & Guilds Initial and continuing professional development (CPD) teacher trainees in universities in the UK, USA, Canada, Australia, New Zealand and beyond. It will also be of interest to staff in the 600 Jobcentre Plus providers in the UK and to many private training organizations. All may find this series of use and interest in learning about FE educational practice in the 24 different areas of these specialist books from experts in the field.

Our use of this somewhat fuzzy term 'practitioners' includes staff in the FE/LSC-funded sector who engage in professional practice in governance, leadership, management, teaching, training, financial and administration services, student support services, ICT and MIS technical support, librarianship, learning resources, marketing, research and development, nursery and crèche services, community and business support, transport and estates management. It is also intended to include staff in a host of other FE services including work-related training, catering, outreach and specialist health, diagnostic additional learning support, pastoral and religious support for students. Updating staff in professional practice is critically important at a time of such continuing radical policy-driven change, and we are pleased to contribute to this nationally and internationally.

We are also privileged to have an exceptional range of authors writing for the series. Many of our series authors are renowned for their work in further education, having worked in the sector for thirty years or more. Some have received OBE or CBE honours, professorships, fellowships and awards for contributions they have made to further education. All have demonstrated a commitment to FE that makes their books come alive with a kind of wise guidance for the reader. Sometimes this is tinged with world-weariness, sometimes with sympathy, humour or excitement. Sometimes the books are just plain clever or a fascinating read, to guide practitioners of the future who will read these works. Together, the books make up a considerable portfolio of assets for you to take with you through your journeys in further education. We hope the experience of reading the books will be interesting, instructive and pleasurable and that experience gained from them will last, renewed, for many seasons.

It has been wonderful to work with all of the authors and with Continuum's UK Education Publisher, Alexandra Webster, on this series. The exhilarating opportunity of developing such a comprehensive toolkit of books probably comes once in a lifetime, if at all. I am privileged to have had this rare opportunity, and I thank the publishers, authors and other contributors to the series for making these books come to life with their fantastic contributions to FE.

Dr Jill Jameson
Series Editor

Series Editor's introduction

Ros Clow and Trevor Dawn begin this new book, *The Ultimate FE Lecturer's Handbook*, with a somewhat humorous recollection from 1982, when Ros first started teaching in further education (FE). At that stage, Ros recalls, she 'did not know what FE was'. However, 24 years later, as a senior lecturer and course leader for the PGCE in Post-Compulsory Education at Oxford Brookes University, the former Chair of the Post-16 Committee of UCET (the Universities Council for the Education of Teachers), Ros is now an acknowledged expert in the field. She is joined in authorship by Trevor Dawn, recently awarded an Honorary Fellowship by Oxford Brookes (September, 2006) for his stalwart' work in the university's programmes for the training of teachers in the FE sector. Trevor is also an advanced expert with many years' understanding of training, teaching and learning in FE, the author of several important publications, notably including *Teaching Young Adults* (2000), co-authored with Professor Joe Harkin and Gill Turner, also of Oxford Brookes University.

In the Introduction, Ros and Trevor describe briefly their early days of teaching in the 1960s, advising us that, between them, the authors of this book have 55 years of teacher training experience in post-compulsory education. This is a fitting introduction to a book that indeed has an ultimate' quality about it, not only in the title, but also because the work provides a testimony to a long legacy of experience and knowledge from many decades of dedicated effort in and for further education and its diverse communities of teachers and learners. Writing from the perspective of advanced professional guides with an overview of the field, the authors provide a handbook for teachers that is rich with detail, interest, humour and in-depth experience of FE. The book gives us a wide-ranging overview of a series of crucial issues for lecturers, forming an appropriate concluding volume to the lecturers' series in *The Essential FE Toolkit*.

The book is structured into four sections, beginning with Section 1 on Teaching and Learning. In Chapter 1: Gaining learner interest and sustaining it, the authors outline the Yerkes Dodson curve principle of arousal and performance to advise teachers on effective lesson planning, based on observation, practice and professional reflection from forty years' experience about the most effective ways in which to ensure your learners are, and continue to be, interested in their lessons, including information on deep and surface learning and current research on learning styles. This chapter, including the story about Amos, sparks the readers interest and prepares us for Chapters 2–10 to come, in which the authors guide us through techniques for group work, using role play, working with learners as tutors, managing gifted and talented learners and team teaching. In Chapter 11, Ros and Trevor outline a range of valuable teaching strategies which provide an authoritative guide to the management of the FE classroom.

The book provides an exceptionally useful overview of practical, evidence-informed teaching techniques in the learning and skills sector at a time when new national Qualified Teacher Learning and Skills (QTLS) Standards are being introduced across the UK. The authors were amongst those providing expert advice to government ministers on the new standards for the QTLS. The *Ultimate FE Lecturers' Handbook* provides teachers in FE with admirably compact and helpful guidance to inspire excellent teaching in the classroom. This handbook is relevant to all those teaching in the learning and skills sector, whether readers are still training to achieve the new QTLS or they have already achieved this and/or an equivalent qualification and want to update and implement new techniques to inform day-to-day teaching practice in FE. This book is essential reading for all FE lecturers.

Dr Jill Jameson
Director of Research
School of Education and Training
University of Greenwich
j.jameson@gre.ac.uk

Acknowledgements

We thank a range of others who helped us to write this book. Firstly ex-students who willingly allowed us to copy their work and use it in whatever way we wanted: Alison Andrews, Anne-Marie Brooke-Wavell, Alan Brown, Andrew Byers, Cheryl Burrows, Ed Cahill, Sheila Gardiner, Donna Gilsenan, Bev Hale, Rebecca Hearn, Caroline Jeffrey, Helen Jones, Helen May, John Mostyn, Claire O'Neil, Nicola Penn-Allison, Lorraine Price, Helen Rainsley and Bob Spence.

Also we are very lucky to have great colleagues, past and present, who offered advice, ideas and support throughout the gestation of this work: Steve Kee, Phil Jones, Chris Higgins, Marian McLachlan, Michelle Paule, Sue Rees, Chris Rust, Mary Samuels and Jayne Stuart. Last but not least Bryony Clow, who tries to keep us up to date in the mobile phone world!

Acknowledgements

Lists of Figures and Tables

Figure	Title	Page
1	The Yerkes–Dodson curve 1908	13
2	The value of the Yerkes–Dodson curve in lesson planning	15
3	The traditional triangle	18
4	The traditional triangle and the Kolb cycle	19
5	The learning pyramid, NTL, Bethel, ME, 1964	24
6	Role-play flow chart	75
7	Simplified ego state model (Joines and Stewart 1987)	147
8	Functional analysis of ego states (Joines and Stewart 1987)	148
9	The KAMIS model of vocational talent	167
10	Totem pole for AVCE health and social care	170
11	Totem pole for NVQ Level 3 early years childcare and education	171
12	Starfish diagram	175

Table	Title	Page
1	The classic Taba model	26
2	Bloom's taxonomy – The cognitive domain	58
3	Some common adolescent stressors	97
4	Symptoms of dependency (Priory Group 2005)	100
5	Tutorial transcription – listening skills	116

6	Tutorial transcription – catalytic and supportive interventions	120
7	Tutorial extract – tutor concerns taking over	123
8	Tutorial extract – gruesome-twosome	125
9	The 4 Cs	133
10	What teachers look for in spotting vocational talent	166
11	Make mine a G&T	173
12	Exercise based on 'Sailing to Byzantium'	208
13	The nature of the AA's business	210
14	Customer requests to the AA	211
15	Match the appropriate pairs	215
16	Advertising exercise	217
17	Graded levels of protest	220
18	Cards for 'the real concerns of religion'	222
19	Cards for the 'fundamentals of business'	223
20	Things which can affect and change our perception of reality	229
21	Issues in modern art	230

Introduction

Who we are

In 1982, Ros was asked if she would do some teaching in FE.
She did not know what FE was (as invisible then as it is now)
despite having done her A levels at Norwich City College
rather than stay on at school. So she made a phone call during
the National Childbirth Trust (NCT) bring and buy sale and
was asked to turn up on Monday to teach two groups for a total
of six hours. No application form, no interview and when she
asked 'What is social and life skills?' she was told 'Oh you'll find
it easy, just filling in cheques and things.'

It was anything but easy. The two groups turned out to be
Mode B Youth Training Scheme trainees. This meant that no
employer would risk employing them, so the college took them
on full-time and arranged work placements. During that first
day they were given a range of diagnostic tests, a tour around
the college and were introduced to their new teachers. Sud-
denly, here was a job that used all the skills and experience
acquired in the previous 20 years: youth club activities, psychology of child development, interviewing skills, industrial
relations, business writing, pregnancy education, teaching and
counselling skills learned through the NCT, assertiveness
training and even tennis!

Nine hours a week on that course soon expanded to include
general and communication studies with construction and
motor vehicle students. Fun was had by all: role-plays of the
miners' strike, saying 'No' to drugs at a disco, choosing a flat to
share, planning menus for the week, sex education, pregnancy
and birth education (one student at this point realized she was
pregnant!), healthy eating, a board game to emphasize the

expectations of the workplace, eating out in the training restaurant, team games (indoor hockey, badminton) and educational visits to Windsor Castle and the local sewerage works. Then one day the manager who had employed her said he knew she was doing well (though no one had ever observed her) but would she please keep to the scheme of work. As she had never heard of a scheme of work, nor had anyone at the college mentioned that there was one, it was suggested that she might like to do teacher training, the Cert. Ed.

Trevor had taught primarily history and English in a secondary school for four years from 1964 (though he had to teach maths, French, games and religious education when required!) before he went into what was then termed further education. He had enjoyed his time in the school but it did not offer GCE O levels and A levels and he needed experience of teaching examination subjects if he was to progress in his career. The Catch 22 syndrome meant that schools that offered GCE wanted experience and how do you get experience if it is not available at your current school? The college of further education had no such inhibitions as most of its staff were untrained anyway and he joined with the expectation that he would gain the experience of teaching examination classes and then apply for school jobs in two or three years' time.

At the interview, he had blithely affirmed that he would be happy to teach English and liberal studies to craft and technician level plumbers, engineers and electricians, and to secretaries; and work with newly arrived youngsters from the Commonwealth; and teach police cadets; and Nottingham Forest youth team players; and evening classes; and OND and HND construction students. When he got the job, he wished he hadn't been so glib. He had to adjust quickly to learners who let him know in no uncertain terms what they thought of the lessons. He also had to convince their employers and their vocational teachers of the value of the lessons. It was not easy but it was absorbing. There was freedom for the team to determine what should be taught. The examination classes were full of students from secondary modern schools who had been denied the opportunity of sitting GCE classes, and adults seeking to gain qualifications for entry to professional courses. They were mostly keen and friendly, with diverse abilities and personalities and a delight to teach. He was hooked and has stayed involved in the post-compulsory sector ever since.

The authors' first experiences of teaching were in the 1960s, 1970s and 1980s, long before teacher training for the post-compulsory sector was widespread. Since then, they have taught in a variety of institutions and phases: schools; industry; health education; adult and community education; higher education; voluntary sector and, most importantly, further education. They met in 1992 when Ros joined the Certificate in Education (further education) team lead by Trevor. Between them, they have clocked up 55 years of teacher training for a range of post-compulsory teaching qualifications. They were delighted to be asked to contribute to this series.

Ros and Trevor see this book as a support for those new to teaching in the post-compulsory sector and also those who, having been in the business for a few years, need to revitalize their professional role.

How to use this book

We would be delighted if you did, but we do not expect you to read the whole book. Each chapter stands on its own and addresses key areas of knowledge and skills, which over the years our students have identified as important in their practice.

Each chapter ends with suggested further reading for those who wish to make a more in-depth study of this area. We anticipate that any chapter could be the basis of an independent study based in professional practice, which would be acceptable as continuing professional development for teachers qualified to QTLS or possibly as an option in the new professional quali-fication. For those who simply feel 'jaded or nonchalant' (van Ments 1999: 29) about their teaching we hope our ideas and principles will reinvigorate you and the experience of your students.

We are very different people and have very different teaching styles so we decided at the outset to write chapters individually, although we have offered suggestions to each other as the book developed. Additionally Ros felt her expertise inadequate in the areas of counselling skills for tutorials and the very new field of gifted and talented learners in vocational education. So two colleagues, Jenny Hankey and Annie Haight, were delighted to help out by contributing their particular knowledge and experience to Chapters 6 and 8.

The book continues with a section (Chapter 11) on teaching strategies where practical suggestions for dealing with typical classroom decisions are explored. We hope you will take advantage of them either directly or as a starting point for your own ideas. They are copyright free.

Ros Clow and Trevor Dawn
Oxford Brookes University

Part One
Teaching and learning

1 Gaining learner interest and sustaining it

Trevor Dawn

Introduction

When I am asked to give feedback to teachers on lessons that have not been as effective as the teacher had hoped, I tend to look at the relationship between the 'ingredients' or the phases of the lesson and the 'recipe' or the order in which the phases have been planned. I often find that there were good ingredients but a poor recipe.

In this chapter we will look at the 'ingredients' of a lesson: in particular, the importance of beginnings to topics or lessons, the balance of teacher-centred and student-centred strategies in any lesson and the ways in which a facilitative approach can overcome apathy, hostility and loss of confidence in learners to effect a better 'recipe' for success.

Preamble – beginnings

The beginning of any enterprise – the launch of a new ship, the start of a play, the opening of the Olympic Games, the start of a lesson – provides an opportunity to lay down a marker for what is to follow. A good start, setting up a mood of optimism and involvement, is often the precursor for a good experience. The beginning gives one an opportunity to send out signals: about style and period perhaps; whether we are to expect something conventional or novel or indeed revolutionary with all the emotional conflict this can generate; or points of reference which frame the context and engage the audience.

The start of a book is another example, especially the first chapter.

This 'first' chapter begins with an anecdote from the 1950s.

Many of the themes that are considered in the chapter have their antecedents in this anecdote.

'...and Amos dropped a plumb-line.'

A dull, grey weight, about three centimetres long and held by string, snaked slowly down from the top of the pulpit to just above the bottom. The youth stopped glancing furtively at the group of girls on his left, across the centre aisle and about five rows further down the chapel (he and his mates always sat on the back row of course) and turned his attention for the first time to the preacher. Had the preacher gone mad?

'Come here', the preacher said, addressing a girl of about ten. 'Come up here. Rub some chalk on the string ... a bit more ... that's lovely.'

'Hold the string tight against the side of the pulpit. Tight. OK.'

'Now you, love (*pointing to her friend*), come over here and pull the string out towards you and when it is taut, let go.'

The friend complied, after an initial reluctance.

'That's it. Lovely. Thank you.' After a small pause: 'You can sit down now.'

Both girls went back to their pew and as they did so the preacher pulled up the string and the weight to reveal a straight, chalked line running half the length of the pulpit. The youth looked at the line and waited for the explanation, for explanation there had to be for such an unusual start to a sermon. Sermons were something you endured, as a rule. They were the unavoidable price one paid on Sunday evenings for the free use of the table tennis table on Wednesday and Friday evenings and the chance to meet girls (the youth went to a single-sex school). But he had no expectations of the sermon itself – until he saw the string.

'A plumb-line is straight and true', continued the preacher. 'A builder can work to it knowing that every thing that follows will also be straight and true. God is our plumb-line.'

The sermon went on to elaborate on the motif of datum lines and plans and the surety of God's purpose being founded on order and design and the good building being in the hands of his followers. But the beginning had served its purpose. Indeed, the group of teenagers talked about it afterwards at the house of one of their company whose mother was generous enough, and slightly mad enough, to allow her daughter to invite twenty friends back to her house after chapel.

This was 1956 and the youth went on to be a history teacher. He too told stories in his lessons in a style that borrowed subconsciously from the circuit preachers of his adolescence.

Although this approach was successful some of the time, the young teacher soon concluded that it was unsustainable over the whole year. Other 'beginnings' would be needed. In comparison with the modern classroom, there seemed to be little else to fall back on, but the variety could be found with a little ingenuity. Every classroom had a chalkboard and he became quite proficient in drawing maps in colour of the three-field system or the outlines of a battle; there were some sets of books (the medieval church, castle, village, etc. and their equivalents in different historical periods); there were sets of historical facsimiles, photographs and copies, called *Jackdaw* folders. Sunday supplements had articles and pictures that could be adapted. The school had a Banda machine for handouts and a 16mm film projector, if one could find a relevant film. Educational television had arrived, but it was scheduled at a certain time for 20 minutes and there was no chance to preview the programme, so it was very much hit and miss as to how the programme, in black and white of course, would be received, assuming there were no technical hitches!

The young teacher therefore soon began to experiment with a range of 'beginnings' ... Sometimes, he would tell a story, like the preacher; sometimes he would bring in artefacts and ask the children questions about them; at other times groups would give presentations about their history project; or he would show a film; from time to time he would organize a visit to a castle or other historical site and use the visit as a springboard for a series of lessons.

The modern classroom is so different from the classroom of the 1960s and the resources for teaching so much more comprehensive and yet, in one fundamental aspect, i.e. the importance of gaining learner interest and sustaining it, the problem for the teacher is the same. In this regard, the beginning of the lesson is as critical today as it ever was. Young adults are no more prone to be automatically interested in lessons now than they were forty years ago. There will always be times when a teacher can 'sell' a lesson but she/he will need to have a much bigger toolkit than storytelling and anecdote to gain and sustain the interest of today's young adults.

The importance of beginnings

If the preachers of the Nonconformist circuits were aware of the need to grab the attention of their audience, they were in very good company.

It is generally accepted that the first minutes of any new experience will have a profound effect upon its enduring impact. We recognize the effect of instant appeal in many ways in society. In forming relationships, for example, we are influenced by what happens in the first ten seconds. This has always been known at an intuitive level, but academics have undertaken studies to prove the importance of first impressions. Nalini Ambady (17 February 2004 Internet) of Tufts University (Medford, MA) has said: 'humans can make a lasting judgement about someone after seeing their face for just a few seconds'. Alongside this 'primacy' effect (Park 1986) is personal construct theory, where we are predisposed to look for humour or gentleness in others and this can be the single most important factor in attraction (Hogg and Vaughan 2005). It is a topic that repays further reading.

The design of book covers helps attract buyers; packaging of goods is a crucial first stage in selling a product.

Shakespeare was a master in this regard. The expectations that he generated in his audience led to his developing a range of dramatic openings unrivalled in the theatre in his time or perhaps since. One of the devices he used, following on from the Greek tradition, was a single figure on stage, but

Shakespeare added subtle variations: a chorus to set the scene for great events to come (*Henry V*); a character commenting on a forthcoming event for the benefit of the audience (*Romeo and Juliet*); a continuity speech (*Henry IV*, Part 1); an immediate glimpse into the machinations of the mind of a main character (*Richard III*). Other devices he used were much more atmospheric, designed to appeal to contemporary interests and tastes: the supernatural (the witches in *Macbeth*); ghosts and spirits (*Hamlet*); exotic or foreign lands that very few in the audience would ever visit, and that includes Shakespeare himself (a shipwreck on an island in *The Tempest*). People came to the theatre to be transported to another world. In addition to the plot and the characterization, Shakespeare was also careful to vary the beginning of his plays so that his audiences were constantly intrigued as they waited for the start of the play as to what was to happen.

One can detect similar processes in music. Take the opening movements of Beethoven's piano sonatas. He would often use an allegro in some form or other for the first movement, as in the Pastoral, the Waldstein and the Appassionata, but in Opus 26 and in Opus 27 (the 'Moonlight'), he starts with an adagio, to great dramatic effect. In Beethoven's case, as with many composers, the change in style and the willingness to challenge convention was not always well received at first hearing. One could go on in this vein for some time, including the field of popular music. One of the factors that led to the success of the Beatles was their willingness to challenge expectations and conventions.

Education can in some ways be seen as analogous to popular entertainment, serious music, commerce and the rest, though there are dangers in taking analogies too far. Education is not synonymous with entertainment, though having fun in learning certainly helps. The analogy is most pertinent in the first 15–20 minutes of the lesson or the topic where, to be effective, the teacher needs to capture the interest of the learners, just as the playwright or the composer or the pop group has to gain and hold the interest of the audience.

This has always been the case with younger pupils. Before the 1970s most young people left school at 16 and most went to work. Post-compulsory education dealt with those who had been successful in gaining high grades at GCE O and A level or who had gained training places in industry and commerce and were sent to college on day or block release. Since the last quarter of the twentieth century, however, when the numbers staying on in education and training beyond the compulsory school leaving age has doubled to more than 80 per cent, some form of post-compulsory education or training is the norm for the majority of young people.

In addition, in the early part of the twenty-first century there has been a major shift in the curriculum opportunities for 14–16 year olds. Since before the 1944 Education Act it has been known that large numbers of students would benefit from a more practical and vocationally based education often involving the local college and employers. The Revised Guidance on the Disapplication of the National Curriculum at Key Stage 4 of the 1996 Education Act now recognizes the appropriateness of beginning vocational education at 14. These vocational courses have brought new challenges to the teaching skills of both secondary and college teachers (Green Paper: *Extending Opportunities and Raising Standards* 2002).

Gaining and then sustaining the interest of an individual learner or group of learners is the first task of the teacher. Get it right and there is a fighting chance that the learner will want to pursue a topic further – get it wrong and apathy or resistance could set in.

What makes humans interested in beginnings?

What Shakespeare and Beethoven knew instinctively has become the subject of academic enquiry since the beginning of the twentieth century. Reasons why we are attracted to a new stimulus and how that attraction leads to some form of engagement have interested psychologists since the development of psychology as a serious subject.

One of the seminal works in this regard was the paper, 'The relation of strength of stimulus to rapidity of habit-formation' by Robert M. Yerkes and John D. Dodson (1908) published in *Journal of Comparative Neurology and Psychology* 18: 459–82.

The basic premise is that there is a relationship between performance in a given sphere and the extent of emotional arousal (or anxiety) in the subject engaged in that performance. It was expressed in the form of an inverted U graph (see Figure 1) where the level of performance on the vertical axis increases proportionate to the extent of the arousal or stress on the horizontal axis, up to the optimum point on the curve. This is referred to as 'eustress'. Further increase in arousal after the optimum point of the curve leads only to a downturn in performance. This is referred to as 'distress'.

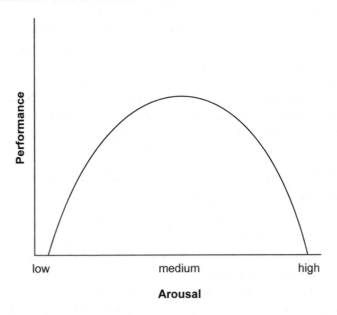

Figure 1: The Yerkes–Dodson curve 1908

The original study was undertaken in a clinical context. Through a series of experiments with mice, Yerkes and Dodson found that moderately stressed mice learnt to complete certain tasks better than those mice which were either not stressed at all, or mice which were highly stressed. Since 1908, psychologists have used the curve in a variety of contexts. Some (Burton 1988, Butler 1996, Hardy *et al.* 1996) have used the principle to explain not only habit formation, but also why the controlling of pressure or stress is vital to success in sports and athletics. Other academics (Hebb 1955, Broadhurst 1959, McCullers 1978) have used the Yerkes–Dodson principle in analysing aspects of motivation and arousal. Loftus and Ketcham (1991) have used it to explain why some eyewitnesses remember selective stimuli in an incident to the exclusion of others.

There has been controversy over the expanded use of the Yerkes–Dodson. law with views varying from Martindale (1991: 130), who asserts that the law 'applies to everything from ... people making decisions ... to rats making brightness discrimination under water', to more sceptical views such as Baumler (1992) who felt that too many claims were being made for the Yerkes–Dodson law and questioned whether the original conclusions took into account all the variables for poor performance. At the time this book was written, there were over 580 entries on the Internet under the heading 'Yerkes–Dodson curve', signifying the extent to which the principle has been applied in cognitive and clinical psychology.

The Yerkes–Dodson curve and professional skills in post-compulsory education

Our interest in the Yerkes–Dodson principle in this book is not based on scientific trials in the clinical sense, nor does it claim to have empirical justification. Our recognition of the value of the Yerkes–Dodson principle is based on observation of practice and professional reflection over a period of forty years. It seems to us that the essential premise of the curve can be applied to at least two facets of teaching and learning:

1   in the context of lesson planning and delivery
2   in managing the syllabus or the scheme of work and enabling the learners to meet their assessment goals

Lesson planning and delivery

In the context of a lesson, the 'performance' that teachers are interested in can be expressed in a number of ways such as: learners paying attention; learners staying on task; the quality of the work achieved; a general willingness to be involved and to do what is expected. 'Arousal' in the same context can also be expressed in several ways: how the teacher presents information or activities to gain interest; the variety and strength of stimuli; attention paid by the teacher to individual needs; curiosity and/ or novelty of approach (like the preacher and his plumb-line); rewards and strokes.

It could be argued that 'performance indicators' such as these can be found in well-motivated learners who cooperate well with the teacher whatever the arousal. Of course, there are variables other than arousal, such as motivation, parental influence, laws of positive reinforcement and so on, which influence performance. But not all learners are predisposed to cooperation and even those who are can easily be switched off if the level of arousal is taken for granted.

In Figure 2, we are interested in the relationship between arousal and performance at the top of the curve. We would

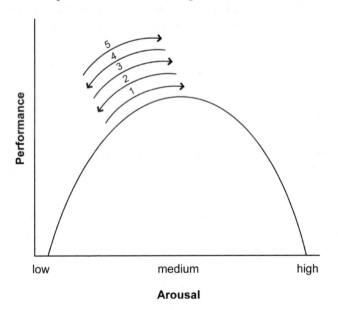

Figure 2: The value of the Yerkes–Dodson curve in lesson planning

argue that peak performance by learners is unsustainable over a whole lesson. What is needed is for the teacher to aim for several peaks of performance through positive arousal (eustress) in a particular lesson, which will also mean planning for periods of reduced arousal. These would allow time for consolidation in the form of discussion or reflection, processing of information or research, testing understanding, application of the new knowledge and so on. This sense of planning can be seen in Figure 2, where we have illustrated the use of the curve through a series of numbers, each odd number signifying a new stimulus or activity with the arrow pointing clockwise, and each even number signifying a period of consolidation with the arrow pointing anticlockwise.

Caveat

Piaget (1966) noticed another phenomenon about the affect of arousal, which they called *assimilation* and *accommodation*. We process all new stimuli either in terms of what we know and feel comfortable with or in terms of having to make some sort of adjustment in order to accept or reject the unexpected or unusual. It is therefore possible that the presentation of new stimuli along the optimum upward line of the Yerkes–Dodson curve might not appeal to all learners, at least not immediately, so you may need to think about how you introduce the idea and what you do if there is resistance.

Managing the syllabus or scheme of work and enabling the learners to meet their assessment goals

The Yerkes–Dodson curve applies also to the way a teacher thinks through the scheme of work. The order of topics and their relationship with each other, the amount of time allocated to them, their role in meeting the expected learning outcomes and their psychological impact on the learners need to be thought through with care. A certain level of stress is useful here, so maintaining a good pace, with plenty of work at the right level and a shared sense of progress, are aids to performance that the good teacher will promote with her/his learners.

Learners in the post-compulsory sector feel reassured when the indicators of progress (performance) are clear and measurable. They may make noises about being given a lot of work, but, provided that the workload is manageable and can be seen to be fulfilling their needs, they will be pleased to be making progress. Distress occurs more often when the pace is slow and the learners are anxious about syllabus coverage or they have perceptions that they are not meeting the standard required. The teacher who conveys a sense of order and is consistent about punctuality, expectations, setting and marking of homework and who gives some thought to the way in which new topics can galvanize a class has every chance of being successful.

We will return to this topic in Chapter 3 when we look at the topic of examination revision.

Gaining learner interest and sustaining it

This is one of the most important elements in the training of those concerned with the teaching and learning of young adults.

One common feature of many lessons that young adults experience is that it is the *teacher* who introduces the topic, often with the aid of PowerPoint or an overhead projector and slides.

This approach follows the outlines of the model in Figure 3, which is set out from the perspective of the teacher in her/his planning. It begins with the expectation that it is the teacher's job to introduce the topic (I 'teach'). After a period of time, anything from fifteen minutes onwards, the learners are set a task (you 'do') and, after they have had time to complete the task, the teacher and the learners go through the exercise together (we 'check'). Assuming the lesson has been successful so far, the teacher moves to phase 4.

We have given this approach the title 'traditional' triangle, synonymous with teaching in the minds of many people. Most young PGCE graduates embarking on their first few days of training have known no other model since Advanced level GCE. At university, it is highly probable that phase 1 (I teach), in the form of a formal lecture, has dominated their educational experience. Weaning them off the notion of the teacher always introducing a topic is one of the first tasks of the PGCE training.

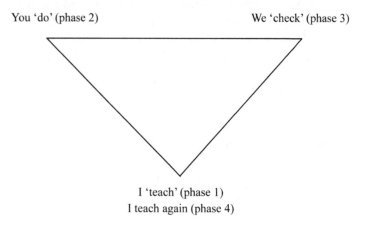

Figure 3: The traditional triangle

Now, there is nothing intrinsically wrong with this model. It has an excellent pedigree and it can be very effective, depending on the skill of the teacher. The preacher in the anecdote at the beginning of the chapter was an expert and could capture the attention of any audience. Indeed, the young history teacher in the 1960s often relied on the traditional triangle to get through to his students. But, if we examine some of the underlying features of the triangle, in particular its relationship to the model of learning styles devised by David Kolb (1984), we notice some interesting issues.

In Figure 4 we superimpose the Kolb model on the traditional triangle (see Figure 4).

From the superimposition, it would appear that the traditional triangle is most suited to two of the four learning styles, i.e. those of assimilators and convergers. Learners with both of these styles are comfortable with abstract ideas, often presented in the form of models and diagrams like the ones in the two figures used here. They tend to latch on well to structures developed by the teacher and can see where the lesson is going from their understanding of the structure. The teacher for her/

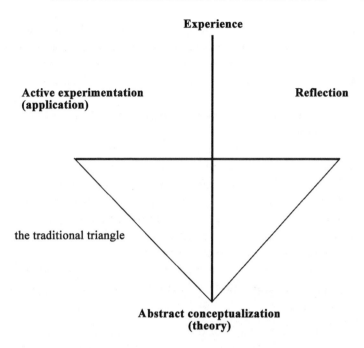

Figure 4: The traditional triangle and the Kolb cycle

his part feels that this approach will work well if it is clearly thought out and delivered with sufficient humour, references to things that might interest the learners, using good question and answer techniques and with good visual aids. More practical or experiential elements are scheduled for phase 2 or later in the lesson, so all styles will eventually be catered for. And this is often the case. It is not the intention of this book to knock the teacher-centred model as such. Meeting the needs of two out of four learning styles is not a bad average.

However, there are some inherent weaknesses in the traditional triangle, which can lead to its ineffectiveness if it is overused or applied to learners who have become disaffected and demotivated.

- It relies on the quality of teacher performance too much. If the teacher has a bad day or fails to inspire, the model is flawed. One has to be conscious of the Yerkes–Dodson principle here.

- It is unrealistic to expect that learners will immediately respond. Often learners fail to see the relevance of a topic when it is presented to them and resistance sets in.
- If the approach fails to strike a chord, some learners can so easily switch off. Bored and uninterested students can easily become 'passengers'. Again, the Yerkes–Dodson principle is important.
- The teacher's structures for organizing and retaining knowledge are assumed to meet the thinking of all the learners. This is not always the case. For example, some learners prefer to use mind maps to organize their notes whereas others adopt a more linear structure.
- There is a danger of condescension. 'They' will not be able to understand unless 'I' mediate the learning.
- It undervalues the potential contribution of each learner's experience and skills in reflection in the shaping of abstract concepts.

One of the advantages of the teacher-centred introduction is that the teacher feels confident that she/he can impose structure and order on the lesson. Teacher confidence in their planning and structure is an essential factor in good teaching. Though this can be a limitation if taken to extremes, it is also extremely valuable if not essential in developing thinking and organizational skills in the learner.

Alternative starting points will only be effective, and accepted, if they display structural characteristics that are as conducive to developing thinking and organizational skills as the teacher-centred models. It is in no one's interests to advocate an inverted, less traditional, triangle, which promotes only experience and active learning without any sort of theoretical context.

Deep and surface learning

Another principle that is relevant here is that of 'personally meaningful learning' (Harkin *et al.* 2001). This idea owes much to the work of Gibbs (1992) who himself builds on the work of Marton and Säljö (1976), Entwistle and Ramsden (1983) and

Entwistle (1987). The process of education may be unproductive and disappointing if the learner can make little or no
sense of it. Harkin and his co-writers (2001) argue that 'if a
student reduces what has to be learned to a series of uncon-
nected facts to be memorised, then a surface approach is
adopted. If a student attempts to make sense of what is to be
learned, then a deep approach is used.' Ramsden (2003)
observes that 'everyone is capable of both deep and surface
approaches from early childhood onwards'. What is important
according to Ramsden is the relationship between the learner
and what he or she is learning, i.e. that the learning is personally
meaningful.

There is no space in this book for an in-depth look at these
approaches. Ramsden (2003: 43–9) and Mark Weyer (2007)
give excellent overviews. We would argue that most educational strategies go either from the specific to the general or vice
versa; and that specific information, therefore, whether in the
form of brainstorming, or processing facts, or talking about
personal experiences is fundamental to the processes of education. What is unacceptable is for the teacher to leave the
learner with the notion that these 'specifics' have a life of their
own. Teachers have the responsibility of ensuring that the
learners have the opportunity to see these specifics in wider or
more 'general' contexts, which 'deepen' understanding. We
deal with this much more fully when we introduce the ideas of
Hilda Taba later in this chapter and again in Chapter 3.

Learning styles and current research

An extensive research project was commissioned by the
Learning and Skills Research Centre (LSRC) to investigate the
current use of learning styles in post-16 education and training
and to analyse the implications for the sector (Coffield *et al.*
2005). The title of the LSRC review is *Learning Styles and
pedagogy in post-16 learning: a critical and systematic review*, wherein
the researchers identified 71 models of learning styles, cat-
egorizing 13 of these as major models which are analysed in the
report with great thoroughness. The description of each model
helps to define what each means by learning style – one of the

main points made by the research is the complexity in defining one's terms – whereas pedagogy is assumed to be, with reference to the report's glossary, 'theoretical and procedural knowledge about teaching'.

The LSRC report and the Kolb cycle

The authors of the LSRC report (ibid. 2005: 71) do not rate Kolb's Learning Styles Inventory (LSI) at all highly. The overall assessment at the foot of table 20 in the LSRC report (p. 71) states 'problems about reliability, validity and the learning cycle continue to dog this model'. We would not disagree with the comments about reliability and validity, even taking into account the improvements made by McCarthy (1990) and the modifications by Kolb himself (2000). The means of gathering via a self-rating instrument and the difficulties in allocating specific characteristics to each quadrant are two design factors that raise doubts about the empirical value of this LSI.

Where we do find the Kolb cycle useful is as a pedagogical tool. It is also effective for reflecting on the structure of a piece of learning. The researchers were unable to find any *evidence* of pedagogical impact, thus adding to the body of criticisms. This is a pity, for it is the pedagogical impact of the Kolb cycle that is most useful in developing teacher skills. For example, in table 20 (p. 71) in the column 'strength' (under implications for pedagogy), 'teachers and students may be stimulated to examine and refine their theories of learning; through dialogue, teachers may become more empathetic with students'. Hidden in a table which itself is only a minute part of a very comprehensive report, it would be easy to underestimate the value of this observation. Yet it is a fundamental step in the process of developing awareness in prospective teachers. They have to start *somewhere* on the road to integrating theory with practice. Their experience as students is likely to have been of a limited range of pedagogic models, along the lines of the traditional triangle. They do not have the luxury of an academic role in this regard, after having spent many years in the teacher training profession.

We feel that the key point here is to get the trainee teachers to examine and refine their theories of learning rather the respective merits of learning style theory. In the first few sessions of training we would rather they become confident in one 'theory' of learning, while acknowledging the need for them to examine the research. All learning is an *experience* of some sort, experience leads to *reflection*, reflection should be placed in the context of relevant *theory* (or several) and these new insights then *applied* or *actively used* in new situations.

The whole point about re-evaluating the traditional triangle is to sensitize teachers to the fact that a lesson can have, potentially, a number of starting points and a variety of approaches. We are aware, as indeed were the authors of the LSRC report (ibid. 2005: § 1, p. 3), of the dangers of 'a type of pedagogic sheep dip', but feel that the most important strategic gain is for trainee teachers to acknowledge the idea of different pedagogic models by contrasting their own experience of being passive with a wider set of pedagogic possibilities. This may leave us open to the charge in table 20 that 'the implications for teaching have been drawn logically from the theory rather than from research findings' (Coffield *et al.* 2005: 71), but in some ways this is an easy jibe. The argument regarding the lack of research findings is the refuge of those who only value what can be proven. Research itself can suffer from paralysis because terminology is too complex, as in the case of learning style definitions and models, or it can oversimplify its analytical findings, as can be seen in table 20 in the LSRC report (2005).

Teachers can see changes in the attitude and behaviour of their learners when the approaches to a topic are more visual, more interactive, more rooted in the experience of all the learners, or more concerned with drawing out ideas and reflecting on them. They are able to reach more learners when the lesson involves more than simply providing learners with a predetermined structure where most of the organization of ideas, if not the thinking, has been done for them. The power of the Yerkes–Dodson curve gives substance to the points we have made, even if it is logically rather than empirically based. One of the challenges for teachers is 'how to structure lessons which enable learners to make personal sense of the meaning that the teacher is trying to communicate' (Harkin *et al.* 2001: 35).

Figure 5, from the National Training Laboratory (NTL), Bethel, ME (1964 footnote) is a further avenue of research to illustrate the gains in extending one's range of openings for lessons.

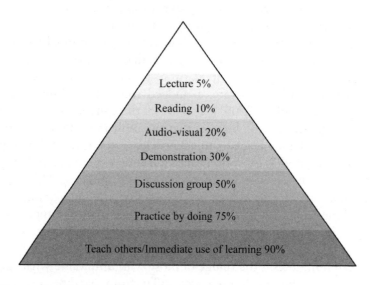

Figure 5: The learning pyramid, NTL, Bethel, ME, 1964

Options for facilitation

There are a number of key questions the teacher can ask in preparing for a lesson where the beginning is based on some form of learner activity. Examples based on these principles will be found in Part Four.

1   What will the learners be doing at each phase (it helps to think of a verb)?
2   What might the learners know already about this topic?
3   Is there something in the learner's life or experience that is tangential or similar or meaningful that can be used as a springboard?
4   Can I organize the learning into some simplified propositions that are self-referencing, e.g. sorting or matching or sequencing or ranking?

5   Is it possible to employ two or more senses in the activity (in line with the Bethel research – Figure 5)

6   How can I manage the Yerkes–Dodson curve more effectively?

Asking these questions will lead to a number of strategic decisions. Would this topic work better if it were presented from the specific to the general or vice versa? What this means can vary, but in essence the teacher needs to decide whether to start the lesson with something concrete and specific, widening the scope by further examples to encompass a deeper understanding, or start with some more general proposition such as a law or a precept or an analytical tool and work backwards from the generality to specific examples.

The preacher knew the answer – he referred specifically to Amos. Emotional intelligence is a key factor here. Most people relate to something that is real and concrete and meaningful and teachers can use this as a basis for widening one's horizons via further examples, and questions. The structure can be agreed and developed on the basis of a mutual journey. One of the analogies we use in training is that of rock climbing. It is perfectly possible to stand at the top of the rock and instruct the climber from above, e.g. 'on your left just above your head there is a handhold . . . yes, about eighteen inches (etc. . . .)' Or, one can stand at the bottom of the rock face with the climber and say 'let us climb the face together'. There are times when each could be appropriate, but with learners who are disaffected, or hostile to education or who have had an unrewarding educational history, 'climbing with' is an important step in changing the learner's mind set.

Prompts and self-referencing principles

Parents, teachers and therapists have always known the value of step-by-step approaches to learning, but how does this work out in practice? One of the choices available to the teacher is the Taba model (Eggen *et al.* 1979, Eggen and Kauchak 1988). The 'classic' Taba approach (see Table 1) consists of seven phases, the first three of which are chiefly concerned with

Table 1: The classic Taba model (1966, 1967)

Data			Organizing framework	Inference			
1	2	3	columns tables models grids charts matrices	4	5	6	7
List	Group	Label		Compare	Generalize	Explain	Predict

establishing what the students already know or acquiring data through the senses and the last four with extending the value of the data to the learners through comparisons, establishing generalizations and so on. For further reading see Harkin *et al.* (2001: 45–7). It is very useful to the teacher to be able to rely on a 'taxonomy', which acts as an information-processing 'map'. We will return to the subject of taxonomies in Chapter 3.

Expectations are quite high in this approach. Not only do you hope that the learners know enough about the topic and are interested enough to take part, but that they will also be able to synthesize their initial thoughts into some sort of structure, even if they need your help. You are asking for *two* concurrent processes: that of generating the data and then processing the information in an ordered way. We should have high expectations, but what happens when you have a deeply demotivated class or one in which the confidence levels are low?

One answer is to simplify the instruction to ONE task i.e. the processing one. This means that YOU supply the basic information and ask the learners to do one of the following:

SORT these cards (envelopes) or pictures into x piles

PLACE these cards in the correct sequence

TELL me three things you know about.... (YOU provide the names)

MATCH items 1–8 with their partner in A–G

ELIMINATE the two irrelevant items from a list of, say, ten or an equivalent set of pictures or artefacts

SPOT the difference(s) in two or more pictures, texts or actions

SELECT a specified number of examples from data supplied by
    the teacher
UNDERLINE a specified number of key words or phrases from
    an article or extract

Examples of these and other activities are to be found in Part
Four.

What you have done is to provide sufficient prompts to get
the activity going and to set up conditions for success. There are
extra bonuses if the items chosen are also topical, visual and
relate to the world that the learners know. You will see
examples in Part Four. It makes good sense here to find out to
what television programmes, magazines and newspapers your
learners have access and for you to access them too. You may
think, as a teacher and a graduate, that you are too well edu-
cated, or perhaps have grown out of, watching reality television
or soap operas or reading magazines such as *OK* or *Hello* or
tabloid newspapers such as the *Sun* or the *Mirror*, but think
again. If you are to relate to the experiences of your learners
and help them to start on a journey that leads them to wider
choices, meeting them where they are is a crucial step. It is the
same philosophy as 'climbing with'.

Prompts define the agenda and help focus the students'
attention on the essentials. It is easier to select from alternatives
than to supply ideas from the top of one's head. One-stage
tasks, especially those that are self referencing, are easier than
two-stage tasks. The idea is to get learners to take part and to
experience some form of success that is immediate and obvious.

One of the key questions we would ask would be about the
verb. Remove all the extraneous elements to some activities,
such as the ones we have just looked at, especially the first task,
and pare it down to one simple action, which the learners can
do individually or in pairs or groups of no more than four.

Closing a lesson

Closing a lesson, like closing a chapter in book, is a key element
in the teaching-learning process if we are to ensure that the
whole experience is satisfying.

The closing of a class requires as much thought as the beginning, but it is often rushed or even omitted altogether. There are several reasons for this: you avoid thinking about closure because you do not have a range of techniques to do it successfully; or you run out of time because some activities took longer than expected; or you need to get to a certain point by today because of some circumstance such as half-term or there is a week's 'residential' impending; or the behaviour of some students in the lesson may be deteriorating and you feel it best to cut your losses; or you are tired and are just relieved to have lasted the lesson.

Closures are valuable for a number of reasons. They allow the teacher and the learners to revisit the aims and learning outcomes and to agree to what extent these have been achieved. Jensen (1988) says 'closure is not part of the presentation, but allows the presentation to have an impact, to "settle in". Closure is the last word, the final thought, the ribbon round the package.' Closures give people with reflective learning styles a forum for their thoughts. They mirror what happens in other social situations, where goodbyes and thanks are part of the social mix. When something is not closed, it can leave people uncertain or disaffected. Jensen advocates allowing five to eight minutes for closure, or about 10 per cent, in a lesson of fifty minutes.

Ideas for closures

In addition to explicitly revisiting the learning outcomes there are a number of ideas you can try. Some of you may do them already.

Round Robin

'Tell us one thing you have learned today or that sticks in your memory; or one thing you feel about the lesson.'

General impact

'Go to x corner if you understood everything and can explain it, y corner if you understood some of it and z corner if you really didn't get it. Now pair off (or threes) with someone from another group and see if you can share what you know, or can resolve each other's questions.'

Checking back
'You have 5 minutes to look through the notes you have made today and are allowed up to 3 questions to ask me and the class. We will go round the class in turn and you cross off questions on your list that have been dealt with.'

Link to homework
You deliberately plan for some key points to be discovered at home. It works best if the tasks are clear and well structured and this needs time at the end of the lesson to ensure that the messages are understood.

Links to past or future lessons
You could prepare a chart to consolidate today's topic within a framework, say, of other ideas in the same 'family', or along a timeline or within a set of similar propositions or as a progression from ideas previously covered.

Preparing for examinations
You could also pose a real or hypothetical examination question as a closure. 'Given what you now know, how might you tackle this question?'

Conclusion

When the authors have been to a lesson observation or have been asked to comment on the reasons why a particular teacher has failed to meet the standards of an inspection, it is very often the case that the 'ingredients' for a good lesson have been assembled. There is often a good mix of teacher and learner activity with well-organized resources and a well thought-out structure. The problem is the 'recipe'. Too many teachers equate teaching with transmission (Harkin *et al.* 2001) and think that they should lead the students through an introduction. So the active and student-centred elements of the lesson are placed later in the lesson, as we see in the traditional triangle. When we have asked teachers about this, they think that they need to ensure that the theory is well grounded before letting the learners loose on some form of development or application. Teaching is associated with leading from the front so that the activities have a firm foundation.

This is fallacious. If we change metaphors for a moment, imagine Andrew Lloyd Webber or Giuseppe Verdi deciding to leave their best tunes till after the interval. There would be no audience. Composers, film directors and playwrights know that an early emotional involvement of the audience is vital for the success of the show. In the same way, teachers need to use some of their best 'tunes' early on. To continue with the audience analogy, learning that has personal meaningfulness is more likely to gain learner interest and then stimulate further commitment than that which is presented in a preordained format.

What is needed sometimes is not transmission, but facilitation. Conditions need to be created whereby the learners can explore a topic individually or in pairs or small groups and rehearse some of their reactions in advance of whole-class discussions and the process of applying structure to process. We will be dealing with this in more detail in Chapter 3.

Further reading

Biggs, J. (2003) *Teaching for Quality Learning at University* (2nd edn), London: McGraw-Hill Education/Open University Press.

Harkin, J., Turner, G. and Dawn, T. (2001) *Teaching Young Adults: a handbook for teachers*, London: Routledge Falmer.

Jensen, J. P. (1988) *Super Teaching: Master Strategies for Building Student Success*, San Diego, CA: Turning Point for Teachers.

Kolb, D. A. (1984) *Experiential Learning: Experience as the Source of Learning and Development*, London: Prentice-Hall.

Ramsden, P. (2003) *Learning to Teach in Higher Education*, London: Routledge Falmer.

2 Using small groups in the classroom

Ros Clow

When I am given a lesson plan for the lesson I am about to observe, my heart sinks if it says something like 'in small groups' and nothing else. In my experience, the trainee teacher has felt obliged to include a group activity somewhere, because they know we teacher trainers like small-group activities, but they have not given it much thought and it could be a recipe for disaster. In this chapter, I shall explore the advantages and disadvantages of using small groups in the classroom and recommend good practice.

Why use small groups?

It is usually easier for quieter, shyer students to express their views in a small group. There is controversy about whether it is necessary for students to contribute in order to learn, but, in general, articulation aids analysis and learning and also of course allows the teacher informally to assess whether each student is understanding key aspects of the lesson.

For almost everyone it is quite threatening to express themselves in large groups. A small group gives individuals the chance to try out ideas before they or someone else share the idea with the whole group.

Early on in a course the small group allows group members to get to know each other better, in a way that would be difficult in the large group, especially if the teacher did not use frequent icebreakers.

Most importantly, small-group work provides a change of activity and focus – a change of state – a chance to move in the classroom, to have a quick word with someone you have not caught up with today, a chance for a quick comfort break or just a break from sitting and listening.

And, in my experience, students are less likely to fall asleep in small groups! As a teacher who has fallen asleep in her own class (while the students were watching a video) this a real consideration!

However, there are drawbacks. Small-group work always takes longer than you expect, especially the setting up. Recently, I moved a group of 27 trainee teachers into six small groups and asked one of the class to time it. Despite the fact that I was demonstrating good practice in the way I set this up, giving clear instructions about where everyone should end up, it took slightly more than three minutes before everyone was seated and ready to listen to the briefing. This time lapse needs to be allocated in the plan. If a plan says 'Group work – 5 minutes', this would leave only two minutes for any discussion.

Occasionally some small groups are dysfunctional. If the group is only operating for five or ten minutes, this is not too much of an issue, although it has to be watched carefully, but if the group is expected to work together for any length of time, this will cause major problems.

And small-group work can be overdone, as can any teaching method. It can be seen as irritating or seem like a 'cop out' for the teacher, as indeed it sometimes is!

Planning small-group work

So if you want to use small groups in your lesson, then it requires a considerable amount of planning.

You need to decide roughly when you want the small groups to run. It might be to provide a change of state halfway through the class. It might be at the beginning of the class, especially if you have perpetual late arrivals (perhaps because of rural bus services). Or it might be at the end of the class to consolidate learning, or to start students thinking about the next topic.

The tasks or topics they are to discuss must be appropriate. It is no good asking a group to discuss something they know nothing about. This is an error I have seen during observations. It is not possible for students to discuss, say, the Poor Law, if they have no prompts or background information. Typically, the group discussions will fizzle out or move back to an earlier topic or settle on what is happening at the weekend. In any case, just asking students to 'discuss' is probably too woolly; it is much more fruitful to ask them to achieve some kind of outcome. Examples are:

- list advantages and disadvantages
- rank in order of priority
- carry out a plus, minus, interesting (PMI) analysis (De Bono 1978)
- create a poster
- create a 'mind map'

You need to decide on the size of the group. Pairs can work very well, and can avoid the need for movement if this is desirable (for speed or because the room is very small for the number of students you have). Six is probably the maximum size for a small group: after that, it becomes too unwieldy and loses its advantages. You need to decide whether you want a spread of ability in each group, or whether you want to give different tasks to different groups and therefore need groups of students with similar abilities together. This is particularly important when some students have literacy problems. In that situation, you need to ensure that at least one member of each group can provide the feedback you want or you could use a learning support assistant to take on that role.

You also need to consider gender mix. There may be a reason to have single-sex groups. In my antenatal teaching, I used to have single-sex groups to list the three things that they are looking forward to after the baby and the three things they are concerned about. This provided a stark contrast in perspective which became the focus of discussion for the rest of the lesson. However, it is my experience that all-male groups tend to take longer to settle down and often, though of course not always, do not work constructively; so I try to avoid them if I can.

You need to prepare a task sheet with written instructions about what is to be done in the group. This does not have to be beautifully word-processed: it is a functional document which makes sure everyone knows what they are doing. It is quite acceptable for it to be written on the whiteboard or flip-chart, but it must be written. This saves lots of queries and is particularly useful for the late arrivals, who can be quietly directed to a group and can become involved without interrupting the group who are already working. The briefing should tell the students what they have to do, how long they have and how they will feed back.

It is also important in the planning stage to decide how you will engineer the groups. There are a multitude of methods for this.

Ways of selecting group membership

There are many ways of selecting groups; using different ways introduces variety and can tell us more about our students too.

Working with the person next to them
This is a quick method of setting up paired work, but it avoids the benefit of an opportunity for movement. It is also difficult for those sitting on their own. Recently, I observed a class where one student was left to work on his own for the whole lesson. In my view, the teacher should have at least given him permission to move to work in a three with one of the pairs. This is probably the place to mention students who prefer to work on their own. There is some thinking, which comes from colleagues working with gifted and talented students, that students should be allowed to work on their own as long as they complete the tasks. This is probably a matter of professional judgement by the teacher depending on the task, the general level of ability of the group and whether there are 'working with others' issues which need to be addressed.

Group counting
Having worked out how many groups you want, you divide the total number of students by that number and then go round saying 'You three (or four) work together'. This means that there is a danger that the individuals will not move, so it is very

important that you make sure they move to sit facing each other. In the main, this will produce friendship groups: they chose to sit near each other, but that may be fine for this class.

Individual counting

This sounds so simple and yet I still make mistakes when I use this in class. At the planning stage, you need to decide how many groups you want. If you decide on four groups, then you go round numbering 1,2,3,4,1,2,3,4 ... As you do this, you need to make sure you have eye contact with each student and that they at least mouth, or, better still, write down the number you have given them. Then you indicate where you want each group to meet: 'Group 1 at the back, group 2 by the window ...' Then you ask them to move and indicate whether they should take all their things with them or not. They will probably get in a muddle, either accidentally because they did not listen, or on purpose, because they want to sit with their friends. You need to keep a watchful eye. With this method, no one will end up sitting next to the same people as they did in the large group and this is the great strength of using 'counting'. I was once asked to observe a GNVQ business class which was completely defeating the trainee teacher. He was so nervous of the group that he could totally dry up and had to sip water throughout. What I observed was that two teenagers in particular were causing all the problems; they chatted to each other about anything at all, nothing to do with the class; they were quite loud; they did not listen to instructions, so had to ask what they were supposed to be doing, but actually they were quite bright and could contribute well to the class, as they both had jobs outside college. I suggested that the teacher next week used the subterfuge of setting up groupwork by counting, in order to separate the two students, and then 'forgot' to ask them to move back to their original seats. An email after the next class told me he had done as I suggested and had had no problems at all during the class; both students worked really well. If only it was always so easy!

Colours

Different coloured handouts, labels or sweets (careful of allergies) can be handed out and then students can be asked to move into 'colour' groups. In this way, the groups can be planned, for instance by allocating colours to name labels given out at the start of the day or lesson or randomly, as in the case of passing a tube of Smarties or a pack of Starburst fruits round.

Profiles

Using 'profiles' can have a multitude of uses in teaching. As a starting point, all the students leave their places and are asked to arrange themselves in a line according to certain criteria. Some criteria can be innocuous. House numbers (and, if your house has a name, count the number of letters in the name) will not provide any additional information for you or students' peers. With a new group, 'birthdays', arranged from 1 January to 31 December, tells them all a little bit about each other and may increase social cohesion. Similarly 'distance travelled to college' may help students find out who lives near them so they can travel together in future.

Once you have a profile, you use counting to divide up the groups. You can use either group counting or individual counting, according to your intentions. This becomes more important when you begin to use more interesting profile criteria.

More interesting criteria will tell you more about the students. So you can ask them to arrange themselves according to how many hours' homework they have done for college in the last week, or how many hours' work they have already done on this assignment. In the latter case, you might use group counting, so that you can give each group a different, differentiated task. If you had asked them to prepare for this lesson by reading a range of sources, a profile which explores how much they have actually done gives you two useful options as you group them. Group counting will give the well-read groups a chance to take their study further and give those who had not found the time to do the reading (I am being very kind here!) time in class to do it. Or, conversely, you can use individual counting to ensure that each group has at least one person who has done the requisite reading.

Other profile criteria might include: how many hours' paid employment have you done this month; number of hours you have spent doing sport this week; number of hours' sleep last night; the amount of kinds of insurance you have, the list is endless. Some criteria are probably too emotive to use. Weight, height, age would need to have very good purposes before you used them. Again, professional judgement will decide which criteria are appropriate for any group.

Self-selection
If you have plenty of time to spare, you can ask a large class to split themselves into groups, with a proviso that each group must be the same size. This happened to me on a 'student-centred learning' course many years ago. We had only known each other for an hour or two when we were asked to do this, and were told we would remain in these groups for the rest of the week. The new friendships meant that it was impossible to form groups of nine without newly found friends being split up. It took over an hour to come to a conclusion, and if I remember rightly the facilitators in the end had to agree to one group of ten and one of eight!

Self-selection of groups can be very problematic, especially if the groups are to exist over a period of time. I learned my lesson on this when I was setting up a manufacturing-based business project for engineering students. The project was to last for all of the middle term; the students had to set up an imaginary company, choose a name, write a company philosophy, design a logo, create accounts, design a product, market the product, design adverts, etc. It was the first time I had run a project like this, so I suggested the students formed themselves into four groups. Three groups, based on friendship, formed themselves very quickly, leaving five individuals to be the fourth group. The lesson was on a Friday afternoon, ending at 5.30pm (they really knew how to timetable general studies!). Each week, I gave a different input and then the groups worked on their project. Within about three weeks I knew I was in trouble! The fourth group included two 'lads' who visited the pub on Friday lunchtimes. If they arrived at all, they were late and smelling of booze. The other three students either went to the pub with them or arrived in class on time but were absolutely clueless as to what they were doing. One of the group was dyslexic and, although he tried to put the project together on his own, he really needed his group to proofread and help. While the other three groups flew, producing accurate and creative work, the fourth group sank without trace. All except the dyslexic student failed the unit.

Since then, whenever setting up any group for longer than a quarter of an hour, I have never let the group self-select. Chances are there will always be a 'fourth group' in any FE class (or elsewhere for that matter).

This does of course raise the really difficult issue of group-based assessment, which really irritates 'good' students but is the lifeline for less able students.

Randomized groups

This can be achieved by handing out sweets as mentioned earlier, or throwing dice, or picking cards from a pack, or taking items from a bag. It adds variety to the class: it is always good for the teacher to be a little bit unpredictable.

Two-stage – rainbow and number – groups

In the first stage of this, you set up the groups according to colours of the rainbow (red, orange, yellow, green, blue, indigo, violet). It is not actually necessary to use all of them. Then as each group is working, you go round and count everyone in each group (1,2,3,4,5,6 – however many there are). After the planned amount of time, you ask everyone to move into number groups. This ensures (if you have done your maths correctly) that there is one representative from each of the rainbow groups in each new group. This can be used to build discussion. Perhaps you give each rainbow group a slightly different aspect of a topic to discuss. So in the rainbow group, you might ask the group to discuss a particular style of garden design applied to a given garden (dimensions, soil type, aspect). When they move to the number groups, in each group there will be one person from each of the rainbow groups who should be able to explain their design decisions for the same garden. Discussion can start after all the designs have been shared and a preferred design selected to be taken forward to a plenary, perhaps as a poster. This is one type of group activity where it may not be necessary to have a plenary, as all the ideas have been shared during the second group.

Delphi technique

Another form of progressive group design begins with small groups discussing an issue. They have to reach consensus on the issue. Consensus means that everyone agrees with what is being said. It is not consensus if they say 'Well, four of us agreed but Jane thinks this is the case'.

You then merge two groups together, they explain and compare their consensuses and have to reach consensus again. Then the process is repeated, with the whole class finally reaching consensus. This technique could be used to establish ground rules for a course; it is used to decide aims of organizations. I recently used it to help university teacher trainers explore what should be included in the various stages of teacher training for the learning and skills sector. It is not a quick process (allow at least 1½ hours) but it does ensure everyone has their say and they thoroughly explore all facets of any topic the technique is being used for.

Parachute discussions

This uses a similar design to the Delphi technique, but consensus is not essential. In this case, you might start with pairs, then make them join with another pair and so on until you judge it is the right time to stop. This can work particularly well in the paired interview icebreaker. The pairs interview each other, then they each introduce their partner in the four, and then each student from the four introduces one of the students they met in the four to the eight. It has the advantage of testing listening skills and using repetition.

Setting up small groups

When you reach the point in the lesson where you want to start small-group work, it is really important that you 'stick to your guns'. I have observed lessons where 'groupwork' is indicated but never happened. During debriefing, the teacher will usually say 'I forgot!' – i.e. they were not following the lesson plan, and probably never did, or they will say that they did not think it appropriate at that time. Of course it is perfectly acceptable to change the plan as we go along, but my suspicion is that at this point the teacher 'bottled out'. Students often complain about being moved into groups. As teachers, we have to be very firm and be very assertive, showing that there is no choice. This can be quite difficult for new teachers, but once they have achieved it with any group, it will happen more easily in the future. Conversely, if the teacher backs down and lets students stay where they are, it will be even more difficult to set up small groups next time.

Once the process has begun, it is important to follow a set sequence. First, the groups are selected as planned. Then you move them into their groups, encouraging them to move furniture so that they can sit in a circle. Never let them sit in a line: always insist they sit facing each other. Sitting side by side is acceptable for pairs, but once the group size reaches three, the teacher has to be firm about them sitting facing each other. If you allow a line, then the students on the ends will be excluded from the group activity unless they have a very strong personality. This is particularly sad when the 'end' students are quieter or for whom English is their second language. The body language and group dynamics of this are easy to observe.

When all the groups are sitting with paper and pens at the ready, this is the time to brief them, using written instructions which maybe you wrote up while they were all milling around!

During small-group work

Not only does it take time for students to move into groups, it also takes time for them to start the activity. It can be useful to refer to Tuckman's (1965) stages of group formation at this point when training new teachers. Depending on the task and the group, there will almost always be a time when the group is 'storming' and it will take time for them to 'form' and 'perform'.

As teacher, you need to go round and visit all the groups and make sure they are clear about what they are doing. This can also prompt them to get on task. Then you leave them alone!

This is often the most difficult thing for new teachers: to absent yourself from the groups. More experienced teachers use the time to do some marking, or reading, or plan the next lesson!

One of the biggest mistakes I have observed is the teacher being drawn into, and in some cases taking over, the small-group discussions. This is a recipe for disaster in many ways. It prevents the group from following their own agenda, it stifles their creativity and inhibits quieter members, as in the larger group. More importantly, it gives the teacher the impression that they have been teaching and those topics were covered. This can mean that the other groups are totally disenfranchised and might miss significant issues, advice or content. Sometimes you have to contribute to a group. Maybe they are confused and ask for your help, or maybe they cannot agree and need guidance. As you interact with the small group, it is quite likely that useful learning points will emerge. There are two ways to deal with this: either you make a note and make sure that you cover these points with the whole class if they do not arise in the plenary discussion, or you ask a student to remind you to mention it to everybody. I have found the latter to work really well; I think it gives an element of responsibility to which most students rise.

As the groupwork proceeds, you need to keep an eye on time. If the groups are floundering, you may want to end the groupwork earlier so that you can mend the situation. If they are all going well, you might like to extend the time they have. Whatever you decide, you need to give warning, e.g. '2 minutes to go'. When time is up, be firm about all groups stopping work and suggest that they move chairs so that they are all facing you. Do not start teaching when any students have their back to you.

It is almost always best for the person who has written the flip-chart or OHT to present the group's findings. Sometimes, groups will try to spread the workload by asking someone who did not write the feedback (and perhaps who has not con- tributed very much?) to present it. This usually does not work and leaves the presenter stranded and having to ask the group what the feedback means.

After small-group work

You have just asked your students to spend some valuable lesson time working on a task for you. It is really important that you show you value what they have done. So, as a first rule, you must let *all* the groups 'show' their work. If you have given each group the same task, then it is essential that you take feedback from the groups, one idea at a time. The worst thing you can do (and I have seen it many times) is to take all the product of one group and then move on to the next group. By the time you reach the last group, they will not only be demotivated, but probably very angry. What was the point of all that effort, if you are not interested in their efforts?

It is often a good idea to give different groups different tasks. For instance, in a lesson on teaching 14–16 year olds in FE, you might ask each group to list advantages and disadvantages from different perspectives: students coming into FE, schoolchildren left behind, parents, schoolteachers, FE teachers, FE managers. It will then be perfectly acceptable to take feedback from each group, one at a time, and in this case the order of feedback is not particularly relevant.

It is sometimes worth planning the order of feedback from groups. If you are asking the groups to explore a particular topic, you might want the groupwork to end on a particular note. You can manipulate this to some extent in the way you take feedback. If all groups have the same topic, say, the advantages and disadvantages of renewable energy sources, you can ask for disadvantages first, so that you end up focusing on the advantages.

Similarly, if each group has a different topic, you can end with the most relevant one, perhaps leading naturally in to the next part of the lesson, so, in the example above, you might end with FE teachers' perceptions before going on to discuss what skills are needed by FE teachers when working with younger learners.

However the groups feed back, make sure you show that you

value their contribution by using verbal encouragement ('good', 'great idea'). Avoid saying anything is 'wrong' if at all possible. On the unfortunate occasion when an answer is totally wrong, you will have to point this out very clearly. Luckily, it will be a group answer so that will spread the blame!

Another trap teachers fall into is to receive all the feedback and then show their own 'one I did earlier'. The use of PowerPoint to prepare lessons means that this seems to be happening more frequently now. What was the point of all the groupwork if the teacher had a nice ready-made list to show them? This is demotivating in the extreme and changes the activity from genuine groupwork to 'guess what's in the teacher's head'. Of course, we will have an idea of what we want to come out of the groupwork and there is no reason we should not have our own list – but not for general consumption. We may need to add one or two things to the students' work, but we do not need to negate it. One of the great strengths of groupwork is that the students will almost always come up with a better list than we as teachers do on our own.

Feedback

Each small group should be asked to provide some kind of product. This might be a list on flip-chart paper, a hand-written acetate, a flowchart, a cartoon, a timeline. The lesson plan needs time to value those products. This can be teacher-led, with the teacher questioning each group in turn and valuing the groupwork by collating ideas into one central list. With more able articulate groups, the most common way of eliciting feedback is to ask a spokesperson from each group to 'talk to' the visual aid they have created.

A different approach is to provide Blu-Tack, Sellotape or drawing pins and when the groupwork is finished, ask the students to display their ideas. Then all the students visit all the displays and make their own notes. I used this method in a lesson on assessment which worked quite well. Students were in small groups, based loosely on where they chose to sit (with late arrivals directed to the smallest groups). I provided a large selection of basic texts that covered assessment and gave each group a topic: validity, reliability, norm referencing, etc. They had to read to make sure they understood and then create a poster on thin card which would help peers to remember what the jargon meant. The posters were displayed and the students then made their own notes on all the key vocabulary of assessment.

The same kind of process can be used with the students creating an electronic version which can be displayed in a shared area on the intranet.

Each group having a different topic does make the plenary/ feedback stage more interesting. Another idea is to ask each group to prepare some kind of creative presentation as a way of feeding back from their group. I have used this a lot when evaluating a course. Each group has a prompt sheet to help them evaluate the course they have done, but instead of delivering their evaluation straight, they present what they think in a much more creative way. Over the years we had, among others, radio programmes, court scenes, raps, chat shows, advertisements and poetry. This is time-consuming, but an excellent way to end a course. It is also easier for teachers to receive criticism in this fun way, yet you can still take away the main messages to improve the course next time.

Assessment in groups

Using groupwork for assessment is more and more common nowadays. There is no doubt that it reduces the marking load of teachers, and with large groups this is not an insignificant consideration. The product can be written, and still taken away for marking, or can be a student presentation, which means the bulk of the marking will be done 'live' during the presentation. Students do not see the overwhelming advantages for teachers as positively. I can remember a very distraught 14-year-old daughter coming home from school announcing, 'They've gone too far in D&T! Now they're making us work in groups!' I also remember attending my other daughter's graduation in Swansea where two students came up to her and thanked her for the effort she had put into their group project as they were sure it had raised their final grade. Research has shown (Lejk *et*

Processing

||||||||||||||||||||||||||||||||||||||||||||||||

F01JEQGAD

Liverpool John Moores University

Customer Number: 18589001	ISBN: 9780826490254
Budget/Fund Code	PSD4 – 2012
Classification	374.0712
Loan Type/Stock	NONE
Site / Location	NONE
Shelfmark	374.0712 CLO
Cutter 1	CLO
PL Category	General
Order Date	02/28/2013
Order Type	orders
PL Intellect. Level	Adult
Coutts shelfmark	Yes

Hand Notes:

al. 1996, Lejk and Wyvill 2002) that group-assessed assignments at university tend to even out the grades; the high flyers are brought down by the groupwork, the strugglers gain their best grades of the course. Race (2005) has written extensively about this and suggests ways in which the individual contribution of each member might be assessed and used to adjust the group grade. During a day course on 'assessing in groups' I tried an experiment. I set up groups of about five or six and gave them a task to complete in 20 minutes. I had written some information on the whiteboard and asked one representative from each group to come out to the front. I asked them to look at the board and pretend I was talking about the information there. In fact, I told them that when they returned to their group, they were to do nothing helpful at all for the entire period that the group was working. This included making no suggestions about the task, not being able to find anything they were asked to get, not contributing to the final product (the groups were creating large posters). I watched the group processes with interest and my 'stooges' did nothing at all. For some, as they later reported, it was extremely difficult, not their usual style. At the end of the group task, I asked each group to give every member of their group a mark out of ten for the effort put in. None of my stooges received less than five out of ten and they had done nothing at all!

Of course, any group project is an ideal opportunity for assessing the 'working with others' (WWO) key skill, but the latter experience makes me think that the assessing should be done by tutors or at least objective observers.

Chris Rust (2001) suggests using yellow and red cards during assessed groupwork. When a group thinks one of their members is not pulling their weight a yellow card is issued to the offender. Another complaint and they receive a red card and have to complete the assignment as an independent piece of work.

Different ways of judging contributions

It is probably worth experimenting with different ways of judging individual contributions to groups. You could have a group mark and an individual mark and just record them as such. The individual mark can be self-assessed, peer-assessed (but see above!), observer-assessed or tutor-assessed.

You can have the two grades as additive. In this case, you need to use percentages in your marking. The group mark maximum is 75 per cent, to which you add a mark out of 25 for the individual contribution.

So, if the group mark is 60 and the person who worked really well in the group received an individual mark of 23, her total mark is 83 per cent. The person in the group who did not attend project meetings and did nothing much at all except be there for the group presentation is awarded only 1 mark so his total mark is 61 per cent. Nothing about this is perfect. The 61 per cent for someone who did nothing seems very unfair.

Other ways of doing this are to award negative marks, so the slacker's grade becomes less than 60 per cent, or to award factors which are multiplied by the group mark. The more complex the marking scheme is, the more mistakes are likely to be made.

A different approach is for the group to list all the tasks needed to complete the assignment and then indicate who did what. This would provide good evidence for WWO, but would be difficult to interpret for summative grades.

Quizzes

A small-group activity that can be used by all teachers is the quiz, especially useful when used for revision for tests and exams. It can be set up in a variety of ways. However it is organized, there are three stages: generating questions; the quiz itself and the final scores.

Generating questions

Of course the teacher can generate the questions, using their own notes or the textbook, but this creates extra unnecessary work for the teacher (see Chapter 6). The whole process is likely to achieve more learning if the students generate their own questions. The one rule of this is that: *They must write both the questions and the answers*, ideally the question on one side of an index card, the answer on the reverse. This can be set as homework or done in the first part of the lesson. Usually, students will need to use notes/textbooks and that is fine.

Alternatively teachers can find questions in pub quiz type books or Trivial Pursuit games if they want to run informal quizzes, perhaps as an end of term activity.

The quiz
Once the teacher has the questions the quiz can begin! Below is a way of organizing a quiz that seems to work well, with everyone involved and listening, as not listening will disadvantage the team.

- Divide the class into teams (three or four in a team is ideal) and spend a bit of time moving furniture so that the teams are clearly defined and can be easily identified.
- The team might like to choose a team name.
- The team must choose a captain.
- The team gives each of its members a number: 1,2,3, . . .

The teacher becomes quizmaster and manages the quiz. You decide an order in which the teams will be asked the questions.

Shuffle the cards and ask the first question to team member number 1 in the first team. If team member number 1 answers correctly, they get 3 points; incorrectly, zero points and the question is then passed to the next team. If the next team get it right, they get 1 point, if wrong, the question passes on to the next team, etc., etc.

The nominated team member can choose to confer with their team, rather than taking the question themselves. At this point, only the captain can answer (so whatever they say is the accepted answer – this is very good to promote teamwork). If the captain gets the answer right, two points are scored by the team. Again, if the answer is wrong, it passes to the next team. You need to remember which team should be asked the next question, though usually the class soon 'get the hang' and will correct you if you make a mistake.

Scores are kept in full view on a whiteboard or flip-chart. It is usually quite hard to keep score and run the quiz, so one of the students will usually rise to the challenge of being scorer. You will end the quiz as fairly as possible, e.g. every team has had three questions and then some basic maths will reveal the winning team. Always have prizes ready for the winning team. I have found unwanted presents very useful in this respect or some sort of confectionery.

Summary

Using small groups in the classroom adds variety, a change of state and is generally motivating and interesting for students. To be successful, groupwork must be carefully planned and this involves a lot of thought at the lesson plan stage. In the classroom, the process of setting up groups has to be led firmly and clearly and groups in action observed carefully. Groupwork must be valued and students given the space to feed back. We must resist the temptation to muscle in on groups and should leave groups to work on their own once we know they are clear about what we want them to do. It is very likely that we as teachers will learn from our students' groupwork, the mark of a good lesson:

> A good classroom ... is one in which things are learned every day which the teacher did not previously know. (Stenhouse 1975: 37)

Further reading

Lejk, M. and Wyvill, M. (2002) 'Peer assessment of contributions to a group project: student attitudes to holistic and category-based approaches', *Assessment and Evaluation in Higher Education* 27 (6): 569–77.

Lejk, M., Wyvill, M. and Farrow, S (1996) 'A survey of methods of deriving individual grades from group assessments', *Assessment and Evaluation in Higher Education* 21 (3): 267–80.

Race, P. (2001) *A Briefing on Self, Peer and Group Assessment*, York: Learning and Teaching Support Network (LTSN).

Rust, C. (2001) *A Briefing on Assessment of Large Groups*, York: Learning and Teaching Support Network.

Tuckman, B. (1965) 'Developmental sequence in small groups'. *Psychology Bulletin* 63 (6): 384–99.

3 The academic teacher

Trevor Dawn

One of the many reasons for the huge expansion of further and adult education since the Second World War has come from the need to satisfy a growing demand for qualifications, originally occupational but now across the whole range of general, vocational and academic courses. Since the Crowther Report (1959) a wide range of vocational and academic courses and programmes of study have been developed in the post-compulsory sector.

In this chapter we will look at the values that inform our understanding of the term 'education' in relation to academic responsibilities particularly in the 16–19 age group and how these values translate into the practical issues of differentiation, inclusion and revising for examinations. We will place this in the wider context of the responsibility of the teacher in this phase in beginning to inculcate a feeling of scholarship and love of learning in their learners and in training them in the traditions and disciplines of academic study.

Introduction

Two recent phenomena, the proposed reform of the qualification structure (The Tomlinson Report (DfES 2004)) and the expansion of higher education, have had a great impact on the development of post-compulsory education.

The former has generated much debate about the relevance of the present fragmented collection of qualifications and awarding bodies to the needs of young people in the twenty-first century. Questions have been raised about the so-called academic/vocational divide; about the danger of over-specialization in the 16–19 age group; about the capacity of the curriculum to produce learners with critical thinking skills; about the need to develop social awareness, enriched personal skills and interests within the framework of a flexible approach to one's own qualifications profile.

The expansion of higher education is one of the issues subsumed within the Tomlinson debate, of course, but unlike the report itself, which has remained at the debating stage and has not resulted in actual changes of policy, the expansion of higher education is a fact. In 2005 the percentage of young people going on to higher education was 43 per cent, a staggering increase from the 15 per cent figure of the 1970s. In the White Paper of autumn 2005, the government has proposed that the percentage should rise further, with some members of the government seeing no ceiling on the numbers and with 50 per cent or more being talked about as a realistic aim. One could argue that the expansion of higher education is a natural concomitant to the expansion of non-advanced post-compulsory education which has seen a dramatic rise in the staying-on rate post-16 so that over 80 per cent of the 16–17 age cohort is in some form of education or training and not far off that figure in the 17–18 cohort (*Youth Cohort Study*, DfES, 2006). It has been a feature of the history of education in this country that developments in one phase have placed pressure for expansion at the next. Wardle (1970) calls this the 'autonomous expansion of education'.

> As a greater proportion of the population receives an effective secondary education there is an increase in the number of people qualified to enter higher education, and not only are these people qualified to enter universities and colleges, but their levels of aspiration have been raised by secondary education so that they expect to do so. (Wardle 1970)

Central to both the arguments for the reform of the qualifications system and the expansion of higher education is the issue of international competitiveness. We need a flexible, highly skilled, highly qualified workforce if we are to compete in the global economy. In some cases, this will mean taking on the competition and performing better in areas of high expertise that are already well established internationally; in other cases it will involve developing new ideas and products that are at the cutting edge of innovation.

The context is important. It is not the purpose of this book to argue the case for or against either the reform of the qualifications structure or the expansion of higher education. It *is* the purpose of this book, however, to equip teachers to fulfil their professional duties in the current climate and the current climate means preparing at least half of our young people for higher education within the current qualifications framework. It is also the purpose of this book to do so with sufficient flexibility and reference to first principles so that teachers are able to adapt to changes in government attitude and policy as and when they occur.

Values and the meaning of education

The issues of qualifications reform and the expansion of higher education present the teacher in the post-compulsory non-advanced sector with a number of challenges, not least the philosophical issue of what in essence do we mean by the term 'education'. There have been a number of Education Acts (1944, 1987, 1996) that have specified the aims of the school curriculum and the parameters of the content at each key stage or equivalent. Notions of breadth and balance, of aptitude and ability, of expected levels of attainment at each key stage, are part of the shared agenda of both professionals and parents. In post-compulsory education, there has been a succession of government-led papers looking at issues such as 'widening participation' (Kennedy 1997), 'lifelong learning' (Fryer 1997), 'skills for life' (Moser 1998), *Inclusive Learning* (Tomlinson 1996) and many more. These have stimulated some of the expansion to which reference was made earlier.

Statements about education cannot be divorced from values. Here is one example. Providing evidence of competence in certain key skills is now a mandatory requirement in the 16–19 curriculum. The reason for the compulsion is because employers, whoever they may be, are said to be alarmed at what they perceive as inadequate levels of literacy and numeracy and they have pressed for the accreditation of key skills in the profile of each young person. There is not space in this book to argue the merits of this decision. What we are saying is that in this case it appears that the role of education is to contribute to the wider needs of the economy, which is a value judgement. There are echoes here of the Callaghan speech at Ruskin College Oxford in 1976.

Where does this leave the teacher in post-compulsory education? There are conflicting values. On the one hand she/he is judged not simply on the number of her/his students who achieve the pass standard, but also on the number of grade A or A star or distinction in vocational courses that are achieved. Reputations of institutions and individual teachers are based on the grade profiles of examination candidates. League tables underpin this. On the other hand, teachers are expected to operate an open access policy where there should be no barriers to participation and where widening of choice is agreed to be a good thing.

In the 1960s and 1970s, educational philosophers such as Hirst and Peters tried to offer clarity about the nature of knowledge and the meaning of the term 'education'.

Hirst (1974) proposed the concept of 'forms' of knowledge whereby we could define subject characteristics and call them history or music or mathematics. This was contrasted with the concept of 'fields', where the nature of one's studies crossed over a number of forms and was therefore a composite. Geography and sociology were two of the so-called 'fields' in Hirst's time, though the number has expanded considerably since then and now includes, among others, media studies, communications studies, information technology, business studies and design. Hirst was seeking to give substance to our view of the nature of educational subjects, to reify something enshrined in the way we have traditionally categorized knowledge. Indeed, our whole library culture, grounded in the Dewey decimal system of classification, relies on a shared understanding of what is meant by terms such as 'philosophy' or 'psychology' or 'physics'. Hirst was attempting to open a debate about the changing nature of knowledge and the problems in having either too narrow a definition or too wide. But he unleashed a storm of emotional reaction largely from those engaged in 'fields' who felt that there was an implied higher status for 'forms'.

Peters (1966, 1967) was interested in the concept of education per se. His analysis of the concept was complex, but among the 'answers' he gave (1966) was that 'it must involve knowledge and understanding and some kind of cognitive perspectives which are not inert'. One of the aims of education was to do something well. Reactions to Peters were equally emotional, with accusations of elitism being raised. Surely education was more than the culmination of years of endeavour for the favoured few? What about the intrinsic value of the processes of education as they were happening: the sense of wonder of a child as she/he discovers something for her/himself, the sense of transformation as one became aware of the power of new learning, the acquisition of new skills and so on. Peters acknowledged that these processes and their attendant outcomes were indeed valid and he has perhaps received less recognition for this than he merits.

As is the nature of educational debate, the arguments remained unresolved and interest in such philosophical niceties has waned. But the issues have not gone away. Take the dilemma of the A/S teacher. Students are now expected to study four subjects at A/S level, though financial constraints limiting funding to three and changes in priorities after the Foster Report (DfES 2005) may alter this. The teacher does not know which students regard the subject as fundamental in a linear progression to higher education, such as A/S English followed by A2 English followed by a degree in English. The teacher also does not know which students see the subject as one of two or three subjects which all contribute to further progress, such as the importance of mathematics to the study of physics, or which students are seeing it as a taster and may drop the subject after one year. To what extent does the teacher attempt to lay the foundations for a continued immersion in the subject, ultimately leading to the Peters concept of 'mastery', and to what extent does she/he make it accessible to those who do not wish to immerse themselves in the process of mastery or who find that they lack the insights and skills to do so?

In terms of 'forms' or 'fields' there are different challenges. At one level, the post–compulsory teacher provides an invaluable service by initiating learners into the culture of the subject. For example, they can help learners get to grips with what it is that economists do; or explain the nature of sociology and explore the ideas of the giant figures who helped shape the way in which the subject is now studied; or clarify how the nature of chemistry is generally perceived and how particular discoveries or laws have influenced our understanding of its dimensions. The transmission of the subject culture is a necessary part of learning, but as the epistemological basis of knowledge expands, we find it increasingly difficult to uphold precise definitions of subject areas. How much of chemistry is now influenced by modern developments in physics? To what extent is our view of history influenced by science, for example in carbon-dating historical artefacts? We would be remiss in our duties as history teachers if we did not introduce our students to a Marxist critique of the English Civil War, even if we did not favour it.

Differentiation and inclusion

One of the functions of the existence of GCE Advanced level or equivalent in the non–advanced sector of post–compulsory education is to set everyone off on the road to potential mastery. Not everyone will see themselves in this light nor wish to stay the course whose ultimate goal is the status of a doctorate, but it is the formal start of the process.

Differentiation

Most people will confess that they did not get on with certain subjects. But the teacher, conscious of the pressures to achieve high grades, is forced to make difficult decisions. Dumbing down is not an option. It must be possible for a student to gain the highest grades or to be exposed to a more testing set of intellectual challenges.

Differentiation by task
In simple terms, this means setting work at different levels so that those with the highest ability are 'stretched' while those

who find a topic difficult are given work that is more suited to their ability. Differentiation in this way can also result from an institutional decision rather than a classroom decision, e.g. setting or streaming.

Differentiation by outcome
In simple terms, this means that the learning outcomes for each examination-style question or essay or assignment are graded in terms of either difficulty or increased complexity or expectations of greater depth. We will develop this notion later when we look at taxonomies of learning.

Differentiation by task *and* ability
It is possible to combine the two so that the interpretation of a task depends on the ability of the learner to utilize different types of equipment. This is often the case in art or design or computing where the ability to use more sophisticated equipment or techniques is as much part of differentiation as the impact of the finished product itself. Sometimes the value of an assignment lies in challenging learners' technical competence as well as their intellectual capability.

Inclusion

There is normally a range of learning outcomes and grade criteria in any subject or unit of study that extends from a pass or its grade equivalent through to merit and distinction or their grade equivalents. The teaching and learning experiences should be planned so that it is possible for a high percentage of learners to engage with the subject at advanced level and with appropriate teaching and support to achieve at least a pass.

There are several conditional factors here that have institutional dimensions. Schools and colleges have a named person whose role is to coordinate the following:

Guidance and advice
It should be 'possible' means just that. It does not mean that all who enrol should pass. Thought needs to be given as to what it

may mean for a student to discover or be advised that she/he is unlikely to succeed in a topic.

Baseline assessment

Initial assessment and previous records of achievement are important here. Advice should be given, and recorded in some cases, as to what is expected in the subject and the difficulties that may be encountered, e.g. that a higher facility in maths or statistics may be needed to cope with the course.

Support

What is meant by 'support'? Again, there should be initial assessment and, in some cases such as dyslexia, a recognized level of support is available and should be applied. There may be physical support too for learners who have difficulties with hearing or sight or other physiological needs.

The more problematic issue is 'appropriate' teaching. How does one teach across such a potentially wide range so that the needs of the predicted A star candidate and the person who attempts but does not achieve a pass are equally met?

One of the ways of doing this is to become familiar with the notion of *taxonomies* and to become more experienced in using them in planning. This point is also emphasized by the Learning and Skills Research Centre (LSRC) findings on post-16 pedagogy and thinking skills (Livingston *et al.* 2004): 'the result of searches made during the project support Moseley *et al.*'s findings (2003) that there are no UK studies in which syllabuses, course planning, assessment tools or learning-related discourse have been analysed using a framework of a taxonomy of thinking skills'. Without a taxonomy, it is difficult to see progression from simple cognitive actions to meta-cognition.

Taxonomies and the structure of knowledge

Some attempts have been made to determine a generalized progression from lower-level to higher-level thinking irrespective of 'forms' or 'fields' of knowledge in the Dewey decimal classification sense. We call this type of classification a 'taxonomy'. Few people have undertaken this complex task and all attempts have received criticism.

The taxonomies that we have found the most useful are those of Bloom (1956) and Taba (1966, 1967).

Bloom's taxonomy of educational objectives

Bloom and his collaborators (1956) produced a taxonomy or classification chart (see Table 1) to demonstrate the relationships between various cognitive acts and their associated action verbs. It is hierarchical in design to represent progression from lower level to higher level thinking.

It is presented here in a précis form (Walklin 1990) in Table 2.

Table 2: Bloom's taxonomy − The cognitive domain

Simple recall of knowledge
Emphasis placed upon remembering facts or terminology without the need to understand that which is recalled.

Comprehension
Elementary level of understanding. The students should be able to explain what they are doing when using information such as a formula.

Application
Having comprehended the meaning of a given subject, the students are able to relate the knowledge to other different situations. They should be able to generalize, using basic principles, and to apply knowledge.

Analysis
The breaking down of a statement or operation into its basic components and the relating of each component to the remainder.

Synthesis
The assembling of a variety of concepts or elements so as to form a new arrangement.

Evaluation
Making value judgements about arrangements, arguments or methods. Highlighting strengths and weaknesses in arguments and assessing the points for and against.

Taba's taxonomy

The basic premise of the Taba model (see Table 1, p. 26) is similar in one sense to that of Bloom, in that it is possible to classify the different 'phases' of learning to produce a progression from the simple to the complex. This becomes important when we consider that the teacher has a responsibility to cater for both inclusion and differentiation.

Note
Taxonomies are a guide to structure, especially to progression and differentiation. We also have to think about inclusion and would argue that taxonomies add a structural dimension to the understandings you have gained from previous chapters such as:

- utilizing the principles of the Yerkes–Dodson curve
- avoiding over-reliance on the 'traditional' triangle
- handling small groups
- ensuring that the 'recipe' for the lesson is such that it will appeal to the whole range of learning styles

What therefore are the teacher's 'academic' responsibilities?

The nature of advanced level subjects and their role in the journey towards higher education have led to the concept of excellence as the prime responsibility of the 'academic' teacher. Ramsden (2003), making a similar point, cites Whitehead (1929: 139–45) as a major figure in this regard; 'his main theme was that a university education should lead students to "the imaginative acquisition of knowledge"'. More recently, the Dearing Report into Higher Education (1997) argued that a university education should 'inspire and enable individuals to develop their capabilities to the highest potential throughout life, so that they grow intellectually, are well equipped for work, can contribute effectively to society and achieve personal fulfilment.'

Most A level teachers have come through the university route and have taken on board the values of scholarship and excellence and are happy to be part of a historical continuum that continues the tradition. Others have challenged this paradigm, arguing that such values are culturally determined. This has led to periods when the traditional view of academic training has been modified and syllabuses have been broadened to introduce new ideas. In the end, the tendency to intellectualize any subject comes through. It is not the purpose of this book to make a case either way and each reader may have a different viewpoint. Personal perspectives will be subordinate to the continuing academic tradition.

To translate these traditional values into a coherent praxis, the teacher needs to deal with a number of practical issues, such as:

1   covering the syllabus
2   preparing learners for the requirements of the summative assessment, usually with an examination bias
3   training learners in:
    ● the academic conventions in your subject
    ● the correct application of agreed bibliographical protocols
    ● the correct referencing of sources
4   developing abstract thinking skills or abstract conceptualization (Kolb, Taba, Bloom, de Bono)
5   ensuring differentiation

What are the main challenges for the teacher?

On a day-to-day basis, there are a number of simultaneous challenges, which influence the ways in which teachers meet their responsibilities and prioritize their practice. Here are some of them:

1   transmitting data and ensuring that learners are familiar with accepted lines of academic enquiry in the subject
2   meeting the learning styles of all the students
3   differentiation by outcome to reflect a five-point grade profile at pass level and above
4   introducing learners to different theories, interpretations and ways of thinking about a given topic or subject

5   motivating learners and remaining true to the principles
    of facilitation
6   initiating and sustaining learner interest

The practical implementation of these challenges
Let us look at these challenges in a little more detail.

Transmitting data – what does this mean for the teacher?
In practice, this means addressing the issue of notes and note-taking:

- If you expect learners to make notes while you speak, you need to allow time for them to do so. Where possible, use some form of structure such as overhead transparencies (OHTs) or PowerPoint slides – indicate where notes should be added.
- Inform learners at the start of the lesson, if you do not expect them to take notes because there is a handout (this could be designed by you or come from other sources).
- As a variation, you may wish to use a gapped handout from time to time.

Introducing learners to a variety of sources
These will include:

- extracts from established texts in books
- articles from journals
- references to official publications and legal documents
- Internet references

Sometimes you will provide the references yourself as part of the flow of the lesson, showing the learners that at particular points the topic can be approached in a variety of ways and that there are a number of valid theoretical perspectives, of which they need to be aware. This is likely to be the pattern in the earlier months of the course. At other times, you will put the onus on the learners to do the research themselves, with appropriate guidance from you, and, perhaps, to inform the rest of the class what they have learned.

Meeting learner expectations
(For this age group, this will also include the expectations of their parents.)

- Learners need to know that you have high expectations and that high levels of academic progress will be made.
- Of course, this has to be handled with tact and in line with the principles of the Yerkes–Dodson curve in Chapter 1. But, deep down, students want to be 'pushed' and will thrive if this is done in a realistic manner and is seen to be fundamental to the whole delivery of the subject.
- They will want to be worked reasonably hard. You will be compared with other teachers, so it is important that there is an agreed policy about the amount of homework or directed study that each subject should be setting.

Initiating and sustaining learner interest
In a standard post-compulsory timetable of three 90-minute sessions per week, you will need to think about some simple patterns of teaching so that the transmitting of data such as notes or the incorporation of established theory does not become so time-consuming that there is no time for intellectual sparring among the learners and of the learners with you.

Here we can see the practical value of taxonomies. They give pointers to the sort of activities that everyone can attempt and find interesting (inclusion), thereby initiating interest, while offering the teacher a template for sustaining interest and stretching those who need stretching (differentiation).

Closing an academic lesson

The same principles apply to the 'academic' lesson as they do to any other lesson. I can still remember, as an A level student, being bowled over by new ideas and the sensation that I was entering an exciting and unknown world. I needed time to digest ideas that had been presented seventy, fifty or thirty minutes earlier which now had to compete with those in the last few minutes as well as with those from previous weeks and from my reading.

The techniques discussed in Chapter 1 will sustain you when you are planning your timings. No matter what the situation, always allow 10–15 per cent of your time for learners to make sense of their new status as their learning develops. This is congruent with the values of deep learning in Chapter 1.

Public examinations

Public examinations in this context mean examinations that are set and marked externally through the auspices of an examination board. It is not the purpose of this book to engage in a debate about the merits of examinations, about issues of reliability and validity, about the morality of placing people under stress and so on. There are other books (Walklin 1990, Minton 1991) that place examinations in the wider arena of assessment methods and offer a balanced critique of arguments for and against. There are further studies, such as Biggs (1996), evaluated in the LSRC report, Livingston et al. (2004), that question the whole relationship of assessment to the development of thinking skills. The evaluation report (Livingston et al. 2004) urges teachers to 'avoid setting tasks which fail to challenge students' thinking'. There is no guarantee that the public examinations will do that but we need to prepare learners on the assumption that they will.

Whatever one's views of examinations, whether one is opposed to them or whether one seeks to reform them in some way, for example in line with the Tomlinson Report (DfES 2004), public examinations are a fact of life for the majority of teachers who teach 16–19 year olds in post-compulsory education. Teachers have to deal with the here and now. There seems to be no prospect that public examinations will decline in importance either in the eyes of government or higher education institutions or employers.

Revising for public examinations

Even before you start teaching a topic and certainly well before the revision stage of the course, you will have collected a stock of previous examination papers and reports of the chief examiner(s). You will have begun to know the structure of the examination in terms of the types of questions set, i.e. short answers, longer answers, multiple-choice questions, answers related to source material, answers linked to previous preparation time and so on.

Joining the local branch of the national association of teachers in your subject will put you in touch with a wide cross-section of fellow professionals from whom you can seek advice. It is also a good idea to become an examiner yourself, even for a few years, to benefit from the experience of other colleagues.

Below we have set out some principles and some hints concerning revision techniques. However, examination revision, like any other part of teaching and learning, is a matter of personal taste and these ideas may not suit everyone.

Principles

1 Make sure you allow adequate time for revision. It is a good idea to build in a little revision throughout the course and not to leave it all till the last few weeks.

2 Your aim should be to empower your learners to be better at revising on their own – teach them techniques and not formulaic answers.

3 Be clear about your objectives – you do not have the time to go through the whole syllabus again, so prioritize.

4 Acquire previous papers set by the same examination board, use the actual questions as the basis for a revision lesson and invent some of your own. Bring common errors to students' attention and demonstrate ways in which to avoid them.

5 Try to have more than one theme for each revision lesson. It is not your role, and not the best use of your time, to go into too much detail. Concentrate on the *structure* of the answer; in particular, get the students to analyse key words in the question to see what the examiners are looking for, then think about the impact of the opening paragraph, then the main headings for subsequent paragraphs, and key facts.

6 Try to think up some different approaches to make

revision fresh and interesting, thus preventing boredom or complacency and minimizing panic in some cases. We will be saying more on this a little later under 'techniques for early revision lessons'.

7   Use timings effectively. In a 90-minute lesson, work out how many topics you could usefully cover and plan accordingly. This will depend on whether you choose short questions worth, say, six marks, in which case you may want several topics, or longer questions worth, say, twenty marks, in which three or four questions in the lesson might be sufficient.

Remember

- For some topics it may be over six months since you first taught it. You do not want to *scare* the learners by exposing too much of what they do not know (you may also be a little rusty or lacking confidence yourself in your first few years of teaching).
- They may not immediately be able to drag much knowledge from their memory banks, so you may need to stimulate their memories by using imaginative techniques. We will be saying more on this in the next two sections.
- Successful preparation for examinations is not a soft option for the teacher. Like any other lesson, revision needs planning carefully and the more you plan, the better it will go.

Techniques for early revision lessons

'Early' in this context means any revision up to about six weeks to one month before the date of the first examination in your subject.

1   Devise some revision sheets on a topic for which YOU have structured the outline of an answer to a specific question from a past paper including *some* of the facts. The students' tasks are a) to give x reasons why you have structured the answer in this way by reference to key words in the question, and b) to supply as much missing detail as possible. You will, of course, encourage them to

give their reaction to the actual structure and to see if they have any alternative ideas.

2   A variation is again for you to supply the outline structure accompanied by a pack of key facts around a particular answer. Then get the students to select what they consider are the most useful facts and apply them to the structure. Once more, you will encourage critical discourse as above.

3   As you get more experienced, you will save some scripts from previous mock examinations and, having ensured that the scripts are anonymous and cannot be traced, get the students to mark/grade them as if THEY were the examiners. You will supply a marking scheme with criteria for each grade. You then act as chief examiner and chair the discussion as to why one should receive an A, one a C and one an E.

4   In the last twenty minutes of a 'normal' lesson, introduce an examination question from earlier in the syllabus. You will need to be strict on your timings. So, start with a five-minute brainstorm for the whole class on facts (or for small groups if you prefer); then five minutes on a whole-class discussion on the nature of the question and what each key word signifies; then get them to try an outline structure of an answer for about seven minutes; then bring the topic a to a conclusion. You can adapt and expand this approach.

5   Acquire some plain white A6 cards. Tell the students they have x minutes individually with no conferring (or pairs with no other conferring if you think this advisable) to write the main points to a question on ONE card only. Get the students to swap cards with each other several times and then to discuss the merits of each card. One advantage of cards is that they can be used as 'crib' cards in the last few days before the exam.

6   A variation on this would be to devise a mind map, preferably in colour, whether on the card or on a sheet of A4.

Getting nearer to the examination

This will vary with A/S, A2 and other examination bodies, but let us say for argument's sake about one month to six weeks before the first examination in your subject.

1 Split the 90 minutes into two, with the first part given over to a timed longer question which you will take away to mark, thus providing a realistic simulation of the examination conditions. It is up to you (and the students) whether you allow 'open' books at this stage. In the second part of the lesson, you can adopt some of the other techniques we have mentioned.

2 Choose a question from a previous examination paper and get the students to devise a marking scheme for it. Ask them to set out the criteria for grades A–E and after a few minutes begin a whole-class discussion. You can use this in conjunction with 1 above.

3 Tell the class 'you have five minutes to plan this question'. If they ask 'why?', tell them that that is about the amount of time you could safely allow yourself in the exam. After the five minutes are up (and you need to be fairly strict on the timings), they swap their plan with a friend and agree a composite plan for the two of them incorporating the best features of each, again taking about five minutes. You can build this up to fours if you wish or simply invite each pair to present their plan for the others to discuss.

4 In groups, students are given a fixed amount of time to devise either short questions (six marks or less) or multiple-choice for other groups to answer, but they must know the answers themselves or they are penalized in some way. They could use books sometimes or memory nearer the exam. How you make this competitive or apply penalties is up to you (or them) but we find that sweets work well (see also Chapter 2).

5 You might also have an activity with a good essay (you might have to write it yourself – or use the board's model answers) cut up into paragraphs for the students to arrange in order. When they've got it right and

know why it's right they can stick it down and take it away.

6   You could also try to find out in advance if there's any particular topic that they found tricky and would like to revise so that you can make sure you're totally up to speed and have it at your fingertips.

7   The Internet now contains specimen examination questions and answers in virtually all subject areas. They can be a boon, but take care. Try to have vetted them where possible so that the students have some guidance as to what is and what is not reliable.

General points on revision

With revision, it is necessary to prune down to essentials and the most effective thing is for you to train the learners to do their own pruning. You cannot be in the examination room with them, so you will need to help them develop the skills and the confidence necessary for them to cope on their own. Systematic exposure to good revision technique is a natural follow-on to the learning checks and emphasis on personal meaningfulness in learning that is at the heart of good teaching. The principles we have outlined and the early training in revision will support you as you seek to prepare the learners to show off what they know.

Conclusion

We have tried to keep a balance in this chapter between values and professional skill, arguing that teachers have to operate successfully in the here and now, whatever their personal beliefs. Transcending fashion and preference, however, teachers have always had a responsibility to inculcate a feeling of scholarship and love of learning in their learners and to train them in the traditions and disciplines of academic study. They are gatekeepers to later generations.

Further reading

Bloom, B. S. (1956) *Taxonomy of Educational Objectives*, Book 1: *Cognitive Domain*, London: Longman.

Taba (1967) in Eggen, P. P., Kauchak, D. P. and Harder, R. J. (1979) *Strategies for Teachers: Teaching Content and Thinking Skills*, Englewood Cliffs, NJ: Prentice Hall.

Hirst, P. H. and Peters, R. S. (1970) *The Logic of Education*, London: Routledge & Kegan Paul.

4 Using role-play

Ros Clow

When carrying out the 'Just teachers' research (Clow 2005) one of the findings that surprised me was that 70 per cent of the respondents (full-time FE teachers) indicated that they used role-play in their teaching. Despite the fact that since my early days of teaching I have regularly used role-play, I had not expected that this was common practice. It was also a matter for concern, since as a staff developer and teacher trainer I was aware that many colleagues were using role-play without a real consideration of its function in any particular lesson and without being aware that it is a very risky teaching method.

In this chapter I shall explore the essential rules of using role-play, examine the many ways I have experienced its use in post-compulsory education and analyse why it sometimes goes wrong. When I began training as an FE teacher in the early 1980s, I was already using role-play with adults in my assert-iveness training courses and with 16–19 year olds in social and life skills classes. I benefited immensely from the Morry van Ments book, *The Effective Use of Role-Play*, which had recently been published (1983). In preparing this chapter, I have reread the book and would still recommend it to those who are wanting to extend their repertoire of role-plays or who would like a variety of structures to use as the basis for in-depth reflection on role-play in practice (van Ments 1999)

What is role-play?

Role-play has so many guises that it is difficult to define absolutely. Van Ments suggests that it is a type of simulation – that is a simplified reproduction of the world. I would agree with this. He also suggests that it focuses on interaction. In this chapter I will use a wider definition. Role-play in teaching is where the learners become resources that can immensely increase understanding in both knowledge and skills. This definition stems from a challenge. For some of the time I was training to teach, I was employed in an engineering department. My technically based colleagues were adamant that role-play could not be used in their lessons, so I had to prove them wrong. I was teaching maths at the time and decided to use 'role-play', or learners as resources, to teach binomial theory. This is what I did.

I asked four students to come out to the front, each to sit on a chair facing the rest of the class. I had prepared slips of paper to act as 'units'. I gave one unit to the student on the right and told him to stand up. All students were told that when they had two 'units' (a 'bit') they had to pass them to their right and sit down. As I passed 'units' to the first student there was lots of passing on stapled-together 'bits', standing up and sitting down, much hilarity, but at any stage I was able to stop the proceedings and the class could write down the binary number (e.g. 1001) according to who was standing up or sitting down, and then the role-players could add up their total number of units. Not the cleanest example of maths teaching, but nevertheless it removed the mystery of binomials, I hope, forever. And I had proved a point! Later we developed complex role-plays to assess HND students' core skills (but more of that later).

Role-play to develop skills

Role-play lends itself very well to the development of social and communication skills. In particular, some skills can only be developed by using role-play. The most straightforward example of this is in teaching assertiveness. In a good assertiveness class, the techniques are explained, the 'wrong' approaches (passive, aggressive and manipulative) described and the appropriate techniques demonstrated by the tutor. Then it is the students' turn. I have seen a tutor then select students from the group and ask them to do a role-play in front of the others. I consider this 'fishbowl' technique inappropriate in this kind of class. Most assertiveness students self-select and come to classes because they are insecure in their communication skills. They could find this approach threatening. Moreover most of the class will just be observing and not practising. In assertiveness training, the techniques eventually have to become automatic and the way to start students on their way to that is lots of practice in class.

So the way forward is to divide the group into pairs (with a three if there are uneven numbers) and give them scenarios in which to role-play and use the different techniques, e.g. broken record; saying no; self-disclosure; giving and receiving criticism and, last but not least, giving and receiving compliments (Dickson 2002).

It was in the last session that role-play provided the greatest challenges. It is not in our culture to compliment each other. The role-play I would set is that each student would compliment their partner and the partner would receive the compliment assertively. At this stage, they would have been in class for about four sessions, so would know a little about each other. The demonstration I gave was that three of them in the group would pay me a compliment (I always enjoyed this bit) and I would give a typical non-assertive, usually passive response.

Compliment: I do like that blouse you're wearing.

Non-assertive response: What this old thing? I got it in the sale, I've had it ages.

Then I would ask them to make the same compliment again and respond assertively. That is to say accept the compliment and maybe build on it. The thinking behind this is that by accepting the compliment you acknowledge the good taste of the person paying the compliment and maintain your own self-esteem.

Compliment: I do like that blouse you're wearing.

Assertive response: Thank you, I always feel good in it.

Easy enough, but it caused so many problems in the 'multiple' role-plays. I had one pair (two men) who could not think of a single compliment to pay each other! And during debriefing, one bookshop manager confessed that she had never once paid a compliment to any of her staff and a different woman dissolved into tears, as it had made her realize that her husband never said she looked good, however much effort she had made before they went out in the evening. And, perhaps most disconcerting, a manager in a large technically based company stayed at the end to say the class had really upset him; I had no idea how difficult it was for him to contemplate telling one of his staff they had done something well!

So here was an example of a short, unscripted role-play on what might have been expected to be a non-intrusive issue, raising all kinds of emotions that had to be dealt with in some way.

When I was teaching social and life skills to teenagers, I used role-play in a variety of ways. One role-play lasted over several lessons. The students were in small groups and given the scenario that they were sharing a flat. They had a budget for all shopping. They had to plan all their breakfasts and evening meals for a week, cost all the ingredients (including the take-aways they liked to include) and then negotiate the menus to agree a shopping list that fitted the budget. This raised all kinds of issues: healthy eating, ability to cook, the enormous cost of takeaways, alcohol and cigarettes. I always enjoyed the fact that they never considered the extras: light bulbs, toothpaste, toilet rolls. Despite the fact that these were disadvantaged students, equivalent of E2E students today, they were totally engrossed for hours at a time with this exercise, going out to supermarkets to cost items, looking up recipes so that they knew what to buy.

Another area where role-play was used successfully was with trainee hairdressers. Communication skills are extremely important for hairdressers. They will need to know to ask about family and holidays with their regular clients but, using role-play, we explored the more difficult areas. Some trainees became clients and were blindfolded while the hairdressers were going to practise how to meet and greet them, guide them to the sink, explain what they were doing, advise suitable treatments and cuts. Always at some stage I held up a sign saying 'Laugh loudly as if you have just heard a funny joke'. During the debrief stage the 'clients' always said that they had assumed that the laughter was directed at them, thus underlining the importance of explaining everything that is going on to a visually impaired customer.

Another session using role-play explored difficult customers in terms of starting to work on the appointment and noticing that the client had 'nits' and difficult colleagues where the hairdresser had BO. In all of these sessions, the role-play helped the students to experience difficult scenarios, discuss and analyse them and make plans about how to deal with them when they happened in the real world of the future.

Customer care skills is another area where role-play can be used fruitfully. This can apply at all levels of ability. I observed an E2E class recently where the tutor role-played being the shop assistant and one or two students volunteered to be shoppers. The tutor did a very bad job of being a shop assistant, committing all the usual errors, much to the delight of his students. They were then able to correct him and tell him how to do it better using their experiences from earlier visits to different shops in the town, where a range of customer care skills had been seen. With more able students, they can put into practice skills they have seen demonstrated and be the 'good practice' shop assistant dealing with a range of difficult customers.

Morry van Ments's rules

When I was expanding my repertoire of uses for role-play I referred in detail to the flow chart provided by van Ments.

Over the years I have distilled this down to six key points that are absolutely essential when using role-play in teaching.

1 Setting the objectives
Although role-play can be a useful 'change of state' in any lesson, if any length of time is going to be taken up by it, then you must be clear about how it will contribute to the overall aims and objectives of the scheme of work. It is possibly the easiest way to introduce experiential learning into the programme and this will usually appeal to some though not all of your learners.

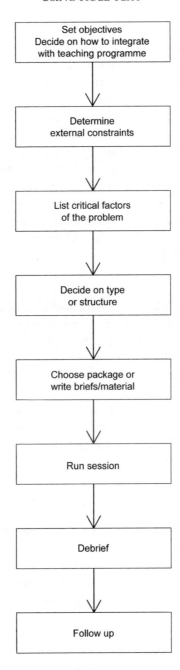

Figure 6: Role-play flow chart

2 Warm-up?

If you are working with a group of students over many weeks or months, then the warmth will come from you (Harkin, Turner and Dawn 2001). By the time you introduce role-play, you should have a good relationship with your students and they will feel comfortable to put their trust in you. You should be able to judge whether you need some kind of warm-up exercise or whether you can go straight to role-play preparation. If you do not know the students well, then you will need to loosen everyone up by using a warm-up. There are lots of ideas around for warm-ups (van Ments 1999: 72, Brandes and Phillips 1979, Ginnis 2002). In the usual kind of lesson where you want to use role-play, you will want the warm-up to take up as little time as possible.

3 Preparation

During the lesson-plan stage, you will have decided what kind of role-play to use. If you are using role briefs, you will have either copied them or written them. If you are using a video prompt, you will have it ready in the right place; if you are going to demonstrate a skill, you will have decided how to set that up.

You will need some time in the lesson to set up the role-play. This might involve moving furniture, role-players reading their briefs, observers finding paper and pens or writing labels for participants. This brings me on to the important topic of role names.

4 Role names

I think it always safer for everyone in a role-play to be given a role name. With short practice role-plays, like the ones in assertiveness, it might not be necessary, but as a general rule, if in doubt, change names. So, whenever a role-play starts, none of the players are using their own name.

5 The session

You will need to manage the session, telling the students when it is starting and being very firm about when it stops. There is no need to say exactly how long it will last, maybe just give an idea: 'about five minutes'. You can leave it to run for longer if it seems to be providing good material for discussion or stop it earlier if students start to sabotage it or lose interest.

6 The debrief

This is the most important part of role-play in many different ways. If you are using role-play in one session, you need to allow time for warm-up and preparation, time for the role-play and time for debrief, perhaps in the ratio 1:2:3. It is during the debrief that the objectives are achieved for the whole group.

During the debrief, you begin to discuss the experiences of both players and observers. You always start with the key players, asking them questions as if they are still in role: Why did you do that? Why did you ignore him? Did it occur to you to react differently?

As you open it up to the others, you make sure that they only comment on the behaviour of the role, using the role name. Then as discussion develops you make sure that you ask the key participants, using their real name, to comment on the behaviour of the roles that they played. In this way, you hope to distance them from the role they played, so that they can view it dispassionately and not be left with unfinished business from the role-play.

The purposes of debriefing (van Ments 1999)

1. Bring players out of role
2. Clarify what happened (on factual level)
3. Correct misunderstandings and mistakes
4. Dissipate tension/anxiety
5. Bring out assumptions, feelings and changes which occurred during run
6. Give players opportunity to develop self-observation
7. Develop observational skills
8. Relate outcome to original aims
9. Analyse why things happened that way
10. Draw conclusions about behaviour
11. Reinforce or correct learning

12 Draw out new points for consideration
13 Deduce ways of improving behaviour
14 Apply to other situations
15 Link with previous learning
16 Provide plan for future learning

If there is not enough time to do the debrief, then it is probably not a good idea to run the role-play.

Even when trying to work exactly to the rules, sometimes role-play can have unanticipated effects. I used role-play on a regular basis when I was teaching A/O level family and community studies. This was an unusual course which had no content syllabus. The exams posed a series of problematic scenarios covering social, economic, political and personal issues and the students had to use well-organized reasoning to identify possible solutions and justify their choice of solution. For part of the course, I used role-play as a stimulus at the beginning of some of the lessons. I wrote detailed role briefs (as suggested by van Ments; see example in Chapter 11), asked for volunteers to play the roles, gave them about 5–10 minutes to read the briefs, ran the role-play, stopped the role-play after 5–10 minutes and then used the rest of the one-hour lesson to debrief and discuss. I used a range of scenarios, mostly to do with family relationships: the daughter discovers she's pregnant by the boyfriend she's just chucked; a mother discovers that her daughter is planning her engagement party and she has not met her daughter's boyfriend yet; a son has been caught stealing from a neighbour's shed; a neighbour complains that she thinks her daughter is being stalked as she has received a pornographic letter and you realize that it is your son's writing on the envelope. Just normal everyday life!

One scenario concerned unemployment (see example briefs in Chapter 11). It was set in a 'steel' town where the mills had been shut down and the man of the household (Graham) had been made redundant three or four years ago. He is happily married, but as time goes by he loses all hope of getting another job. His wife does voluntary work at the local community centre and to her surprise she is offered a full-time paid job as deputy manager of the community centre. She is delighted: all their troubles are over. The interaction starts with her coming home to tell her husband what has happened. Other players included a daughter still at school, and a son who thinks he will have to move away to find work when he leaves school.

My students were great. They played their roles really realistically; there was lots of angst and shouting. I stopped the role-play, as it appeared to run out of steam. Debriefing followed and then good discussion on family roles and the needs of unemployed men (this was the early 1980s). That was Monday. When I walked into the building to teach on Thursday I was met by a deputation of students asking me to sort out Shane, the student who had played Graham. He had been shouting and yelling at them all week and they felt he was still in role. He was intending to go into the police at that stage and normally was quite quiet and good company. I did my best and began this lesson with further debriefing. I hoped it worked, but the last I heard of Shane was that he was a professional footballer playing for Portsmouth!

What I had not known, nor could I have, was that Shane's father was very much the role model for Graham. I later discovered this was the way his father behaved most of the time. The problem is that, however well you know your students, you will never know everything about them. This is why role-play can be risky. It is excellent at enabling students to 'feel, react and behave' (van Ments 1999) but, just occasionally, it presses a button you did not expect.

This also happened when I was using role-play in the training of antenatal teachers. Basically, this was a telephone skills training session. The first contact with National Childbirth Trust antenatal teachers was usually by phone and much of their work continues over the phone. We used standard telephone skills, role-play technique: the teacher was playing herself, and the caller had a role brief, complete with role name. The first scenario was a pregnant mother making contact to ask about classes. She did not want to know anything about drugs or caesareans as she wanted a completely natural birth. This was quite a common scenario and all went well with good debriefing and discussion afterwards. The second scenario was more difficult. This was a phone call from the hospital after a baby had been born with Down's syndrome. The baby's father wanted to leave the baby in hospital as he was not the perfect baby expected; the mother was understandably distraught and phoned the NCT teacher for advice. I chose one of my trainee teachers as the NCT teacher. She was very promising, happily married and had had three children and I expected her to cope well with the difficult scenario.

As usual, we set up the two participants back to back so as not to be able to use body language and the role-play started. We were well aware how difficult the role would be for the 'mother' so she had been chosen carefully too. About 5 minutes into the role-play, my trainee burst into tears, apologized and said she couldn't do it, picked up her things, told me she would write to me and left! So much for debriefing! We continued to the end of the study day, all feeling a bit shaken. When the letter came, it transpired that while she had been training with me she had become pregnant. Her husband was adamant he did not want another baby and she had had an abortion. She thought she had dealt with it, but the role-play was too close to home and aroused feelings she had been denying. She apologized for not telling me. She knew that I would not have had her in either role if I had known the situation.

Whole group role-plays

Role-play can be used where all the students in the group have a role and they can use role-play to explore issues where no absolute answer is possible. The first time I used this was on the topic of health economics, with a low-ability teenage group. At the time, there was a national appeal to raise thousands of pounds to pay for a liver transplant for a young boy. The students were very sympathetic to this but could not understand why the 'government' could not pay for it. There was no way I could have delivered a lecture or even a discussion on this, as they had very little life experience to bring to the issue. I set them up as the local health authority council, each bringing a request for funding over the next year. There was an available budget and they had to decide how to spend their money. Each student had a role name and a card describing a patient or a health or care issue which needed funding. The kinds of requests for funds covered a range of issues: a liver transplant for a young boy, an old people's home place for someone's gran who had Alzheimer's, abortions for unmarried mothers, vaccinations for all the children against polio/tetanus, dialysis for someone's mother, a heart transplant for a 70-year-old man, etc. Each request had a sum of money against it (made as realistic as I could), a good reason why that request should be allowed – and the budget did not cover all the needs. Looking back on this, I realize how well these youngsters responded to this kind of role-play, took it mostly seriously and came up with credible solutions. We outlawed the suggestion that everyone over 60 should be put down! But I am afraid the liver transplant boy was relegated to a TV appeal for his operation – it was just too expensive for the HAC.

Another whole-group role-play with a similar group put all of them in the role of employees in an IT company (they were on an IT course). They each had their role name and a card which gave them their holiday entitlement and a reason for needing to take their holiday at a certain time of year. They had some large copies of the calendar for the coming year. The scenario was that their boss wanted them to negotiate their next year's holiday within the company rules that there must always be a certain number of people at work. This provided good practice at talking, listening, stating a case, negotiating and an insight into the real world. I had set it up so that three or four people, all for very good but different reasons, had to take their holiday at the same time and this would leave the office understaffed. This meant that they had to renegotiate several times. I always think that it is good to realize that in life there is seldom one correct answer.

Another example of a whole-group role-play was with national diploma engineering students, in their general studies class. This was an example of a public enquiry used as the focus of a role-play. The purpose was to illustrate 'vested interests' in the real world, in this case using the Newbury bypass as the planning issue. This was many years before the bypass was built, but I was able to obtain maps showing the three possible routes: one a tunnel through the centre of the town; the second a road to the east of Newbury which gave the nearby town of Thatcham, which had a not insignificant industry base, good access to the road and the third, the western route, which cut through areas of natural beauty and would be within hearing distance of the Watermill Theatre. Each student was given a role name and a role which meant they would speak at the enquiry for or against a particular route. So, in this case: a resident who lived near the proposed tunnel site; a parent who objected to the tunnel route bringing even more lead pollution to the children's park; Friends of the Earth who objected to the western route because of damage to the countryside; a representative of the theatre complaining that the traffic noise would interfere with all their performances; a member of the landed gentry to state that the eastern route was impossible because the racecourse was in direct line; an RAF officer arguing that the cruise missile bunkers could not be moved to accommodate the eastern bypass, plus many others. This was an able group, all engineering apprentices at local engineering companies, and they put their cases well. After the role-play, we were able to discuss what had actually happened and why the western route had been chosen – a useful lesson in the relative power of different sections of society.

Other types of role-play can introduce students to specific technical roles needed in their vocational area. An HND construction group becomes a project management team planning a particular building, the new art block to be built in the town-centre campus of an FE college. The project team all took specific 'real' roles and met over several weeks. They collected information from college management, art teachers and the students' union, and technical documents. There was a chair and a minutes secretary. The tutor observed their meetings and was able to assess each individual's contribution.

Similarly it is quite common for law students to role-play a court scene. This is called a moot and everyone will take on the various roles of the courtroom. As in all these whole-group role-plays, preparation is key and participants have to be given, or given the opportunity to obtain, enough information so that they feel confident to take on their role in a way that enables everyone to benefit from the learning aspects of the role-play.

Role-play in assessment

Role-play can be an added extra for assessment, or in some situations it provides the most valid method of assessment available. In the latter case, competence-based qualifications will always need to be able to fall back on role-play for certain performance criteria. If you need to demonstrate ability to deal with a difficult customer, despite the fact there are plenty of them around, you may need to use a simulation including role-play in order to be assessed as to how you deal with them. It is often the most difficult scenarios that need role-play as a fall-back: a nurse breaking bad news to a patient or patient's relatives; a client becoming upset during counselling; dismissing someone from their job. As always, this needs to be set up with sensitivity and it is essential that the students trust the tutor.

As mentioned earlier, I was able to build a complex role-play into assessment of the HND in software engineering and HND engineering (software). They were two different courses! The scenario was based on a business which grew orchids. Their commercial greenhouses had been destroyed in the recent hurricane and they were looking for a company to erect new greenhouses with state of the art technical features. Preparation for the role-play included: drawing a map of the site, showing the proprietor's house and the greenhouses; researching the temperature, humidity, nutritional and watering needs of orchids and taking two other colleagues from the engineering and science department to be on the panel with me. The staff role-played the proprietors and an orchid expert.

The students were put into groups by their tutor and given an appointment when they could meet with us. They had to prepare questions and then had about 20 minutes to find out as much relevant information as they could. Essentially, they had to design a rooflight that was controlled by temperature and humidity sensors and an alarm system which summoned the proprietors if there was a danger of damage to the orchids.

They had a week in which to review their information and then they visited the panel again with their initial ideas and had a second opportunity to find out what they needed to know. Thereafter, the project ran all term and we were invited to demonstrations of all their opening windows (which they were very proud of!)

Of course, their tutor could have just written out the specification and a briefing sheet and technically they would have achieved the same thing. The role-play allowed us to assess their communication skills (especially their questioning skills), their teamworking skills and their ability to analyse a design problem. And they took on the professional engineering role. They arrived dressed in suits and behaved as if they were electronic systems engineers. Once again, role-play gave a taste of the real world (and BTEC liked it too!)

Occasionally, I used role-play without having prepared it. On one occasion, I was teaching general and communication studies to motor vehicle technicians. It was the time of the miners' strike and I planned to lead a discussion using newspaper cuttings and TV coverage. It became clear that the students had no empathy at all with what was going on and could only see the issue from their own distant perspectives. So – a change of plan! I made each student take on the role of a different faction of the dispute (Nottinghamshire miners, miners' wives, local police, London police, bus drivers, Welsh miners, the government). We used the classroom as a map of England and Wales and then began to develop the stages of the dispute. This totally changed their attitudes and they were able to see why everyone was so upset.

Role-play for work-based skills

Role-play is the favoured method for teaching interview skills. This is from both perspectives. As a young personnel officer, I was sent to London to learn how to interview. An excellent course was organized, during which we role-played being an interviewer and were videoed. I think all interviewers (and teachers) should see themselves on video. On this course, the video of my efforts (and everyone else's) was viewed by the whole group. I am still cringing from my dreadful repetitive mannerisms with the pencil to this day!

Role-play can be used in all aspects of interviewing. Practising using politically correct questions and good equal opportunities practice works well in interview role-plays. Also, of course, it works the other way round. Many courses give their students job interview practice by inviting in experienced interviewers who put students through their paces and then give them feedback.

I was also involved in training FE teachers to carry out training needs analysis in local businesses and adapted an excellent residential course to use with colleagues. After a day's input on techniques, we split the FE teachers into groups of three and asked them to prepare to visit both the general manager and the manufacturing manager of the company. Briefs were given to two 'actors' who came into the hotel to play the roles. In truth, they were not real actors but friends of mine when I had worked in industry. They were total strangers to the participants. Following the opportunity to interview the managers, the groups spent till the early hours of the morning preparing a presentation of their training needs analysis (TNA), matched with what the college could offer them. On the final day, all three groups delivered their presentation to the two managers, followed by debriefing, discussion and analysis.

I received a lot of criticism that one of the 'managers' had been very curt and opened the interview with 'I don't know what I want, you tell me what you can offer!' Later, one of the participants rang me to tell me that he had just carried out his first TNA and was greeted by the identical attitude that he had had to cope with during the training! And he had coped well – thank goodness.

Earlier in the chapter, you may have noticed that, when setting up multiple role-plays in assertiveness, I suggested that uneven numbers were accommodated by a group of three, and not by the tutor joining in. This is because, other than during ice-breakers, I think it is a bad idea for tutors to become involved in role-plays. This is particularly the case when tutors take on roles very different from their own. Here, I speak from experience.

When I was relatively new to teacher training in FE, I was involved in planning and running a residential weekend for the City & Guilds 730 course. We decided to take role-play as our theme for the weekend, looking at van Ments's rules, asking students to devise role-plays and inevitably to participate in them. As a special treat we decided that on the Saturday night we would do a whole-group role-play which explored challenging behaviour in the classroom. We asked for a volunteer to be the teacher. Lorraine volunteered straight away. Most of the rest of the group and my two co-tutors were given role names and short briefs as students. Four students and I were observers. The tutors (one male and one female) had ended up with the roles of teenagers who were 'seeing each other' (this was a long time ago!) and going through a bit of a drama. A bit of a drama was exactly what it was! They threw themselves into their roles (I later discovered they had 'am dram' backgrounds) and were as difficult and obnoxious as any students I have ever met. The role-play was just getting into its swing when the 'teacher' burst into tears and said she could not go on. Luckily for me, one of the observers was a psychiatric nurse with lots of experience in psychodrama: he was able to suggest a way forward. He asked me to take the 'teacher' and the two tutors away while he debriefed the rest of the group. I think it was a helpful suggestion, anyway!

I worked at debriefing the key players, eliciting apologies from all and doing my best to mend the situation. A bottle of whisky was also consumed, but this is not essential to the exercise! However, although we all ended up friends, the rest of the group were in high dudgeon and threatening to leave the course, which by this time was due to meet the next evening (Monday). We carried on with the planned programme, but the negative atmosphere was tangible. After lunch, I decided to make a last-ditch attempt to repair the situation. I took the whole group and used a variation on the icebreaker 'fears in a hat'. I gave out slips of paper and asked everyone to write whatever they wanted to say on a slip of paper, as many as they liked. I collected them in a hat. I then read each one out, without comment, and then in full view screwed each comment up and threw it into the bin. A kind of visual punctuation – this episode is now over. And it worked. We lost no students and all continued with the usual expected enthusiasm of trainee teachers and trainers till the end of the course.

So what lessons did this emotional lesson teach me?

It is not a good idea to let tutors assume roles in role-plays. Everyone can become focused in their role, including tutors. What we had in the 'challenging behaviour' role-play was a mixed-power scenario. It is bad enough dealing with challenging behaviour without the naughty students normally being your teachers.

It is also probably not a good idea to attempt role-plays when students and tutors are already tired, especially on residential courses. The residential situation is difficult for many students. Our group were spending first nights for many years apart from partners, or had left husbands to look after children for the first time. The role-play in the evening was an additional stress.

In this situation, it had been useful to have observers, especially an experienced one. It would have been much better for the tutors to have been observers.

Later stories I heard about role-plays having undesired effects were always during residential courses. Particular care needs to be taken in this situation.

Summary

Role-play is an exciting, motivating teaching method that is used in a wide variety of ways in almost every curriculum area. It is ideal for developing certain kinds of communication skills such as interview skills, telephone skills and group interaction skills. It can be used for students to experience the kinds of role they will adopt in their work role. It can be used as a way of enabling students to empathize with others outside their experience. It works well as a stimulus for discussion and analysis. It also has its place in the assessment of vocational and key skills.

It needs to be planned so that it is a step along the way to achieving the aims of the learning programme. In the session it is used there needs to be time to prepare the role-play, run it and, most importantly, for the debrief which must be skilfully managed by the tutor.

As van Ments says it is good to revisit role-play as a method if you have become 'jaded and nonchalant' (p. 29).

Further reading

van Ments, M. (1999) *The Effective Use of Role-Play*, London: Kogan Page.

The Morry van Ments book is the best publication available on role-play. If you wanted to develop your use of role-play in your teaching and base a CPD module on it, it would probably help to reflect in depth on the experiences you encounter. Research evidence shows that reflection is deepened when a framework is used to provide a structure for reflections and questions that will challenge our thinking. These articles suggest frameworks to support reflection and to help practitioners self-assess their reflection.

Bain, J. D., Ballantyne, R., Packer, J. and Mills, C. (1999) 'Using journal writing to enhance student teachers' reflectivity during field experience placements', *Teachers and Teaching: theory and practice* 5(1): 51–73.

Brookfield, S. (1995) *Becoming a critically reflective teacher*, San Francisco: Jossey-Bass.

Hamlin, K. D. (2004) 'Beginning the journey: supporting reflection in early field experiences', *Reflective Practice* 5 (2): 167–79.

Johns C. (1995) 'Framing learning through reflection within Carper's fundamental ways of knowing in nursing', *Journal of Advanced Nursing* 22: 226–34.

Kreber, C. (2004) 'An analysis of two models of reflection and their implications for educational development', *International Journal for Academic Development* 9 (1): 29–49.

Part Two
Working with learners

5 Learner characteristics

Trevor Dawn

Everyone who teaches has at some time been on the 'other' side, i.e. they have previously been students, in some cases with little experience of anything else other than education. As a student, you judged teachers by the selfish yardstick of what they did for you; how well they taught, how well you learned, whether the lessons were fun or interesting, or dull and boring, just as one might judge, say, a doctor by how they treated you in your illness or the shop by how well it provided a service. You compared one with another and they did not all find favour. You probably took little or no account of your teachers' workload or health or personal circumstances. Your reactions were most unlikely to have been very charitable or tolerant if they were unable to cope with episodes of misbehaviour by your fellow students, more so if you happened not to like the teacher.

The situation looks quite different now since *you* are the teacher. Your students are likely to judge you in the same way as you judged your teachers and perhaps be as uncharitable as you were. You have to accept that they will treat you like they treat their dentist or the bus driver and expect you to perform to a high level more or less all the time.

Whatever their opinions, you have the responsibility for motivating and enthusing all the learners in front of you. Some of the students will have characteristics and experiences that are similar to your own, but a large number will be different: in social background and opportunity, in how they learn, in geographical heritage, in family position, in first language, in the way they have benefited from their previous education and so on.

In this chapter we will look at the way in which your

experience and understanding of learner characteristics develops over time and examine the role of research in helping you to gain deeper insights into the behaviour of the people you teach. These break down into two main groups: adolescents and adults, though there are some overlaps between them. In this series, Amanda Hayes has examined the characteristics of adult learners and explored ways of teaching them in her book *Teaching Adults in FE* (2006), so we will concentrate on adolescence in this chapter. We also refer you to James Ogunleye's book on 14–19 teaching in the Essential FE Toolkit Series (2006). James's book complements and extends our discussion here.

Adolescence

This book does not attempt to be comprehensive in its coverage of this topic. The focus is on reminding the reader of some of the ways in which an awareness of adolescent feelings and concerns will help you become better teachers and to relate more appropriately to your learners. It may also inspire you to read more deeply into some of the texts from which we have quoted.

Every year for the past ten years, at the start of the Cert. Ed. course, we have asked over 150 trainee teachers, arranged in small groups, for single words or phrases that evoke the essence of their adolescence. By and large, it is a fun activity. Their responses tend to home in on the music, the fashion, the television programmes, especially the comedies, the escapades which meant deceiving parents about what they were actually doing and the formulation of their own identity. But adolescence was also seen as problematic with examinations, acne, dissatisfaction with one's body, low self-esteem, lack of privacy and pangs of love identified as the angst that went alongside the fun. What unites all the responses, from whatever the era, is that adolescent experiences are ingrained into our very being and can be recalled with great clarity many years later. Part of adolescence remains with us throughout our lives, often to the embarrassment of our children when we re-enact our youth in front of them, say, at a wedding or a party.

Definition of adolescence

It is not easy to define adolescence. It is a biological, a sociological and a cultural phenomenon.

Biologically, it is synonymous with the hormonal changes that come with puberty and with growth and changes in one's physical make-up. These vary from individual to individual, but can start as young as 9 or 10 and go on till mid teens in sexual and hormonal changes and till late teens in terms of height, body shape, facial hair, muscle tone and so on.

Sociologically and culturally, adolescence is also a protracted affair. In the same session, at the start of the Cert. Ed. course, one of the activities we use is the adolescence 'test'. Try it for yourself.

At what age is it legal to:

- work night shifts
- consent to have heterosexual sex
- consent to have homosexual sex
- admit to criminal liability
- buy cigarettes
- smoke cigarettes
- buy alcohol in a supermarket
- be sent to a young offenders' institution
- receive your National Insurance number (NI)
- join the army
- ride a motorcycle above 50cc on the public highway
- drive a car
- be assessed as a mature student for grant purposes
- undertake paid employment such as a paper round
- witness a passport photograph

The answers range from 10 years old in the case of admitting to criminal liability to about 23 for being classed as a mature student (five years of independent living). You should not be asked to witness a passport photograph unless you are a 'professional' person which is unlikely to happen before the age of about 22 (after a minimum of three years higher education plus one year professional training) and is more likely to be nearer 30. Adolescence in its social context can extend in some cases over a period of 15–20 years, a fact that advertisers and mar-keting people have come to exploit.

But it isn't a fixed period, any more than a historical period such as the thirties or the sixties is fixed by the decade per se. The archetypical sixties did not really start till perhaps 1963 and lingered on in some ways till the mid-1970s beyond the formal end of the decade. The Priory Group (2005: 16) makes the point that the adolescent period can seem very short in some cases, especially in sexual development, activity and orientation where the adolescent period lasts perhaps three or four years from the first encounter to an adult-style relationship involving cohabitation, perhaps children, and all that that entails.

In biological terms, our developments in adolescence re-define us as adult as opposed to child. Our bodies become 'adult', with knock-on effects on our personality. One example is where increased testosterone tends to make male behaviour more aggressive. Cairns and Cairns (1994) note: 'the abrupt rise in arrests for violence begins at about age 11, rises sharply, and peaks at ages 17 and 18. Seventeen and 18 year-old males constitute the age group that is most likely to be arrested for crimes of violence' (US data). Biology affects girls too. Blake-more and Frith (2005) recount the case of a girl who was: 'coy in the company of adults but in the company of peers she was outgoing. In photographs she no longer smiled unselfcon-sciously but looked sullen and posed or avoided the camera altogether. She always wanted to look different: prettier and thinner than she thought she was.' If you have teenage children or work with them, you do not need books to apprise you of the personality roller-coaster of adolescence.

The brain also changes in adolescence. Blakemore and Frith (2005) devote a whole chapter to this factor. They state that MRI scans can now reveal 'higher gray matter volume in the frontal cortex and parietal cortex in younger children. The older group, by contrast, had a higher volume of white matter in the same regions', though slightly different for girls and boys, in whom it is sharper and peaks later. According to Blakemore and Frith, this involves a decrease in synaptic density, i.e. the number of synapses or information junctions per unit volume of brain tissue and an increase in axonal myelination or the transmission of electrical impulses down the neurons. The implication, say Blakemore and Frith, 'seems to be greater control and better planning of the complex actions necessary in both work and social life'. Biologically we are ready to be stretched intellectually and perhaps socially. This insight is not new, though the scientific underpinning for it is. In the 1948 *Handbook of Suggestions for Teachers*, published by the Board of Education, changes in the adolescent brain were acknowledged: 'to some extent he is able to suspend judgement until he knows all the facts of the situation. He is learning to carry in his mind a number of outwardly dissimilar ideas, to abstract from each such elements as they have in common and to make simple generalisations about them.'

In cultural terms, adolescence denotes a series of 'milestones' that change our status. We receive our NI number, pass our driving test, take out our first independent hire purchase agreement, have our first experience of sexual intercourse (in some cases get married), receive our first pay packet, vote in national and local elections and so on. With each instance, there comes a new initiation into adulthood. This can lead to a certain amount of turbulence if the drive to full adult status is slowed down by existing restrictions and prohibitions in other areas of one's life.

Socially, adolescence is also a time for preparation, though it is not always embraced as such, despite the findings of Blakemore and Frith. While we are in the very process of being adolescent, we are also expected to lay down the foundations for leaving it. We do not really want to – many of us that is. We like it here: we feel we have the right to place the emphasis on enjoying ourselves before settling down; we take it for granted when the tone of the law is more tolerant if we make mistakes; the majority of us rely on the safety net of parents if we get into difficulties. Others of us, however, have no choice – we leave our adolescence before we are ready, being thrust into responsibility too early, say, in terms of an unwanted early pregnancy or supporting a family that is in crisis. Some feel they have to leave home because conditions have become intolerable. There are cultural differences in quitting adolescence across the world and some of these impinge on our society, for example, in the age of marriage. But for the majority of young people in this country, adolescence means putting responsibility on hold.

Adolescence and mental health

Biological and sociological forces collide in adolescence. Sometimes it is proper and it feels right to act as we once did as a child; at other times, we want to be treated as adult. Adult attitudes to adolescents also change: we are expected to be grown up, accept responsibility, plan for the future, control our emotions. This is difficult enough for any teenager, but for some it is a nightmare.

An independent study of adolescence commissioned by the Priory Group was published in 2005. Entitled *Adolescent angst*, its findings are based partly on fieldwork conducted by LVQ Research, The Children's Omnibus, into the views of 1,000 representative adolescents aged 12–19 which took place from 19 to 26 March 2005 and 16 to 28 June 2005, and partly on other sources such as the Mental Health Foundation, the Institute of Psychiatry and the Office of National Statistics. One of the study's major claims is that 'the mental health of British adolescents has declined over the last 30 years – a unique trend in the developing world, since other countries experienced stable levels of child and adolescent mental health problems during this time' (p. 5). Using data from the Nuffield Foundation's time trial, the study claims that the data suggests that 'behavioural problems have doubled and emotional problems like depression and anxiety have soared by 70 per cent' (Nuffield Foundation 2004).

Some of the statistics from the Priory Group's study make sobering reading for the teacher in post-14 education. According to the study (Table 20, reproduced here as Table 3), any one of us can be faced with a class whose make-up is as in Table 3. There are other findings in the study about drugs, alcohol and sex, which also make interesting reading and are highly relevant to this book, that are not in Table 3.

Allowances for accuracy have to be made of course for the

Table 3: Some common adolescent stressors (Priory Group 2005: Table 20)

Stressor	Age 14	Age 15	Age 16	Age 17	Age 18	Age 19	Average
Bullying at school	27%	27%	21%	21%	28%	32%	**26%**
Suffering from peer-group pressure	22%	33%	32%	20%	26%	27%	**27%**
Difficult relationship with one or more teachers	52%	56%	44%	35%	31%	37%	**42%**
Money worries	20%	33%	44%	41%	53%	60%	**42%**
Difficult relationship with parents	22%	37%	33%	33%	35%	31%	**32%**
Stressed about schoolwork	53%	58%	65%	47%	53%	50%	**54%**

nature of the sample and the fact that the type of questions used could have been open to interpretation. But even if a 10 per cent downward readjustment is made to accommodate any doubts about statistical validity, there is no escaping the conclusion that angst exists in a high percentage of our young people, though the spread of such angst across our group of stressors will vary by age or type of stress. Anything from one-third to a half of your class may be having difficulties with you or some of your colleagues, perhaps the same ones who cause about half the class to have anxieties about the work they are given (whether because it is too difficult, not hard enough, not relevant to their lives, not interesting, etc., is not clear).

The message appears to be that anxiety of some description may well be latent in many of our students and that we should be on the lookout for signs that the anxiety is affecting their work or their emotional well-being or both. Not all teenagers will behave this way. Kroger (2004), in discussing the 'turmoil' theory of adolescence, presenting storm and stress as normative features of the teenage years, warns that there is little evidence for psychopathology or even storm and stress among large sections of the adolescent population of the United States. The

Priory Group's findings, however, would suggest that the incidence is high enough for one to be on one's guard.

Teachers and adolescence

How do you come across to your students?

The point has been made quite strongly that the way you now view your teenage students can be informed by your studies of adolescence and that it is part of your job to find out more about the subject and to learn how to react professionally.

However, the reverse is not true. It is not part of the teenager's 'job' to study you, though they will all have their view about you, and all their teachers. Is the 'you' they see what your friends see at the badminton club or in the staff workroom or at home? It is highly unlikely, however adult or natural we think we are. We have to consider our authority and how we use it (a topic which is covered in full in Chapter 7), an authority that does not exist in other aspects of our lives. We are perceived as having more power and status than our students, which affects how they see us. With the younger age group, 14–16, we are in loco parentis. Even with the older students, we sometimes have to represent the organization in ways that we would rather not do, especially soon after a staff meeting when agreed protocols for certain contingencies have been set up by majority vote. One may lose popularity, hopefully temporarily, by enforcing such protocols, for example on eating and drinking, or litter, or punctuality with classes where the enforcement is seen as too much like school.

We may also be tested on our attitudes, having to take a view on things which teenagers regard with a different set of values to our own. We are expected to discourage the use of drugs, even class C, even if we are users; we cannot be seen to condone bad language, even if we do resort to it in the staff workroom. We are the embodiment of a certain type of adulthood, one that has achieved something through commitment to the very process that the young person is going through. Your manner and behaviour says: 'this is professional, responsible adulthood'.

But this sounds so stuffy – and the danger is that in some

cases it will be seen as stuffy. So we also need to show discretion and humour even when we differ from our adolescent students about values. We may well have power and status but flaunting them unnecessarily will only alienate the students. Research cited in Harkin *et al.* (2001) indicates that leadership that is in tune with each particular group of students is more effective than one that is authoritarian. We could also examine how many of the checklist for successful learning for adults as expressed by Hayes (2006) could be applied to adolescents – see below.

Checklist for successful adult learning (Hayes 2006)
- value adults' experience and their accumulated knowledge
- help them make connections between what they already know and what they are currently learning in your class
- challenge them to try something new, but do it sensitively
- encourage them to be autonomous learners through your style and methods
- develop an environment of equal status, as adults may not respond well to being told what to do and how to do it by you
- develop interesting ways to draw out theory from practice
- never make assumptions about adult students' skills or understanding, always check learning is taking place
- remember to plan for and recognize the wider personal and social benefits of learning
- see the whole person and support them in managing the different demands in their lives

If one of the roles of the teacher of adolescents is to help them make the transition from childhood to adulthood, then treating them as adult and therefore adopting many of these practices is part of the package.

Reactions to changes in behaviour

In addition to the changes in behaviour that one could encounter with any teenager, teachers should look out for changes that emanate from drugs or substance abuse. According to the Priory Group's findings (2005) you should be concerned if you notice a fair incidence in a particular student of the symptoms in Table 4.

Table 4: Symptoms of dependency (Priory Group 2005)

- drop in academic performance
- change in groups of friends
- delinquent behaviour
- deterioration in family relationships
- change in eating or sleeping habits
- persistent cough
- runny nose
- red eyes

They may not be drug-related but: 'be on your guard' is the message.

What else have you noticed about adolescents?

Perhaps the classic text is Horrocks (1976). He formulated six points of reference as follows:

1   A time of increasing awareness of self; he gradually works towards the self-stabilization that will characterize his adult years.
2   A time of seeking status as an individual; there is a tendency to attempt emancipation from childish submission to parental authority and a period of developing vocational interests and striving towards economic independence.
3   A time when group relationships become of major importance; he tends to desire intensely to conform to the actions and standards of his peers.
4   A time of physical development; in this period there is a rapid altering of the body image and habitual motor patterns.
5   A time of intellectual expansion; he is asked to acquire

many skills and concepts useful at some time in the future but often lacks immediate motivation.

6   A time of development and evaluation of values; his life is accompanied by the development of self-ideals and acceptance of self in harmony with those ideals. It is a time of conflict between youthful idealism and reality.

In general terms, what Horrocks identified thirty years ago still applies today. However, there are some additional factors to consider:

Technology

One of the things that older people notice about the young is their love affair with the latest technology. You may share some of the same attraction, depending on your age and/or disposition. The young especially like gadgets that can be carried on their person and are instantly accessible.

Ownership of, and proficiency with, the latest technology is one of the defining characteristics of adolescence, especially in the twenty-first century. It can be both a badge of individuality and a means of social interaction. The individuality comes through in terms of which brand is preferred, what extra or special features are included, and how it is used. The social interaction, notably through the mobile phone, is vital in terms of making (and breaking) arrangements, in networking, in maintaining one's social circle and as an expression of social conformity, but it is also important as a focus for shared interests, giving a guaranteed topic of conversation through comparison and the capacity to show off one's competence.

Unlike earlier technologies, the mobile phone has become indispensable to young people in the very way they conduct their lives and, through the G3, this trend will continue as the century progresses. Teachers would be advised to view the young and technology, especially their mobile phones, as a fact of life and to see how they can incorporate some of the more positive features into their lessons (see Part Four).

We need to exercise some caution. Technology can have its down side. We have all of us had to deal with students texting when they should be working (or listening) or accessing dubious websites or plagiarizing from the Internet. Some become over-reliant on technology and cannot check the veracity of their technological information by other means. Indiscriminate use of Internet sources is a good example. Some are reluctant to undertake activities that are 'low-tech' because they may have high status through their competence with technology but feel exposed without their technical 'prop' or the low tech seems less exciting.

On balance, however, the embracing of new technology invariably means working with the grain as far as adolescence is concerned. You will become increasingly sensitive to both possibilities and dangers as you gain in experience.

Language

Teenagers have always been noted for having their own language. They adopt the latest slang to distance themselves from adults, defining 'their' culture and 'their' generation as different from anything that went before. Whereas fashion can sometimes be derivative, retro or even throwback in style, language is rarely so, evolving as it does more from things that immediately impinge on life. Language that was in vogue even 10 years ago now seems dated. Teachers constantly have to readjust. One gets accustomed to being baffled by what the young are saying, though they will almost always enlighten you, with amused patience, if you ask.

Multiple influences abound. The broadcasting media have been prominent organizations for spreading the new terminology. It can be a good use of your time if you occasionally watch the sort of programmes that interest your students, not to show that you are up to date with the latest slang, but to absorb some of the contextual influences that go with the language. The media reflect the changing nature of society, especially the impact of mass migration, the development of second and third generation multi-ethnic communities, and the phenomenon of social mobility. Teachers need to be aware of the world their students are living in. The young, exposed to a variety of language use, especially that which derives from urban situations, adopt and repackage language in a way that seems bewildering to the more conventional adult, but this can be a source of inspiration. Nothing demonstrates this more than texting. The need for abbreviated codes has resulted not only in the fusion of numbers and words and the emergence of accepted conventions but also the invention of textonym code such as 'book' for the term cool. This can be used by the teacher to advantage, for example in key skills or in rapping (see Part Four).

Vernacular language

You will hear language that is taken for granted by the young which was socially unacceptable when you were young. In the media, it can be used for characterization in a play or a film or is present for dramatic effect or is a catchphrase and can be justified on those grounds, but it does present a challenge for the teacher. It is often difficult to know when to object to what sounds like swearing when the young seem oblivious to its implications and use it as a matter of course. This has always been so and it is perhaps part of the role of the teacher to confront the young when you feel that they have overstepped the boundaries of acceptability. It may be an individual decision, but you will know when to intervene, for example regarding swearing that crudely refers to parts of the male or female genitalia or sexual intercourse (for instance use of the 'f' word or the 'c' word are unacceptable) or when the mode of address is aimed at belittling or humiliating another person. It is part of the role of the teacher to exemplify the sort of standards that obtain in polite society, similar to the watershed idea on TV. This may come across as dated, but there are times when it is both expedient and desirable to represent respectability.

Subcultures

Subcultures exist in all societies and social networks. Who mixes with whom and why is an interesting topic. The outward manifestation to the teacher in the classroom can come through gender or ethnic groupings, with certain students always sitting with the same close set of friends in class and in the refectory. In such cases, it is not unusual for seating preferences in the classroom to be expressed and acted upon and for some reluctance to be shown when you try to get different people to work together. With some classes, it is wise to expect that there will be subgroups or cliques and that early action to break down barriers and create an open classroom climate will prove to be worthwhile in the long term (see Chapter 7).

In some cases teenagers may find that their social network varies little from college/school to leisure and that they are comfortable with a restricted social circle, the more so, perhaps, if that social grouping is seen as different and exclusive from the norm and that they can identify with its culture. The boundaries are often age-specific, not extending much beyond a two-year band either side of their own. Dress codes can become important as an expression of the subgroup's membership. The influence of the group will extend not only to fashion but also to what interests them in the lesson, the language they use, to you and among themselves, how they work and sometimes to their mood.

This is not always the case. You will come across other students who have a much more fluid and dynamic set of social networks that operate beyond the restrictions of gender, ethnic and age boundaries. Some students are much more open to experimenting with social networks. Influences that originate from music and fashion also impact upon relationships and social networks. In urban contexts in particular, the college may well be an area where the young come face to face with aspects of cultures and subcultures that they may have seen on television, perhaps in the soaps or reality TV. One of the reasons why students choose college at 16 in preference to school is to enter into a more diverse society that is more representative of the adult society that they see around them. It is a good preparation for both higher education and the world of work.

Working with the grain

In your first year or two of teaching, concentrating on the content of the lesson tends to come before both process and rapport. What does this mean? Quite simply a lot of work is needed just to have enough content or material to occupy the class. It is not unusual for a one and a half hour lesson to take up to six hours to prepare. Everything from schemes of work to lesson plans to teaching notes to resources has to be built up, much of it from scratch. This is not to say that new teachers pay *no* attention to the subtleties of teaching strategies or the reactions of the class, but that it is natural to devote the bulk of one's energy to the acquiring of teaching and learning material.

In the second and subsequent years, you are more experienced and have, hopefully, a little more time to stand back from concentrating on good-quality content with its accent on academic or vocational integrity and to look at the wider issues. Your training in reflective practice, your lesson evaluations and your discussions with your mentor will have alerted you to some of the changes that you need to consider. Some of these changes will be to the content itself, of course: you may have misjudged the level, or the pace, or the ability of some learners; you may have emphasized some aspect to the exclusion of something equally important. You may have discovered new sources of information or a recent publication or invention has changed the way your subject is perceived. Other changes, however, will be concerned with process (see Chapters 1 and 11) and some changes relate to what you have learned about how *you* relate to the students. What have you learned about them and, just as importantly, about yourself?

You are part of the equation. How you see your learners and how you treat them has a profound effect on their attitude to you. It is easier to work with the grain than rub against it. The traditional triangle (see Chapter 1) is a case in point. It is more productive to plan lessons that meet the needs of learners with different learning styles than to teach in ways that marginalize some of them. If you have high expectations and high levels of trust, most students will rise to those levels, though not always as quickly as we would wish. In effect, you are training your students in how to conduct themselves in adult situations and therefore they need to be socialized into gradually accepting responsibility for their behaviour. We will return to this in Chapter 7.

Conclusion

It is a fact in all non-repetitive jobs such as teaching that experience gives you access to new insights that can only come with experience. What you learn first time round has to be modified the second and subsequent times, because on each new occasion there are different variables with which to contend.

Nowhere is this more apt than when we teach the same subject for the second time to a class we thought had identical features to its predecessor. After a while you can feel confident about some generalizations, but there will always be surprises that force you to make adjustments.

Research and personal experience show that adolescence is a time of angst, but not for everybody and not for all of the time. You need to be aware of the signs when they occur, but not to see problems round every corner.

Adolescence is a time of growing independence and maturity, but vestiges of childish and childlike behaviour will come through and need to be addressed with sensitivity.

It is natural to want to be seen as approachable, but you also need to act as a foil, i.e. someone who will objectively confront the young with the consequences of their behaviour or the existence of alternative points of view.

Further reading

Blakemore, S.-J. & Frith, U. (2005) *The learning brain: lessons for education*, Oxford: Blackwell.

Horrocks, J. E. (1976) *The Psychology of Adolescence* (4th edn), Boston, MA: Houghton Mifflin.

Kroger, J. (2004) *Identity in Adolescence: the balance between self and other*, London: Routledge.

Priory Group (2005) *Adolescent angst* www.prioryhealthcare.com/adolescentangst

Strauch, B. (2003) *Why are they so weird? What's really going on in a teenager's brain?* London: Bloomsbury.

6 Tutorials: working with the individual learner

Ros Clow and Jenny Hankey

In the 'Just teachers' research (Clow 2005), one of the most significant findings was that all full-time FE teachers in the survey carried out one to one tutorials. This was shown to be a development in the role over the last twenty years, at least for those working on vocational courses. From our experience as external examiners and from our roles as trainers/staff developers in FE colleges, we know that it has not necessarily been the case that training for the tutorial role is included in all initial teacher training courses.

Indeed the word 'tutorial' has a range of meanings in FE colleges. We have been timetabled for 'tutorial' yet found that this involved taking the whole group without having any kind of plan as to what they should be doing. During those sessions, the students were expected to attend and work quietly on coursework, although they could use the 'tutor' as a resource if they were stuck and needed help. The help available depended on the match between the coursework and the tutor's knowledge base.

More recently, the whole-class tutorial is more likely to have a scheme of work which addresses social and progression issues and is often centrally devised by the college. Typically, the tutorial curriculum will cover applying to university, writing CVs, drugs, alcohol and smoking education, sexual health, citizenship, etc. There is an expectation that all course tutors will be competent to deliver this kind of curriculum.

We have also been involved with 'group tutorials'. In this instance, the group is usually a subgroup of the whole class and there is no specific plan except that the students can ask for guidance. This format is common on teacher training courses and in HE, supposedly as a way of individuals gaining tutorial support as cost-effectively as possible. An advantage of this arrangement is that several students may have the same questions to ask. Also, they might be stimulated by the interactions around them. However, this is not our preferred method of teaching. The whole experience can be exhausting and messy, although students seem to like it.

In this chapter, we will concentrate on the one to one tutorial in its different guises. There seem to be four different kinds of one to one tutorial although they can segue from one to another.

- academic tutorial
- individual learning plan (ILP) session
- personal tutorial
- disciplinary tutorial

In the academic tutorial, the teacher and student work together on academic matters. Usually the student will have prepared work for the tutorial; certainly this will make the tutorial more effective. The work might be a plan for an essay, a portfolio of evidence for a particular NVQ unit or the collection of all tutor feedback on assignments so far in the course.

Recent years have seen the proliferation of individual learning plans, often directly related to funding and inspired by inspection. Colleges have created systems and formats to help teachers. The tutorial consists of establishing what has been achieved to date and ends with an action plan which will move the student towards successful completion. In effect, these are managerialist tutorials and, although they appear to be high-quality interactions, experience (and more recently, research into using ILPs with learning and sector skills sector trainee teachers (Hankey 2006)) shows that the ILP process often precludes the delivery of effective tutorials.

In some institutions, especially HE but more and more in FE, students are allocated a personal tutor. It is the student's role to initiate contact and the tutor may not be known to them. However, this is the person they need to talk to if they are struggling with the course or have personal issues that need addressing.

Nuts and bolts

Whatever kind of individual tutorial, there are practical and temporal considerations that need to be decided, usually by the tutor.

Frequency

On most courses, there will be a required amount of tutorial contact. This may be one or two tutorials a term. It would be expected that the teacher would have these hours timetabled, but experience in FE shows this is not always the case. Sometimes there is a class tutorial slot and the teacher is expected to supervise the whole group while carrying out individual tutorials in the same room (Green 2001). Sometimes tutorials are carried out during the tutor's 'free' time, e.g. lunch breaks.

The tutorial relationship has to involve multiple meetings. For this reason, it is usually better for the tutor to be a teacher who teaches the students on a regular basis. The only case where this would be inadvisable is where there is a personality clash between the student and the assigned tutor. In these cases, the system should allow for the student to request another tutor. And only that! Experience shows that students can ask to change but not who they want to change to. In this way, they have to be really sure they want to change, no matter who else they will be assigned to.

Tutorial appointments can be made by the tutor, or students can be asked to 'sign up' on a list which indicates available times. In this way the tutor limits the length of the tutorial.

There are a wide range of institutional approaches to the tutorial, especially for full-time 16–19 year olds, in *Successful tutoring* (Green 2001). One scheme involves personal advisers who are not teachers and are paid on a lower pay scale. We are hesitant about this approach, as this means that the 'tutor' is not one of the student's teachers (although they may be timetabled to supervise the class once a week!) and would need a lot of experience before they could really understand the course the student is on. It also denies any teachers who work in that college the rewarding experience of working in a tutorial relationship with their students.

How long is a tutorial?

It is unlikely that a real tutorial can take less than 15 minutes. Even an ILP session would be difficult to slot into such a short time. A proper and worthwhile tutorial, as we will explain later, needs to allow for both conversation and silences and is unlikely to last less than 25 minutes, and so is better planned for a 30-minute slot. This is particularly the case when working with adults, who generally both value and benefit from individual tutorials.

Physical arrangements

Although well aware that timetabling and rooming constraints will often dictate where tutorials are held, nevertheless all professionals should be trying to achieve the ideal space for tutorials. Probably the perfect space would be a bespoke interview room, with a computer with Internet connection. The reason for the latter is that quite often tutorial issues can be sorted by interrogating the intranet or World Wide Web on the spot. It can also be useful to be able to make telephone calls to sort out issues during the tutorial. Tutorials should never be interrupted by telephone. This can be achieved by putting the phone through to voicemail or just explaining at the start of the tutorial that you will be ignoring the phone.

Furniture is also important. Ideally, both tutor and tutee should be on chairs of the same height positioned at about 90° to each other. In tutorials which involve looking through written work or portfolios of evidence, it is useful to both be able to look together at the work on a table or desk.

If the tutorial is taking place in an office or interview room, a decision has to be made about whether to close the door or not. Closing the door creates privacy and cuts down on distractions. A note on the door can indicate 'engaged' and keep visitors away. The student may prefer to keep the door open for reasons of their own. However, one issue that needs to be considered is that of safety. When working with a student who can be aggressive, it may be inadvisable to close the door. While keeping the door open will protect against harassment allegations.

If you have no access to a private office or room, then you

will need to look for acceptable alternatives. An empty class-room or a corner in the refectory can suffice. What will not suffice is an inhabited classroom or even worse a staff work-room, with other staff present. These environments do not provide the privacy that is essential for tutorial. They may (only may) allow you to complete ILP paperwork, but there is no way that tutees in those environments will disclose anything that discomforts them. Over the years, we have had tutees disclose intensely personal information: a teenager who had had seven of his close friends and relatives die in the previous six months and who was, unsurprisingly, feeling suicidal himself; female students with histories of anorexia, bulimia and alco-holism; students having affairs with peers; students having affairs with staff; students having just discovered they are diabetic; students with sons addicted to heroin and students experiencing racial harassment. We have no doubt that none of this would have been disclosed in a noisy staffroom. And yet these dis-closures provided a turning point where we could really action-plan and ensure appropriate support was accessed.

Questioning

There are two essential skills for tutoring: questioning and lis-tening. These are also essential skills in teaching, so there can be an assumption that trained teachers will automatically be able to carry out effective tutorials. Perhaps strangely, this does not seem to be the case. Perhaps while teaching we assume a 'teacher' role which enables us to use questioning skills: recall questioning, open questioning, probing, to promote learning? Often these skills seem to desert the teacher once they assume the tutor role. Certainly over years of marking tutorial tran-scripts, 'counter-productive questioning' (Mackay 1995) seems to flourish in the tutorial.

As a way of refreshing questioning skills in an appropriate way for leading tutorials, it is useful to look at counselling skills. The tutorial is not a counselling session, but the skills and theoretical approaches used by counsellors can develop our tutorial skills especially if we apply the theory to transcripts of recordings of tutorials.

Further tutoring skills

Structuring

Given that the amount of time tutors have to spend with individual students tends to be severely limited by the constraints of budgeting and timetabling, it can be useful to think about the structure of a tutorial as having distinct phases and outcomes, in the same way that we consider planning lessons. One model which we have found useful is an adaptation of Egan's model of skilled helping (Egan 2002). This adaptation divides the tutorial into three separate phases and in our experience provides a helpful structure, whatever the focus of the tutorial.

Phase 1 − The student's story
This phase involves placing the focus clearly on the student and listening to the student's concerns and issues. This is a time for the student to talk − about work, personal issues, anything that they want to bring to the tutorial. A general, open question along the lines of 'how are things with you?' will often be sufficient to begin the tutorial.

Phase 2 − Options and alternatives
In this phase, desired outcomes are explored. The student may want to complete a piece of research, put together a portfolio or find a part-time job, or the tutor may wish to point out the consequences of particular actions, but this is a stage of joint exploration and consideration of objectives and solutions.

Phase 3 − Putting it all together − the action plan
This is the final stage of the tutorial at which specific actions are agreed towards the accomplishment of objectives. The notion of SMART targets can be helpful here. If the agreed steps of the action plan are formulated in a way which makes them *S*pecific, *M*easurable, *A*chievable, *R*ealistic and *T*ime-related, the student is clear about what exactly has been negotiated and the process of reviewing progress at subsequent tutorials is facilitated.

At this point, it is important that the agreed actions are recorded and a copy of the action plan is retained by both tutor and student. The recording might take place on a tutorial record sheet or an individual learning plan (ILP), and would ideally be signed by both tutor and student, indicating agreement with the planned actions. It is also helpful to indicate a date for the next tutorial to review progress; many learners respond well to deadlines. Apart from considerations of auditing for funding claims, the written action plan is a document which can be consulted by both parties and progress can be tracked against the targets, resulting in a consistent approach to learning over the duration of a programme.

Listening

Whatever the function of a tutorial, whether it be part of a disciplinary process, a review of academic progress or a meeting requested by a student to discuss personal issues, the first skill that the tutor must use is that of listening. A tutorial is a time for students to raise individual concerns which it may be inappropriate to raise in class, and for the tutor to work towards understanding the student in order to facilitate individual learning. Listening, in the sense of active or professional listening, as opposed to the listening which occurs as part of interaction in social life, is also one of the skills which can be taken for granted, or perceived as an aspect of individual personality – one either is, or isn't, a good listener. In fact, listening is a skill which can be developed, as other skills, through practice and reflection.

A typical list of skills might include those of *attending*: indicating by aspects of non-verbal communication that we are interested in, and listening to, what the student is saying, and elements would include the following:

1   Maintaining appropriate eye contact. In the dominant culture of Britain, there is a sense that eye contact is an indication of interest and attention. Some sources even specify that a 'normal' percentage of time spent in eye contact during a conversation would be between 60 and 70 per cent, while fixed eye contact, where we don't look away from the person we are speaking to, is interpreted as aggressive. On the other hand, we can

interpret lack of eye contact to mean that someone is shifty or dissembling – the 'she wouldn't look me in the eye' syndrome. It is important to note that different cultural norms apply, so that for some of our students, making eye contact with an authority figure would be considered a mark of disrespect.

2   Posture. We are advised that a relaxed and open posture signals to the student that we are ready to listen and open to hearing what they have to say, whereas a closed and tense posture can signal anxiety and lack of assurance in the tutor role.

3   Head movements. Stillness is generally advocated, as jerks, twitches, looking around can indicate lack of interest or unwillingness to listen.

4   Facial expression. This should be appropriate to the story we are hearing from the students, and it is suggested that mirroring the student's expression is a good way to signal that we are listening to and understanding their concerns.

5   Orientation. We need to be able to see our student, yet sitting directly opposite can be a confrontational position, so ideally, as stated above, we would sit at an angle of up to 90 degrees where eye contact is still possible, even though there may also be the sharing of documents.

6   Proximity. How physically close we get to our students in tutorial can often be dictated by the size of the space in which the tutorial is conducted. However, the distance at which we are comfortable with other people is culturally, as well as individually, defined. As a generalization, English and Scottish people tend to be more distant than, for example, people from Arab cultures, and misunderstandings or discomfort can arise from lack of understanding about the appropriate distance to maintain. Mehrabian (1972) suggests that, typically, white Anglo-Saxon cultures like to have between 15 cm and 1 metre of personal space, while W. H. Auden in 'Prologue: The Birth of Architecture' (1966) suggests he requires '30 inches' of personal space (76 cm for those of you who don't remember Imperial measurements!). We would suggest that, no matter how reassuring a tutor

wants to be, it is better not to touch students during tutorial, as touch can be misconstrued.

Lists like this always leave us feeling 'yes, but ...'.

I know that these are good dispositions for attending to students, that tutors who consciously adopt them find them useful, and that we should think carefully about how our body language is being interpreted by learners; but we also think that a tutor who is timing the frequency of eye contact, or sitting uncomfortably because they don't wish, for example, to cross their legs and appear 'closed', is not an effective tutor. To simulate naturalness is not to be natural. The key seems to be to have a reflexive awareness of the effect our appearance, movements and seating arrangements have on students and to be prepared to learn, practise and adjust accordingly.

Along with attending skills, further active listening skills might typically include the following:

1   *Not interrupting*. This is self-explanatory. A tutor who interrupts is not allowing the student to express their concerns, and is perhaps engaged in following their own train of thought rather than focusing on issues important to the student.

2   *Using minimal encouragers*. These are the vocalizations, the umms and ahs that we typically use to indicate that we are still listening and are interested in what is being said. These are the sounds that we make when listening on the phone and an absence of these can indicate to the student either disinterest or lack of understanding.

3   *Repetition*. Repeating a significant word, or the final word of what the student has said, can encourage them to continue, without the tutor interrupting with a question, which, if ill-judged, could block the student and change the course of the conversation.

4   *Paraphrasing*. This can be used to check that you have understood the student's intended meaning.

5   *Summarizing*. An important skill to use in order to recap and pull out the main points of the tutorial and facilitate joint understanding. It is good practice for either the tutor or student to make a summary of the discussion for

the tutorial record or the student's ILP, and for both to sign agreement of the issues covered and of any targets or plan of action.

Again, we would wish to enter a caveat here, in that while these are important skills for a tutor to use, when they are not used well, for example, if the paraphrase is as long as the original utterance, or if repetition is overused, the effect can be to create a parody of a conversation and can hinder communication rather than facilitate it. The key to successful use of these skills is practice and reflective self-awareness.

In Table 5 (below) there is a transcription of a section of a tutorial which will illustrate how important it is to listen, and how easy it is to pursue our own agendas as teachers and tutors, rather than listening to the concerns of our students. The tutorial transcript runs down the left-hand side of the page and a commentary on listening skills is on the right.

Table 5: Tutorial transcription – listening skills

Tutor: Hello (name). Thank you for handing in your project. How have you found it so far?	*A good opening. The tutor is welcoming and asks an open question to encourage the student to talk.*
Student: It was very difficult, Miss. I am not sure about how to map it.	*Elicits a response which shows that the student has concerns he would like to raise (mapping the project).*
T: OK, but we will go through that in a sec. Umm, firstly do you know how many words it is?	*The student's response is ignored. Both in terms of the general difficulty of the work and the specific concern about mapping. Tutor has her own agenda which she pursues by asking a closed question. Repetition of the student's words on a rising intonation 'map it?' would have helped the student continue and articulate his concerns, as would use of an encouraging 'mmm?' An opportunity has been missed to explore and perhaps deepen the student's understanding of the work.*
S: No, no I haven't added it up.	
T: Do you know how to get the computer to do it?	*Tutor pursues her preoccupation with length of work completed. Another closed question.*

S: Yes, using the word count, yes.

T: Yes, you need to find out the word count and just write it on.

Continuing pursuit of tutor's agenda.

S: On every page...

T: No, just the total. See this one here, she has just done an index. Umm, terms of reference, that's easy enough, and a manager's authenticity, which I can do for you. Also executive summary and then they have just started to go through each section.

Tutor responds to student's question but then continues with her agenda which has moved on to look at the work of another student. The focus of a tutorial should be the tutee and his work.

Tutor is talking, not listening and not checking student's understanding of what she is saying.

S: So my introduction is not long enough.

Student attempts to re-focus tutorial on his own work. It appears that he has interpreted the tutor's focus on someone else's assignment as a criticism of his own.

T: Hold on, I'll have a read through in a sec ... analysis of the current system, recommendations, and they have just done an implementation and review of how they would put their ideas into practice. And then she has put some appendices in, some information that refers to the text, and that is her mapping document. Right, so what you have done then is a methodology, that's fine, that one is OK, ummmm, executive summary, right then, you can write this one at the end. So if I put ...

Tutor doesn't respond to his concern but continues to focus on the work of another student.

Still no response to the student's question.

Tutor rather than student focus.

S: It says keep it brief, and I don't know how brief.

Student tries again to elicit a response to the earlier question about length of introduction.

T: Well, that's OK. Just a paragraph that sums up what you have done. For example, I have suggested the following things that would make the hotel run a lot more smoothly.

I'm not sure that this question is answered.

Tutorials are often conducted in circumstances where time is at a premium and there can be a concern to make sure that the specified content is covered, to the detriment of the individual student who may have specific and personal issues they would like to raise. In this extract, the tutor was speaking approximately four times more than the student was. It is important in tutoring, perhaps even more so than in classroom teaching, that we 'ask', rather than 'tell', so that we start with the student's view of their learning, rather than the vision that we want to impose.

Making interventions

If listening is one of the key skills used in tutoring, it cannot be the only one. A tutorial is a dialogue and the good tutor makes appropriate interventions, at appropriate times, to facilitate learning and development. A framework which we have found useful in thinking about what we say in tutorial is John Heron's six-category intervention analysis (Heron 1975). Heron studied interventions employed during counselling sessions and developed a taxonomy for the analysis and categorization of such interventions. Tutoring is not counselling, but Heron's framework is applicable across a range of settings and can provide some valuable insights into why some of the things that we say to students in tutorial can be helpful, and some things do not act as the catalysts for development that we might hope.

In broad terms, interventions are categorized as being either *authoritative*, of the 'I am telling you' kind, or *facilitative*, of the 'you tell me about it' kind.

Authoritative interventions are further broken down into three types:

- *Prescriptive* interventions, in which the tutor is giving advice or directing the student to a particular course of action. These interventions are made from an 'expert' standpoint, so should relate to aspects of academic progress on which the tutor might legitimately claim to be expert, e.g. 'you must get your assignment in by the deadline or marks will be deducted', rather than to personal issues on which no one can be anyone else's expert – e.g. 'well, you obviously need to divorce her', is not helpful.

- *Informative* interventions in which we provide information or instruction. A positive aspect of this intervention is that information can be given to the student on which they can base their decisions – e.g. 'if your assignment isn't in by the deadline, 5 per cent will be deducted from your mark for every day that it's late'. Less positive informative interventions can also be made when too much or partial information is given, so the student becomes confused.
- *Confronting* interventions provide a direct challenge to behaviour, attitudes or belief. This can involve giving direct feedback which invites the student to consider aspects of their performance or of themselves which they may have taken for granted or not noticed – e.g. 'do you realize that you put an apostrophe before every "s" in that essay?' or 'on the one hand, you say you missed Trevor's class because you were at the dentist's, on the other hand, you were sitting in the row in front of me at the cinema all yesterday afternoon'.

Facilitative interventions also have three categories:

- *Cathartic* interventions. These interventions may be used to help someone work through often painful emotions which may not have been previously acknowledged. As such, we would suggest that these are interventions to be approached with extreme caution and perhaps used only by tutors with appropriate counselling training and supervision. It is an irresponsible act to encourage the unleashing of emotions which could overwhelm both the student and tutor.
- *Catalytic* interventions. These encourage reflection, self-direction and problem solving and are particularly useful in promoting learner autonomy – e.g. 'can you tell me more about ...', 'why do you think that?'
- *Supportive* interventions. The tutor bolsters the confidence of the student by focusing on areas of competence, by signifying approval and acknowledging effort and achievement – e.g. 'this is a very good report', 'I'm glad

that things have worked out for you'. This intervention can also run through all the other categories.

None of these interventions is intrinsically better or worse than the others. The concern is to use them appropriately so that the student is helped to develop and progress. Again, it might be useful to see how they are used in practice, so the following is another partial tutorial transcript; this time the tutorial is with a student teacher following a lesson observation. The transcription starts partway through the tutorial.

Table 6: Tutorial transcript – catalytic and supportive interventions

S: So, if I'd had more time I would have prepared it differently ... mmm it's the first time I've done groupwork with them ...	
T: How would you have prepared it differently, what would you have done?	*Catalytic intervention to promote exploration of alternatives*
S: When they were studying the OHP they were nicely concentrated, their thoughts were concentrated, so I think what I would have done is ... do a short OHP, direct them, give them an activity ...	
T: Mmm	*Minimal encourager, so the student's analysis of the lesson is not interrupted*
S: Keep that, but make it sharper, because I tended to say OK I'll give you 10 minutes and then I'd give them another couple of minutes ...	
T: Yeah ...	*Another encourager, no interruption*
S: Stop that, feed back, make them be quiet while the others feed back, make it a lot snappier	
T: Yes, I think you're exactly right	*Supportive intervention, to affirm the worth of the student's suggestions*

Balance

Having read hundreds of tutorial transcripts provided by student teachers, we would suggest that, on the whole, the majority of tutors are predisposed to be very supportive of their students. However, for tutorials to be successful in promoting development, it is also important to provide the student with challenges to help keep them motivated and ensure that they progress. The skilled tutor will work to ensure that they achieve the optimum balance between these two aspects of the tutorial process, as elements of both are essential. From mentoring theory (Daloz 1986), we know that continuous support, unbalanced by elements of challenge, encourages students in the belief that their current situation/level of work cannot be improved upon, so development is unlikely; they are constantly reassured that they are working well, the student and tutor both feel good about the work and targets are not set, so development is stifled. On the other hand, challenge, unmitigated by support, can lead the student to despair that nothing they do is ever good enough, so they may as well give up. In both cases, learning is inhibited rather than fostered. Too little support or challenge can leave the student in a fog produced by lack of feedback. They don't know what they are doing well, nor where improvements could be made, so are left without direction. There can never be a formula for finding the right balance, so the tutor needs to be sensitive to the individual needs of the student and to gauge the levels of support and challenge according to the situation and the moment.

Values and attitudes

In the same way that we have individual approaches to teaching, the style adopted by tutors in tutorial will vary according not only to the skills and knowledge of the tutor but also according to their personal values and attitudes. Here, again, theories developed in counselling can provide insights into tutoring. Carl Rogers (Rogers and Freiberg 1993), acknowledged as the founder of the 'client-centred' school of counselling, suggested that the key to facilitating significant learning rests upon certain attitudinal qualities that exist in the personal *relationship* between the tutor/facilitator and the learner. He suggested that there are three core conditions underpinning the relationship:

1   *Congruence*: the notion that the tutor is genuine, is being herself, 'without front', and is, in the context of tutoring, meeting the student in a direct personal encounter on a person–to–person basis.

2   *Acceptance*: this relates to the idea of the tutor holding a warm, positive and accepting attitude to the student. The student is accepted for what s/he is, not what the tutor would like her/him to be. I think that here it is important to make a distinction between the idea of acceptance and the idea of approval. There is no suggestion here that where a tutor is able to experience unconditional positive regard for the student as a fellow human being this necessarily entails approval of their behaviour.

3   *Empathic understanding*: this is the idea that the tutor attempts to understand deeply the student's world, to experience it *as if* it were her own, without ever losing the 'as if' quality of the understanding. This is an understanding which is not based on analysis or evaluation but accepts the inner world of the student.

Tutors, however, are not counsellors, and if these core conditions for the facilitation of learning and change seem, for some tutors, either too difficult or too inappropriate to reach, it might be useful to look at some of the pitfalls of tutoring which should be avoided as being generally unhelpful to students. The following are adapted from the work of Henshaw (1973).

Tutoring pitfalls

Eight potential pitfalls in tutoring are described, and in some cases illustrated below. These are examples of the sorts of behaviours and attitudes which should be avoided if tutoring is to be productive of learning and development.

1   *Over-clarification*. Anxiety or desire to be helpful can lead the tutor to ask too many 'clarifying' questions or to

propose quick solutions to what they perceive to be the problem, so that concerns the student might have are lost. In this way the tutor imposes her/his understanding and structure on the tutorial and blocks the student exploring her/his concerns. The tutorial extract in Table 7 demonstrates how the tutor's concerns can completely dominate the interaction:

Table 7: Tutorial extract – tutor concerns taking over

T: It would help me to know what support you have, is your company keen to help you? S: They are supportive they send us on courses in finance . . .	*A closed question, focusing on support from one quarter. A more open question 'what sort of support might you be able to call on?' would help the student articulate their ideas*
T: That's good, do you have support from your manager and colleagues? . . . S: Yes, yes	*Another closed question attempting to further clarify the sources of support (a minimal encourager here may have helped the student explore more deeply the support offered by the company)*
T: What about your family, I know your family are a long way away, are the people that you have here, are they supportive? S: Yes, yes	*A third closed attempt at clarification*
T: So you have time to study at home? S: Yes, yes after work	*Fourth closed clarification of specific nature of support*
T: And your husband is happy if you say I have to read this book . . . S: Yes, yes, absolutely	*Fifth closed attempt (overtones of sexism, possible cultural imperialism)* *Sixth question on the same subject*
T: So outside of here you have a support network? S: Yes, yes	*The student may well be wondering if the tutor is listening*

2   *Storytelling.* In the desire to communicate understanding, possibly even empathy, the tutor says 'Yes, I know exactly what you mean, a similar thing happened to me

(my son, my neighbour ...).' The effect of this is to stop listening to the student and shift the focus to the tutor and her story. This is rarely an effective intervention, as circumstances and people involved will be different. The student probably needs to have *his/her* story listened to.

3   *Tolerating silence.* In tutorials, as in class, it is important to be able to gauge the quality and the appropriate length of silences. Students may need time to reflect, to formulate and then articulate what they want to say. A tutor who cannot tolerate silence may break the student's train of thought and block communication. If you find it really difficult to remain silent, counting slowly to 10 in your head can help.

4   *Being judgemental.* '*A spell in the army would do you the world of good my lad*' is stereotypical, but the gap between the student's culture and the tutor's may mean that the tutor presses for their own preferred solutions based on their own values rather than those of the student. '*You'll just have to forgo your football/clubbing/etc. until you get this assignment finished*' is equally likely to be an unproductive intervention. Solutions to problems should be jointly explored and agreed.

5   *Forming a 'gruesome twosome'.* A most unproductive tutor–student partnership can be formed when there is collusion in a mutual admiration society, the 'good' tutor and the 'good' student congratulating themselves (silently) and each other (loudly) on the success of the partnership and the mutuality of their shared world view.
Student: 'No one has ever understood me like you do.'
Tutor: 'You always grasp these things so much more quickly than the rest of the group.'

The tutorial extract in Table 8, part of the same tutorial as Table 7, illustrates this pitfall:

Table 8: Tutorial extract – gruesome-twosome

T: What did you think of yesterday's session?	*Open question*
S: It was very interesting, very enjoyable. I don't know what I got out of it. No, if you'd come in and said we're going to do time management and we're going to look at Covey and this is what we're going to do, Ugh, oh no, because I wasn't feeling a hundred per cent yesterday, but it was a nice little bit of here we go, right, do this, well, OK then, do this, huh? I didn't come here to work, (laughter) what do you mean, move? But yes, I enjoyed yesterday	*Collusive laughter*
T: Oh good	
S: But I must admit I enjoy your sessions, whether it's because we're alike in some ways	*Beginning to establish shared values/attitudes*
T: Like in our intolerance of noisy students	*Tutor builds on this mutuality*
S: Yes, that's right, it really does get to run you down doesn't it . . .	*Beginning of a mutual admiration society which could run on unless a change of focus is achieved*

6   *Lack of trust in learner autonomy.* For some tutors, the need to feel omni-competent or indispensable can lead them to attempt to take charge of the student's development. This can be manifested by unreasonable and unrealistic offers of help – 'don't worry, leave it to me, I'll sort out your *referencing/punctuation/maths teacher/social worker/landlord'.* This can lead to student over-dependence, when what is needed is help to cope with their own life/learning rather than having it taken over by the tutor. In some cases, the tutor can experience such a 'buzz' from helping that they fail to refer a student to an agency which is more equipped to provide the skilled help needed by the student.

7   *Time.* This is one of the most difficult issues in that tutors tend to feel that they would be better able to help

students if they had more time to spend in one to one tutorials. When a student asks to speak to their tutor outside a scheduled session, one of the first judgements to make is whether their concern can be dealt with on the spot or whether an appointment needs to be arranged. A pitfall to be avoided is encouraging a student to begin speaking when the tutor is concerned about their next lesson, attending a meeting, picking up photocopying. Whatever the issue, the student will not feel listened to, and if the student has come with something that they find difficult to say, they may never get started again if interrupted in mid-flow. A helpful reply to a student's '*can I have a word?*' is not necessarily '*of course*'. It is much more helpful to say: '*I can't talk to you now, but I can see you for 5/10/20 minutes at break/lunchtime/4 o'clock*'. The student can then make a decision about how long they might need. It is not part of the tutor's role to be constantly available to students, and, sometimes, the possibility of having to forgo their own breaks in order to see their tutor can encourage students to be more resourceful and independent. The student who genuinely needs a tutor is usually happy to agree to a later meeting.

8   *Promising confidentiality*. This is an important and particularly thorny issue. Students who reveal to their tutor information about their past or current circumstances or their innermost feelings, often do so in the belief that they are sharing a confidence and that this is necessary for help to be obtained. They often trust the tutor, assuming the information will remain confidential – '*I don't want this to go any further*'. **Tutors are not in a position to guarantee confidentiality**. While it is to be hoped that a tutor would not gossip about a student, even under the guise of sharing information with colleagues, in some instances, conversations must be reported, for example if there are child protection issues involved. A helpful guideline to follow is to make sure, before the student tells their story (and there is usually some preliminary hedging, as in the example above, which signals what is

about to happen) that they are aware that confidentiality is not automatic. The student can then make an informed decision about what they say. If a tutor feels it would be helpful to a student to share information with colleagues, the student's permission should be sought, and an explanation given for why sharing information might be of benefit. It can also be helpful to the student who wants to talk in confidence to refer them to a student counsellor whose regulatory body will have formulated guidelines on confidentiality.

Boundaries

Inevitably, tutorials will raise issues which we as teachers are not qualified to deal with. One of the most difficult aspects of this is that we have to ask the tutee to move on. They have to tell their story to a new person, probably a stranger, and they might be reluctant to do this, having screwed up all their courage to be honest with you. We can ease the transition by knowing exactly the right service they need, making appointments for them, even going with them to their first appointment, but what we cannot do is become the expert they need. We have to explain clearly the areas of demarcation and be prepared to withdraw if they do not take our advice. These are hard decisions, but essential for us to continue in our role of teacher – we are not counsellors. Referral of a student to another agency is something which needs to be handled with sensitivity, openness and honesty. One of the issues of which it is important to be aware is that referring a student can make them feel bad: it can make them think that their problem is too awful even for their competent adult tutor to cope with. For this reason, referral must be discussed with the student. Once the tutor has explained clearly the reasons for wanting to refer, the decision must be the student's. Referral should only occur with the informed consent of the student.

Part of our tutorial kit, hopefully supplied centrally by the college, should be a list of local referral points: learning support, dyslexia advice, the Samaritans, Citizens' Advice for debt counselling, housing organizations, and especially counsellors. It is, however, part of the tutor's role to double-check whether the individual or agency to which you want to refer your student does in fact provide the necessary and appropriate services. This is particularly important if you are referring outside the college or workplace, as it is not always possible to determine the orientation or even reputation of an agency from its title. Some, for example a number of agencies which offer support in pregnancy, can have very specific aims, which may not be appropriate to your student's needs.

It might also be a good idea to give the tutee your suggested next port of call in writing, on the action plan described above, because there might be a delay between this appointment and their decision to take your advice.

Further considerations

Tutoring students, particularly those who bring personal difficulties to tutorial, can be an emotional and draining experience. We have described above how it is important for tutors to monitor the limits of their expertise, but it is also important to monitor the effect that tutoring needy students can have on us. Again, we can learn from counselling theory. The psychodynamic notion of projection suggests that powerful emotions can be projected from one person to another. Most of us have experienced as part of everyday life the feeling of being affected by other people's moods: we can feel low after talking with a friend who is depressed or have our mood lifted by joining a happy, joking group of friends. Similarly, in tutorial, a tutor who is open and receptive to the feelings of their tutee may find themselves being used as a container for the student's mental pain (Salzberger-Wittenberg et al. 1983). The tutor may leave the tutorial feeling bad, particularly if the student's story chimes with personal experiences and feelings from her past or present, while the student leaves possibly feeling better at having unloaded their difficulties. It is not a good idea for us to allow ourselves to be treated as a kind of emotional dustbin. This is unhelpful to the student, who cannot, in reality, dump problems, and to the tutor, who has to work hard to overcome the effect of the evoked emotions. It is important to monitor the effect that some kinds of tutorial can have on the tutor and for the tutor to reflect carefully on the nature of what they are feeling and the reasons for the feelings. It can sometimes be helpful for the tutor to talk these emotional aspects of tutoring through with colleagues or with the college counsellor. Most college counsellors are happy to work with their teaching colleagues and support them in the emotional aspects of their tutoring role.

Tutorials as inclusion and differentiation

The tutorial is by definition the best place to support the individual student. Paul Martinez' and Felicity Munday's work (Martinez and Munday 1998) demonstrated that tutorial support was a *'major factor in retention'*, (p.95). The essence of inclusion is that students are encouraged to complete their qualification, giving them the option of returning to learning in the following year or even after a break. Once a student 'fails', the barriers are up and the chances are that it will be very difficult for them to pick up their learning later. All qualified teachers in the FE sector subscribe to the value of inclusion but sometimes this can lead to huge problems with disaffected students who could complete their qualification (usually at Level 1 or 2) but who have not really applied themselves all year. We have observed tutorials, in the summer term, where the teacher is working flat out to 'support' the student and yet I am doubtful whether the student really deserves so much support. This can extend to additional sessions during the teacher's breaks, strong guidance on where to find information that should have been researched months ago and re-teaching sessions the student did not bother to turn up for. Our concern about this is not the ethic, because we do believe in inclusion, but the health of the teacher, who will already be timetabled for many more hours than a schoolteacher. This is an example which possibly borders on supererogatory professionalism, teachers offering a service which is 'beyond the call of duty'. How far does a teacher go to support a student? There are no clear guidelines for FE teachers. Research (Clow 2001) and our experience provide examples of teachers giving students their home or mobile number, buying students breakfast, advising on treatment for head lice, organizing for smelly students to use college facilities to shower, taking students' clothes home to wash them, even standing in for parents in life-threatening situations. This is all a matter of professional judgement and will be dependent on the neediness of the students involved.

Using theory during tutorials

There are dozens of theories that relate to how people learn. Some such as VAK (Ginnis 2002) have a high profile in the school sector, others such as the Honey and Mumford learning styles work are used in the training sector. FENTO standards specifically mentioned that learning styles should be taken into account, likewise the new standards for Qualified Teacher Learning and Skills (QTLS). No specific theoretical approach is mentioned and the recent thorough analysis by Coffield *et al.* (2005) suggests that no single tool is properly validated.

Nevertheless, teacher training over the years has advocated using learning theory as the basis for planning lessons. At the risk of being branded heretics, we suggest that whatever theoretical approach is used in the design of lessons, the best outcome that can be expected is that for any individuals in a group of students, at least part of the lesson will appeal to them, interest them and motivate them to continue with their learning.

The one to one tutorial session where the tutor is using good questioning and listening skills is a much better scenario for the application of learning theory. In our view the choice of theory will be personal; what is important is that a theory is selected to allow a structured evaluation of the interaction. The Theory Into Practice (http://tip.psychology.org/) site lists 50 theories of learning. We have selected some examples of theories below that we or our trainees have found useful, in that they provide a structure which can be explained to the student and may help them to move forwards in their learning:

Kolb's experiential learning cycle

The Kolb learning cycle (see Chapter 1) has long been a favourite theory that we use in the design of lessons. It may be best used as a check that the students will, during the lesson, be pushed to complete at least one cycle. The most common gap in the cycle is the lack of opportunity for students to reflect individually as part of the learning process. Too often, they jump from concrete experience to some sort of group discussion without the opportunity to think about their own ideas and impressions. It can also be a useful theory to apply when working with individual students.

Some years ago, Ros was planning some staff development on how to do tutorials. She wanted to use video and used a simulation to create film of bad practice. She decided to video two real tutorials, and then edit them to create clips to demonstrate good practice. She asked Phil, an experienced and well-respected colleague, if she could video two of his tutorials with HND engineering students. At the time, he was using the BTEC common skills as the basis for the structure of his tutorials, asking the students to self-assess themselves against the 18 competences in the seven skills (Edexel 2000). As she observed and filmed the tutorial, she was amazed at some of the tutees' deficits. She then realized that each tutee was struggling because they were leaving out specific stages of Kolb's cycle.

Both students, Andy and Brian, were on a full-time course in an area of low unemployment, and both were struggling with the course. It is probably fair to say that if they had a better academic history they would not have been on this course. In effect they were not good at learning at this stage in their life (aged about 18). Phil reviewed each of the common skills in turn. He had prepared good open questions for each criterion. When he asked Andy whether he was keeping a diary, Andy looked totally bemused. Phil meant to explore whether Andy was planning when he would work on his assignments and whether he was doing any kind of reflection. Andy answered 'Well my Mum gave me one for Christmas but I haven't written anything in it yet'! Phil went on to explain how Andy might organize himself better by using a diary, and how he might note things he did not understand to be able to ask teachers when he next saw them.

Brian's tutorial faltered in a different place. The question that foxed him was the one about using the library. He looked blank, admitted he had never visited it and that he was not using any books to help him complete assignments, just using class notes. Phil handled both students and their difficulties well. As Ros began to reflect on them and to review the video she realized that this was an example in which Kolb's cycle could explain the fact that these two students were not successful learners. Andy was just ploughing on doing coursework, if and when he could find the time, without taking time out for reflective observation. Brian had a depleted model of abstract conceptualization, as he was not using any reading to support the learning process.

Brain-based theories

In the last forty years, a panoply of theories have emerged that can be useful during a tutorial. They can be used to make tutees aware that there are a variety of ways to approach the task in hand. For some, this is in effect giving them permission to use their strengths, however bizarre the methods might seem at first. Once they have made progress, they can begin to develop the weaker areas that were holding them back in the past.

Left and right brain

In the late 1960s Sperry, while researching the cerebral cortex, put forward the theory that the major intellectual functions were divided between the left and right hemispheres. The right hemisphere was considered dominant in rhythm, spatial awareness, gestalt (wholeness), imagination, daydreaming, colour and dimension; the left in words, logic, numbers, sequence, linearity, analysis and lists (Buzan 1989, Buzan and Buzan 1995). More recent research has shown and continues to demonstrate that this is a simplistic representation (Blakemore and Frith 2005). However, the concept that the school curriculum up to the age of 16 concentrates and benefits those with left-brain strengths, but that right-brain mental skills are just as important in more advanced study and the workplace, can be liberating for students who have found school de-motivating.

Mindmaps

Tony Buzan's work on using the full capacity of the brain to improve thinking and learning skills led to his ideas on Radiant Thinking and in particular his Mindmaps (Buzan and Buzan 1995). Teaching trainee teachers to create mindmaps can also be a liberating experience for them, and one they can pass on to their students. The Buzans' approach to mindmaps, while being very effective for more intellectual pursuits, is particular and complex. It is unlikely that students working on Level 1 and 2 courses would be able to achieve the map in an unsupported environment. We, or more truthfully, some of our trainee teachers, have developed a simplified rule system for helping students create mindmaps: the 4 Cs (see Table 9).

Table 9: The 4 Cs

a Centre	Ideally with a picture and a short written title
Colour	Each arm of the diagram in a different colour
Capitals	Despite the advice that all resources for students should use lower case, this is an exception. Capitals take more time but ensure that spelling is clear
Cartoons	Include as many pictures as possible, to illustrate key points

Note taking

Mindmaps can be used for making notes from lectures, books, Internet, TV programmes. The emphasis here is on *making* notes. The easy access to information on the Internet is fraught with problems. Research (Howe, cited in Buzan and Buzan 1995: 51) has shown that being given notes (which in effect downloading pages from the Web is) is the least effective method of recording information for presentations or exams. If students can be persuaded to review lessons by creating mindmaps and then adding more information from additional reading, the personal involvement should increase their learning.

IT and mindmaps

There are now various software packages that can be used to create mindmaps and this might suit some students better. 'Inspiration' is the most frequently provided, but '2simple' is designed for primary school children and might be useful with some students. Alternatively the more sophisticated graphics programmes can be employed, such as Adobe Illustrator.

The key with all of these ideas is that learning requires effort and does not (unfortunately!) usually happen by osmosis. Or does it?

The most recent research in cognitive neuroscience does suggest that sleep following attempts to learn will improve performance. In Stickgold's experiments, it was found that a nap of 30–60 minutes immediately following learning significantly improved learning performance on wakening compared to the pre-sleep performance (Blakemore and Frith 2005: 175). This improvement was not achieved by just having a break. Many research projects now underline the importance of having enough sleep when in a learning situation. This suggests that this may be an issue to check up on with students who are struggling at college. Adults need seven and a half hours a night, adolescents nine hours, children need more. Motivation comes from success, so each time a student achieves, the chances are that they will stay the course.

Planning written work

Another key use of mindmaps is in planning. The first stage is to collate everything you know already on a mindmap and then add to the map as you read more, or just remember things that escaped your memory the first time. Then you can add a sequence to the map to structure the assignment, essay or presentation – or even the chapter of this book.

Multiple intelligences (MI)

In the 1980s Howard Gardner published his theory that there existed a small number of relatively discrete 'intelligences' (Gardner 1993). Two of these, logico-mathematical intelligence and linguistic intelligence, were the focus of standard IQ tests, but the others (spatial, bodily-kinaesthetic, musical, interpersonal and intrapersonal) were less valued, though combined in each individual to create an 'intellectual repertoire' (White 1998). In the same way as the left/right brain skills illustrate that there are a variety of ways of learning that the brain can provide, the MI theory offers methods that appeal to those with different strengths. Again, there is an element of giving permission to try different ways of learning. If talking out loud or audiotape recording help you learn, then that is fine. If dancing round the room to a rap written to remind you of the principles of electrical power generation helps you, great!

It was no coincidence that the original IQ tests focused on words and logic; these are key areas for success in life and work, but by working through their different strengths, students can be supported to achieve in all areas of 'intelligence'.

The tutor's role is to suggest ways in which strengths can be used to surmount the next educational hurdle.

Neuro-linguistic programming (NLP)
NLP, first developed in the 1960s, is widely used as a therapeutic technique (especially in the treatment of phobias) and in communications training. Some aspects of it are also useful when working one to one with tutees. NLP suggests that each individual has sensory system preferences: visual, auditory, kinaesthetic, olfactory and gustatory. The latter two are absent from Gardner's intelligences, a point made by White (1998). They probably have little relevance to the school curriculum (hence the development of VAK) but there are vocational areas where smelling and tasting are very significant and are probably not valued or developed as they should be. This deficit was clearly demonstrated during the Jamie Oliver Channel 4 television series *Fifteen*. Jamie set out to select fifteen unemployed and/or homeless people to train as chefs. His selection test was to ask each applicant to taste different foods and describe what they could taste. His problem was that nearly all of them struggled with this task and had no vocabulary to demonstrate their tasting/smelling skills.

We can identify these preferences from clues that the individual unwittingly presents: eye movements and choice of vocabulary.

Language clues

The words we choose tend to link to our preferred sensory system (O'Connor and Seymour 2002). By reading this chapter, or handouts that you have written, you could tell the preferred sensory system of the author. The clues are in the words chosen: appeal, link, strengths, escaped, stay the course, collate, focus, illuminate.

You might hear 'kinaesthetic' students use: link, strengths, escape, stay the course or:

- I can handle it
- I haven't quite grasped that
- I feel more comfortable with that option

Students with a visual sensory preference might say: see, look, focus, illuminate

- I see what you mean
- Let me see if I can remember
- Of course that's my view

Those with a highly developed auditory representational system might use: sound, hear, quieten, voice, tune into.

And students might say:

- That sounds good to me
- That rings a bell
- He likes to voice his opinion

By listening to our students' choice of language, we can gauge their preferred representational system and this can have two benefits. First, we can change our language to 'fit' theirs, so easing communication between us. Secondly, it gives us a clue as to how to attempt future explanations. A strongly visual student will be helped by us drawing large diagrams, using images and colour. Yes, the mindmap is a good candidate here!

The auditory student will benefit from clear explanations; maybe you should ask them to explain it back to you, and the kinaesthetic student may benefit from moving around or by linking new knowledge to emotional experiences of the past.

Asking a student the question, 'What did you think of last

week's lesson?' can be a good starting point for working out their preferred system.

NLP has also established that our eyes move in different ways according to what we are trying to think about. This also gives us clues to how a student is thinking. If you ask a student what they thought of a certain lesson, you can judge to some extent which system they are using to recall it. If their eyes go up (or are out of focus concentrating on the distance) they are visualizing the lesson. If their eyes move horizontally they are recalling what they heard in the lesson, using the auditory representational system. If their eyes go down it is a bit more difficult; either they are recalling, through their kinaesthetic system, how they felt during the lesson, or their physical movements, or they are having an internal dialogue as to whether they should tell you the truth or not! When eyes move down to the left-hand side this signifies an internal dialogue and might be an indicator that the next words spoken will be a lie! A follow up of 'What did you really think?' can be very illuminating! These ocular accessing cues relate to most right-handed people, but the kinaesthetic cues can be reversed in some left-handed and some right-handed people. The eye movement gives us a clue, but we will always need to check out our assumptions by questioning.

Rapport

Other techniques which stem from NLP can be useful in one to one situations. Mirroring the student's mannerisms can consolidate the relationship between tutor and tutee. And pacing, where the tutor speaks at the same speed and pace as the student, can be used to calm an agitated student. The tutor starts to speak as quickly as the student and then gradually slows down, bringing the student in to a calmer mode of communication.

Matching/mismatching

Another concept that has been helpful for tutors and tutees has been that of students who learn in overtly different ways. A Matcher will take every new idea, appraise it positively, look at different ways it might be useful, look at how well it fits into earlier ideas. We love these students! They are a joy to teach.

But some students are Mismatchers (Jensen 1988: 46). Each new idea you present is appraised negatively. They question, challenge, find as many ways as possible of showing your ideas to be erroneous, always look for the exceptions to the rule. And then just when you think that teaching was probably not the career for you, they accept your idea and happily move on to shred the next theory or principle you present. This is the way they learn. They do not have a personal vendetta against you and just realizing that can help us cope with these students. They do often irritate the others in the class and this can cause group dynamic problems too. It can be a good idea to present these ideas to them during tutorial so that they understand what they are doing. They are often confused by the way they need to challenge everything while the others just sit back and accept everything.

Serialist/holist learners
Another useful theory is Pask's work on Serialist and Holists. His theory was developed during the 1960s when trying to simulate thinking on the enormous computers of that time (Pask 1976) He proposed two different basic preferences in thinking. Holists like an overview before they start; they like to know where they are going. Serialists find an overview irritating and want to get going straight away; they work away one thing at a time. Again it can be useful for students to realize that there are different approaches. Recently, we had a trainee teacher who was upset that her mentor did not have a proper scheme of work and that she had only about a week's notice of what she had to teach and no idea of how that would link to her next lesson. When we explored this, we found that she was Holist in her approach. She always wants a complete overview of where she is going, so in fact she was more unsettled by this example of poor mentoring than another trainee might have been.

Emotional intelligence
Daniel Goleman's book on Emotional Intelligence (1996) also offers ideas that can help with tutorials. In particular his six

steps, 'traffic light' approach (p. 276) can be a tool that students might be offered to help them control their aggressive actions.

Red light	1	Stop, calm down and think before you act
Amber light	2	State the problem and how you feel
	3	Set a positive goal
	4	Think of lots of solutions
	5	Think ahead to the consequences
Green light	6	Go ahead and try the best plan

Posters outlining this approach are now widely used in early-years institutions. With adolescents, cognitive neuroscience research has shown that the changes in the prefrontal cortex mean that the ability consistently to inhibit behaviour, especially risky behaviour, is lacking. Traffic lights serve as a reminder that there are other ways to behave that might have better consequences.

Goleman also mentions Csikszentmihalyi's concept of 'flow'. Flow happens when an individual surmounts a challenge and loses themselves in what they are doing. It is what athletes call 'the zone', when time stands still and they perform at their best, 'stretching beyond their former limits' (1996: 90/95). We would like all our students to experience this! And sometimes when you question them about doing an earlier piece of coursework or practical exercise they realize that they have experienced it – it is when actually doing the studying provides its own pleasure. In order to enter 'flow', you have to accept a challenge, for instance to put time aside and force yourself to sit and write for a period of time. They key is that the challenge is just far enough ahead of your previous performance that you can manage it. I think that the common student retort 'This is boring' is the opposite of 'flow' and is a signal that the challenge is too great, and therefore they are afraid to start. Our role is then to break down the challenge into more manageable parts, so that they can cope with the steps to reach the desired end result. This might be a key part of the tutorial process.

Conclusion

Tutorials are key events in the learning process. In the Martinez and Munday (1998) study, staff agreed that tutorials should:

monitor and support student achievement
develop close, supportive relationships between staff and students
clarify learning aims and career goals through ongoing personal and academic guidance
develop learning styles and study skills
identify personal problems and blocks to learning and make prompt and appropriate referral

In order to work effectively as a tutor you need to

prepare space and time for the tutorial
guide the tutee in how they should prepare for the tutorial, preferably in writing
equip yourself with excellent questioning and listening skills
have access to a range of theories that can assist you in structuring and correcting the learning experience
know where you can refer students when they need more specialist help that you can offer
have a system of recording what happens in tutorials

Further reading

Buzan, T. (1989) *Use your head*, London: BBC Books.

Buzan, T. and Buzan, B. (1995) *The Mindmap book*, London: BBC Books.

Ginnis, P. (2002) *The Teacher's Toolkit: raise classroom achievement with strategies for every learner*, Carmarthen: Crown House.

Green, M. (2001) *Successful tutoring: good practice for managers and tutors*, London: Learning and Skills Development Agency.

Hart, N. (1996) 'The role of the tutor in a college of further education: a comparison of skills used by personal tutors and by student counsellors when working with students in distress' *British Journal of Guidance and Counselling* 24 (1): 83–96.

Nelson-Jones, R. (2004) *Practical Counselling and Helping Skills* (4ᵗʰ edn), London: Sage.

Novak, J. D. and Gowin, D. B. (1984) *Learning How to Learn*, Cambridge: Cambridge University Press.

O'Connor, J. and Seymour, J. (2002) *Introducing NLP: Psychological Skills for Understanding and Influencing People*. London: Element.

For more about Mind Maps™ contact:
  The Buzan Centres Worldwide plc
  Tel: 0845 0099555
  Website: www.buzancentresworldwide.com

7 Managing behaviour

Trevor Dawn

Introduction

When we think back to our own education, we can all remember the teachers that maintained good discipline and were respected; and those that were a soft touch whom we ran rings round and, by extension, we did not respect. Students today are equally aware of the same things. They know that you do not mess around in Mrs X's or Mr Y's class, often for different reasons. The styles of Mrs X and Mr Y may well vary, but central to both, and at the core of the relationship between teacher and class, is something deliberate and well thought out – a sense of what sort of classroom the teacher wants and clear principles as to how this will come about. There is this notion of the 'ideal', not that we can define all of its characteristics, but we know it when we see it. The management of learner behaviour is often equated with the concept of control.

This implies that a classroom climate that is purposeful and happy does not happen by accident. A few charismatic teachers, or those lucky enough to have always taught in a school or college where the vast majority of the students are disposed to behave very well, may never have had to sit down and think how they are going to handle a range of demanding behaviours. For most teachers, however, this is not the case. Most of us are only too conscious of the thin line between order and anarchy. Some days we only just avoid disaster; some days we 'lose it' – our self-control, our composure, our authority – and wonder how ever will we recover. In despair, we turn to colleagues who may or may not know what to do, or are too concerned by their own problems to offer much support. In many cases, we take the problem home with us and brood on our inadequacy, comparing ourselves unfavourably with the ideal, feeling a failure. For many, the loss of control and respect in the classroom is the final straw in a sheaf of pressures that wear one down and some teachers are forced to take time off work as a result of stress in order to recover. Some never do recover, and quit teaching.

This chapter will not provide answers to all problems and situations. What we will try to do is to attempt to synthesize some of the principles that make Mrs X and Mr Y good role models. To do this, we take a holistic approach to disruptive behaviour by addressing the emotional context of teaching; by examining the bases of teacher authority and control; and by demonstrating how the whole gamut of teacher training and experience can be applied to classroom control so that teachers feel that they can be self-supporting. Our basic philosophy is: 'if some teachers can succeed in establishing a happy and productive environment for learning, why not all?'

What is disruption?

In Chapter 5 we recognised that the 14–19 age group is one of volatility where the tectonic clash of childhood and young adulthood often results in volcanic explosions of behaviour, even in the most placid young person. The teenage years are notorious for mood swings, for rebellion and rejection of authority, for disinclination to conform and so on. Sometimes these behaviours are affected by something that happens in or is caused by the college or school environment itself; sometimes the behaviours result from diet and the effects of too much sugar, additives and junk food in general; some are as a result of the emotional 'baggage' entirely outside the classroom that a particular young person is carrying and cannot yet deal with.

It is important to recognize that there may be a variety of reasons why a student is disruptive and that we should stop to think about her/his viewpoint as well as the effect of the behaviour on ourselves (see also Chapter 11: 'Manchild' – p. 224). Whatever the cause, whenever these behaviours come up against the teacher's desire for order so that learning can take place, disruption in some form or other is often unavoidable. It goes with the territory.

Nor is the issue new. There are studies from the 1960s (Curtis 1966) and the 1980s (McManus 1989, Montgomery 1989) that chronicle the existence of disruptive behaviour in schools since the Second World War. McManus (1989) in fact traces the origins of troublesome behaviour back to Cambridge University in the thirteenth century. These books are comprehensive in their coverage and both Montgomery and McManus refer to government reports and trade union surveys to highlight the seriousness of the problem. It is not the intention of this book to duplicate such thoroughness. We take it as a given that teachers do experience troublesome and disruptive behaviour.

It is very difficult to define disruptive behaviour accurately for a number of reasons:

1   Teachers' notions of order are subjective. Some allow a certain amount of chat when the students are engaged in activities or exercises; others want silence and enforce it. Some demand unconditional respect even if they do not earn it.

2   Levels of teacher confidence and experience can also affect attitudes. Some feel that a situation is getting out of hand when their expertise is mildly challenged, whereas others see this as a sign that there is something to work with and that it is better than apathy.

3   Environmental issues such as the shape of the classroom or its location in respect of the sun or its size in relation to the size of the class do have an impact. We have all experienced being cramped for space with a class of 28 in a room big enough for 15.

4   The time of day (or year), the teacher who the class had before you, the length of the lesson, all impact on behaviour. A two-hour key skills lesson from 6 till 8 in the evening for a group of day-release students who have been at college all day can be a discipline disaster waiting to happen.

5   The mix of individual students contains so many

variables in terms of behaviour. We all know that a particular class would be so different without two or three characters. Many young people may have had negative experiences of education and see no reason to be well-behaved for you.

6   Adolescence is a volatile time and the teacher is often at the receiving end of external 'baggage' in the form of attitudes and feelings that need to be acknowledged as part of the nature of teaching.

Both McManus and Montgomery concede that it is very difficult to state a precise, objective definition for troublesome or disruptive behaviour that can be used in all cases and that takes into account all the variables above. We would suggest that the nearest common denominator, albeit subjective, is the DES (1979) definition in Montgomery (1989): 'that which interferes with the learning and opportunities of other pupils and imposes undue stress upon the Teacher'.

Manifestations of difficult behaviour

When you decide to become a teacher, you sign up to a role where you are challenged in a variety of ways. A lot of these are relatively minor. Over the past fifteen years when we have run workshops on troublesome and disruptive behaviour for teachers in post-compulsory education and training, we have asked practitioners to brainstorm in small groups (on flip-charts) what they see as disruptive behaviour.

Not surprisingly, given our difficulties in arriving at an agreed objective definition, everyone sees the problem in a different light. It is often cathartic, too, when participants realize that other people have had similar experiences and concerns to theirs, even if the manifestation is different. Here is but a small selection of the low-level disruption that is wearying and a nuisance but all too commonplace in teaching situations. These examples are in no particular order:

- individual students arriving late, often in dribs and drabs
- students talking while you are talking

- students with no paper, books, pens nor anything which signifies they are ready to work
- mobile phones not switched off
- texting under the table
- extraneous noise
- gratuitous insults and point scoring
- sexist, racist, homophobic comments
- going off the subject on the slightest pretext, often referring to another authority such as newspapers or television or other teachers for corroboration
- items being thrown across the room
- attention-seeking behaviour, such as playing to the gallery or leaning back on two legs of the chair or loud yawning
- thoughtless ritualistic behaviour such as the constant flicking on and off of a biro or strands of hair or the loose edge of Formica on a desk
- students deciding they cannot be bothered to do anything and who need to be chivvied along all the time

Teacher behaviour

So far in this chapter we have concentrated to a large extent on the impact of student behaviour on the teacher. It is time to look at the effect of teacher behaviour on the students.

Here is an example of what we mean. We call it flip-flops.

Flip-flops

Sometimes the action of the teacher increases the likelihood that there will be disruption in the class. The flip-flop will cause this problem whether students are 14–16 year olds or mature adults at an evening class. It is a mistake we often observe.

A typical situation would be where the teacher initiates the expectation by saying 'after this we'll have a break'. Then the teacher becomes carried away with enthusiasm for the excellent activities/inputs they have devised and moves on from 'this' to another topic or even worse begins to talk about something interesting. It does not matter how interesting the following activities or teacher talk are, the students have mentally, if not physically, started packing up for their break. They become agitated. At best this is dead learning time; at worst chaos reigns.

Early studies of behaviour (Thorndike 1924, Watson 1931, McLelland 1961) have alerted us to the recognition that behaviour is not a neutral phenomenon. People do not live in a non-contextual bubble, but are influenced by their environment. Certain behaviour becomes habituated because it is reinforcing to the individual (Watson) or it satisfies some form of drive (Thorndike) or is linked with the need to achieve (McLelland). Later research introduced an interpersonal dimension through the development of the theory of transactional analysis (Berne 1966, Joines and Stewart 1987, Hay 1992), suggesting that some behaviour is in fact reciprocal. In ego state theory, for example, 'A' influences the way 'B' behaves and vice versa.

Ego state theory

There is not space in this book to consider all aspects of ego state theory. There are many very good books on the subject (Joines and Stewart 1987, Hay 1992, Napper and Newton 2000) which would repay serious study for those interested in pursuing transactional analysis (TA) further. Some devotees of TA might argue that a serious study of transactional analysis would cover most of what teachers need to know to deal with behaviour.

Here we wish to highlight one aspect of TA (ego states) but first a quick reminder of the basic idea. According to ego state theory, in any given situation we have a choice of behaving in one of three ego states: parent, adult or child (see Figure 7).

P **parent ego state**
   behaviours, thoughts and feelings copied from parents or parent figures
A **adult ego state**
   behaviours, thoughts and feelings which are direct responses to the here and now
C **child ego state**
   behaviours, thoughts and feelings replayed from childhood

Figure 7: Simplified ego state model (from Joines and Stewart 1987)

This does not mean that we *are* parents or the children in a particular situation, but that we revert to responses and behaviours learned in the past, very often in childhood. We might find ourselves saying, when at our wits end, 'because I say so' and realize that we are replaying, without thinking, situations that 'parent' figures played out with us in the past. Similarly when hurt, we might react in a petulant or submissive manner, again replaying past scenarios.

As far as the parent state is concerned, there are two subdivisions which have been called *nurturing* and *controlling* (Berne 1966, Hay 1992), each having positive and negative facets. As far as the child is concerned, there are also two subdivisions, namely *adapted* and *free* (see Figure 8 below).

CP NP

A

AC FC

CP = Controlling parent; **NP** = Nurturing parent; **A** = Adult; **AC** = Adaptive child; and **FC** = Free child

Figure 8: Functional analysis of ego states (from Joines and Stewart 1987)

We would like to suggest that teaching could be seen as an inherently parenting activity. It is natural for teachers to *nurture* their charges by building up their confidence, giving them positive 'strokes', helping to sort out difficulties and so on. The tutor role in particular lends itself to such behaviours. It is also natural for teachers to want to be in *control* by enforcing standards of behaviour (even if the ground rules have been negotiated) and by managing the learning process.

There are dangers in overdoing the parenting role. Over-nurturing can lead to dependency, which can be disastrous in later life. For example, one can so spoon-feed students that they cannot cope without the 'parenting' figure in the exam room or at university. This is an example of *negative parenting*.

The main focus in this chapter is to alert readers to the dangers of the over-controlling parent state. It is possible to want to have things too tightly controlled. Most ego state theorists advocate flexibility, shifting ego states from time to time based on a conscious judgement of what might be appropriate in a certain situation. It is likely that Mrs X and Mr Y, our ideal teachers, know when to lighten up (positive free child), and when to devolve responsibility to the students for a particular action or activity (adult). In the volatile 14–19 age group, there are strong forces pulling students back towards their childhood and others forward towards adulthood. It is sometimes good tactics to build in fun and lack of inhibition into a lesson, legitimizing the value of free child. It is equally part of one's role to develop the 'adult' skills for future growth by activities and expectations that increase self-reliance and self-discipline. This does not mean we have to abandon either nurture or control, but we should be careful not to operate in too narrow a spectrum of behaviour.

Authority in the classroom
In this section, we want you to consider how an analysis of power and authority in the classroom can enable teachers to feel more confident about their classroom control.

Without authority there can be no learning.

When we have run workshops on handling disruptive students, we have been surprised how little thought teachers have given to the question of where their authority comes from. It is assumed that it exists, though you might not think so, from the number of times it is challenged in one day! Sometimes, the best places to look for books on the subject are in the business and management studies section of the library rather than the education section.

One model we use is the five-point analysis of power bases developed by French and Raven (1958) to which we have added a sixth – 'negotiated': Reward, Coercive, Legitimate (position), Referent (charismatic), Expert, Negotiated (the added one).

The concept is straightforward. In order for someone in authority to exercise that authority, there has to be some theoretical and/or practical justification for that authority. In other words, what is it that makes one subscribe to the authority in question? Let us apply each one to the teaching situation.

Reward

We agree to conform because we will be rewarded in some way.

Rewards that are in the gift of the teacher have always been part of the teaching/learning process. Positive reinforcement of appropriate behaviour through verbal and social approval, by ticks and positive comments on student work when it is marked, through prizes and other tangible tokens of reward, are all things with which we are familiar as teachers and as learners. It pays to become proficient in the use of rewards. Praise and social approval plus immediate feedback on work produced should be part of your teaching style from the outset. You will learn that immediate gratification in either tangible or social form can gradually be replaced by delayed gratification via the end of module test or the final exam. We see this in our own lives, of course, where delayed gratification comes through the monthly salary cheque or perhaps in achieving goals which lead to a bonus.

You will come across other forms of reward later in the chapter when we consider the principles of classroom management.

Coercive

We agree to conform because we fear the consequences if we do not.

Rewards alone do not always produce desired behaviours, despite their benefits in educational, social and vocational contexts. For example, the rewards for not drinking and driving were insufficient to deter offenders and so more coercive measures were needed.

In educational settings, sometimes sanctions are needed. Most, if not all, colleges and schools have booklets that contain a code of conduct with clear statements about the rights and responsibilities of both students and staff, with an indication of the sort of sanctions that could be applied to students who consistently breach the code. It is helpful when all colleagues follow the agreed procedures and work as a team.

Every teacher can set the tone where the lines are drawn in the sand and students know that they should not cross them. These are often drawn up with the students in the form of ground rules, which we will look at under the heading of 'negotiation'. Things such as a consistent upholding of rules on lateness or absence, strict application of deadlines for handing in work (unless a written permission for extension has been signed), being consistent in dealing with antisocial behaviour or sexist and racist language, all help set the tone of behaviour and relationships that aids learning. These signals of order and respect make it less likely that you will have to refer explicitly to the code, but it is there to be used and one should not be afraid to do so.

There are dangers that one could be over-zealous in upholding rules and standards of behaviour, leading to what could be seen as 'authoritarian' behaviour. It is then possible that you will find you have lost more than you gain. If you go through all the stages of the college code, it can be a very lengthy process and you may find that you have a whole class that is hostile. You may feel you were in the right but that may not be how it comes across to colleagues or students. Sometimes a quiet word or a referral to the student's tutor will produce a more lasting effect.

Legitimate (based on one's position or status)
We agree to conform because we accept the right of someone in that position to tell us what to do.

There was a time – probably the apocryphal era when two people could go to the pictures, have drinks and supper and take a taxi home for sixpence (pre-decimal, of course) – when positions in society such as doctor or policeman or teacher had a certain cachet of respect. For example, people did what the policeman told them to do with little or no argument. This is no longer automatically the case in society, teaching being no exception. But vestiges of it still linger on in folk memory and the skilled teacher learns how to exploit this.

Students are normally disposed to adhere to your instructions, such as 'I want you to work in pairs' or 'you have ten minutes to do this', etc.; they will accept the way in which you organize the sequence of topics in the scheme of work; they go along with your lesson planning; they keep the noise down when you ask them. There is an acknowledged contract between you and the class that you have the authority to control the way in which the learning is planned and delivered. Learners feel safe and therefore likely to cooperate when they see examples of good organization and good habits.

Such authority has to be exercised responsibly, taking into account the sensibilities and feelings of the class, or else it could crumble when challenged. We can no longer rely absolutely on compliance and would be ill-advised to do so, but we can subtly use it alongside the other bases in this section.

Referent or charismatic

We agree to conform because of the personal qualities of the person in charge.

There are natural leaders in all walks of life. There are also people with big personalities who seem to attract followers. Teaching is no exception. We can all remember teachers who were very effective whatever they did, through some inner flair or charm or appeal.

There is no reason why all teachers could not exploit their personal qualities, but this has to be a matter of personal choice. We have found that allowing the students to glimpse some aspects of our natural personality can be a valuable aid to good discipline, as long as it is used with discretion. You only have to think about what happens on Children in Need day, or on an educational visit or on a staff–student event to notice the change in students' perceptions of you when they see you as a rounded person with a positive free–child attitude. They also respond well when they know what you stand for in matters of morality or politics and that you are true to your convictions. You might be one of the few adult role models who offer an objective or disinterested reference point in their lives and show them what the adult ego state might mean.

Little things are more important than you think. Some

modest forms of self-disclosure, for example which football team you support or whether you have children or what television programmes you watch, provide points of social contact that can be useful in spare time, such as chatting to one or two students in the five minutes or so before the whole class arrives. Varying your appearance from time to time shows you to be someone interesting and allows further social interaction. It soon becomes clear when to draw the line, because *you* can always decline to go further. There are always some students who will push to know even more about you, but you can usually disarm that because you are secure enough in your personality to handle this, just like you are in any work–related situation.

The point here is that personality is not neutral. You are not a robot. Whether you like it or not, students will see you as you present yourself to them. You have the choice whether to think about this in advance and work out something or leave it to chance or present something contrived and false. There are pros and cons in all of this, so you may as well think through how you want to present yourself and work on it. You may as well be proactive and have some control over it.

Expert

We agree to conform because the other person knows more about x than we do or has more experience and we would be stupid not to be influenced by them into compliance with what they say or advise.

You may remember in Chapter 3 we discussed the proposition of R. S. Peters (Peters 1967) that education is about mastery in a given area. This proposition is part of the cement that holds society together. If I am ill I will more than likely go to a doctor, if my heating system breaks down, to a plumber, if I am selling my house, to a lawyer. We would accept that there are some people who can do these things for themselves, but few if any of us has not sought expert advice at some time.

When we do so, we need to feel reassured that the expertise has been guaranteed in some way, usually by qualifications, and, that being the case, we go along with what the expert says. This applies very much to teaching. Students expect that the person in front of them will have both subject expertise and pedagogic expertise. Expertise can be a powerful basis for authority, but, again, discretion is needed in its exercise. It is not a shield of inviolability to insulate the teacher from challenge or criticism. It only works when the expert can explain the reasons for her/his opinion in an objective and open way, with a clear outline of alternative interpretations to empower the client or student to gain full benefit from the expert.

Expert power is close to legitimate power and reward power. In assessing learning, teachers fall back on their expert status and their opinion carries great weight. It is true that they are subject to checks and balances in double marking, external examining, appeals procedures and the like, but on a day-to-day basis the expert influence of the teacher is strong. So, discretion is needed. Expert power is a boon but it can also be a barrier. One can set one's standards so high that only a few students reach them, with resulting loss of confidence in many cases. Expertise can be worn like a badge. I am Doctor so-and-so and am to be deferred to in all matters.

We have found that expert power works best in a climate of reflective practice where students are encouraged to revisit their newly acquired knowledge or skills and to test out their cumulative understandings with other learners and with the teacher. We will return to this in more detail in the Conclusion.

Negotiated
We agree to conform because our consent was secured.

In a democracy, the consent of the governed is a cornerstone of the system. Authority works much better through agreement, e.g. to conditions of employment, to the election of office holders, to the use of delegated powers and so on. It is also axiomatic that there are channels for reviewing the basis of consent, such as elections or fixed-term agreements that need to be reviewed on referring something to an outside body.

Some of these characteristics apply equally to teaching. Consent, in the form of ground rules, is a sensible tactic. Teachers need to be clear what is non-negotiable and it is probably best to try to anticipate most of the points the students might suggest. It is also acceptable to assert the right to add one or two of your own requirements to the negotiations, usually those that you anticipated but which did not crop up.

It is worthwhile thinking through the procedure for arriving at a whole-class consensus. There are a number of models. One such is the cascade, where you might ask groups of four to draw up their list of ten points on a flip-chart and then factorize how many times the same point occurred across the groups. This is usually about 5–7 items. You can then reconvene the groups and ask them to rank the merits of all the other views not on the composite list and put these on the flip-chart. It is usually clear by then what the consensus is. There are other variations. You may feel brave enough to leave the room (if the door has a window for you to look through) and stand outside for a few minutes and let the class decide.

Ground rules should be visible on the wall in the room, certainly for the first few weeks, so that the teacher and the class can refer to them at any time. This often helps to enforce agreements such as not interrupting others when they are speaking, or not demeaning others' contributions. Sometimes it is worth revisiting the ground rules to see how things are going and to renegotiate some.

Negotiation is not confined to ground rules. You can always offer choices about how an assignment might be delivered, about the most appropriate time for an assignment deadline, about choice of project, about classroom layout, about music (if you allow it), about the running order for presentations or feedback from groups, about roles or responsibilities (duty chef in the kitchen, who is the model this week, who needs to act as supervisor, etc.), about work placements, and so on. It costs nothing and it trains young people in the art of seeking consensus, which will serve them well at work.

What can we learn from an analysis of authority bases?
The main point is this: *the wider the basis of authority, the more effective you will be.*

The key is to work across all the bases with forethought and sensitivity and not to get stuck in only one or two of them. Forethought implies that you have worked out to some extent how you want to be seen, what you can and cannot do, what sort of relationships you wish to have. Sensitivity implies that you are observant, that you watch for signs that your approach is successful or needs modifying, that your strategies are for the long term.

Key principles in handling disruptive or uncooperative behaviour

The first priority of any teacher is to establish a good classroom climate

- negotiate ground rules
- ensure there is a basic 'Maslow' structure in place (Maslow 1943)
- make the work you set the students relevant and interesting
- revisit the ground rules

With most classes, these measures will lead to a positive climate, with relatively few problems.

But if things start to go wrong
These pointers are in no particular order.

Stay calm
at the time of the incident(s) and the next time you see the class. You have the inner strength, so don't let it faze you.

Relate appropriately
You will expect to develop a pleasant and productive working relationship, but it may take some time with certain groups or individuals. You have to set the tone and shape the students' behaviour.

Avoid a 'theatre'
Go into detail with the individual or individuals about an incident or issue after the lesson if at all possible, or at least without an audience.

Be assertive
You have every right to say what behaviour is acceptable or not. The key is HOW you say it. Try not to be judgemental. Deal with the behaviour, but do not demean the person. Leave the door open for future, improved relationships.

Use the college code
Some incidents are so serious that the code has to be invoked.

Much disruptive behaviour is more wearing and low level than serious, so other pointers in this section may prove to be more useful. However, the college code is always there to be used if necessary.

Do not blame yourself
Disruptive behaviour happens to ALL of us. It goes with the territory. Usually it does not last long. The majority of the students are on your side and want you to succeed.

Promote and reward positive behaviour
No put-downs: no sarcasm.

Set some assessed work early, mark it immediately and give the students the results as soon as possible. Make the tasks success-driven, i.e. set at a level which is likely to lead to success. Successful work creates an intimate bond between the teacher and each individual learner. Your written remarks are personal to each learner and can help build trust and confidence.

Look back to Chapter 1. Use prompts to define the agenda and help focus the attention on the essentials; present a selection from alternatives; devise one-stage tasks, especially those that are self-referencing, which are easier than two-stage tasks. All of these will allow the teacher to praise what the learners have done. All the learners can take part and experience success that is immediate and obvious.

Be consistent in your behaviour
Be punctual and well-organized. Clarify both tasks and instructions, e.g. time allowed, what the final product might be,

who works with whom and so on. Clearly spell out your expectations of the task and reinforce them from time to time.

Avoid mood swings (this links to *Relate appropriately* and *Be assertive* of the principles covered earlier). Think this through and ensure your behaviour complements other aspects of your professionalism.

Avoid threats and references to the disciplinary code unless there is no other way. Be assertive, set the tone and be consistent.

Turn disruption to your advantage

Disruption is a form of communication – it can be a cry for help. The individual may well be in crisis, short-term or long-term.

Students may find it is difficult to do what you are asking. You need to be aware of this, perhaps using more visual prompts or more single-stage tasks in the early days to ensure success.

You may well be being tested to see how your approach conforms to or differs from the behaviour they are used to from adults. They may have had unhappy brushes with authority in the past and you are being tested to see how you will react.

One of the most vulnerable aspects of teaching is the first ten minutes when you are trying to clarify instructions for a new task or trying to get across vital information. If individuals are bent on sabotaging you, this is a good time for them. Minimize the amount of time needed to get the majority working by, say, giving out instruction sheets or having the instructions on the whiteboard, and you can cut down the disruption.

Use all your options

You always have the advantage of surprise for the next lesson (like the white pieces at chess!). No matter how disastrous the lesson, you will have time to regroup by the next time you see the class.

You are the professional and have a whole toolkit of teaching strategies at your disposal – see Part Four, Chapter 11 for further ideas. You can also refer to Harkin *et al.* (2001) and to Wallace (2007) in this series.

In your position as the teacher you have the opportunity to change any or all of the following for next time: the type of tasks or activities; the instructions given in the form of envelopes or hidden on display boards rather than verbally; the way you organize group structures and group dynamics; the classroom layout; the nature of the rewards; the timings of each phase of the lesson.

Conclusion

There are no magic solutions that guarantee one can handle all types of challenging behaviour in all situations.

No one would pretend that even the most experienced teacher does not experience some difficulties. It can be an emotional battle. Often one feels hot and bothered when loss of control seems imminent.

The key is not to lose one's nerve and to accept that some turbulence is unavoidable, particularly when working with 14–19 year olds. It is rare that the worst of it lasts for long, although we have all had classes that remain difficult for the whole year, no matter what we try. In such cases, all we can do is give our best professional service and accept the fact that things are difficult. It happens in all walks of life: a play has a bad run, a good business fails to spark, colleagues fail to get on and, likewise, sometimes your relationship with a class is flat.

If a class is particularly difficult to control, try to resist the temptation to put everything right straightaway. It is more realistic to aim for incremental gains in cooperation so that the situation improves over time. In the period when things are difficult, you will glean a lot of information about all the class members which will help you to determine your tactics for putting things right when you decide to be proactive.

Classroom discipline does not come in its own box with its own label. It is the result of a compendium of influences: through interesting lessons with an accent on enjoyment and success; through a relaxed environment where the learners feel valued and supported; through the establishing of boundaries of acceptable behaviour; through a philosophy which asserts that respect is earned, not demanded, and is mutual.

Adhering to the basic principles outlined in this chapter will help you to think through how you want to be proactive in establishing a positive working climate and how to react when things go wrong. Useful though this book may be, it is no substitute for enrolling on a good programme of professional training where you can discuss issues with your colleagues and your trainer.

Further reading

Hay, J. (1992) *Transactional Analysis for Trainers*, London: McGraw-Hill.

Joines, I. and Stewart, V. (1987) *TA: A New Introduction to Transactional Analysis*, Nottingham and Chapel Hill, NC: Lifespace.

McManus, M. (1989) *Troublesome Behaviour in the Classroom*, London: Routledge.

Montgomery, D. (1989) *Managing Behaviour Problems*, London: Hodder & Stoughton.

Pelzer, D. (1993) *A Child called 'It'*, Omaha, NE: Omaha Press.

Working with Younger Learners. Support modules for post-16 staff: http://www.lifelonglearninguk.org/currentactivity/14_16_modules.html

8 Teaching gifted and talented learners on vocational courses

Ros Clow and Annie Haight

Introduction

In Autumn 2003 the DfES awarded Oxford Brookes University a contract to develop an Aimhigher workshop to visit all regions of England in 2004, delivering a programme to support teachers of gifted and talented students on Level 3 vocational education courses. This one-day workshop represented an unusual continuing professional development event, focusing as it did on the conjunction between Level 3 vocational education and the particular version of gifted and talented education emerging in England for the past five or six years.

The workshop was developed through the collaboration of two teams within the university: the Gifted and Talented (G&T) team and the Post-Compulsory Education (PCE) team. For the past four years, the G&T team had designed and delivered the Master's-level, DfES-funded National Development Programme for Gifted and Talented Coordinators in secondary schools under the Excellence in Cities (EiC) initiative, as well as other CPD modules on gifted and talented education. The PCE team trained teachers for the learning and skills sector, particularly FE, and also delivered degree and Master's level programmes. It was quickly evident that our different focuses involved separate theoretical foundations. Over the next few months we shared our different approaches, discovering areas of similarity (Bloom *et al.*'s taxonomy) and aspects of the G&T literature that lent themselves very well to vocational education.

This chapter describes the theory and strategies that we presented to teachers in the Aimhigher workshop, and goes further to develop a model of high ability in the wider post-compulsory context. We believe this model can help with the recognition of gifted and talented learners and may explain why youngsters who appear mediocre in the compulsory school system may 'fly' when they begin vocational education.

The English approach to gifted and talented education

In 1999 the Labour government mobilized the pursuit of gifted and talented education, with the introduction of the Gifted and Talented strand of the Excellence in Cities initiative, a programme designed to redress social, economic and educational disadvantage and raise standards in inner-city areas. This project was extended to primary schools and to areas of rural deprivation in 2001 and to former Education Action Zones in 2003, with the new partnerships being known as Excellence Clusters. As a key component of the Labour government's social inclusion agenda, the G&T initiative is intended to promote social mobility and allow young people from 'non-traditional backgrounds' (i.e. with no family history of higher education) to access university education and graduate job markets. Since 2001 the Aimhigher initiative in schools (originally called Excellence Challenge) and the Widening Participation agenda in universities have supported this objective by seeking to raise the expectations of young people with the potential to attend university, thus contributing to the government's target of 50 per cent of 18–30 year olds in higher education by 2010 (Blair 2001, DfES 2000a).

For schools eligible for the G&T initiative, funds are available until 2006 to provide a range of interventions to identify and support the achievement of the most able. A multi-dimensional approach is taken to identification, with an expectation that a norm-referenced cohort, representative of the wider school population in terms of ethnicity, gender, socio-economic status and special educational needs, will be identified. There is explicit guidance stating that underachievers should be targeted as well as high-performing students already fulfilling their potential.

There is generally a three-part approach to provision for this cohort (and, in many schools, for other students outside the named group, who could benefit from it):

- extra-curricular enrichment such as after-school clubs, master classes, summer schools, Open University courses, collaborative programmes with local FE and HE institutions, and individual mentoring
- structural and administrative approaches such as setting by ability or other pupil-grouping strategies, and early entrance to GCSE and A level exams
- classroom strategies such as effective differentiation

The last aspect is considered a priority, as the initiative seeks to embed sustainable, classroom-based approaches which will continue after funding is withdrawn. The emphasis on personalized learning in the 2004 White Paper is also explicitly intended to help sustain appropriate provision for high-ability students (among others). Students considered to be among the 5 per cent most able in the country are invited to join the National Academy for Gifted and Talented Youth (established in 2001), which facilitates individualized learning plans and offers access to enrichment events, university-level summer schools and subject experts.

G&T provision is often accompanied by Aimhigher and Widening Participation opportunities designed to raise aspirations to higher education, such as 'taster days' and visits to universities. The success of the initiative is generally viewed in terms of good exam results and places taken up at university.

Definitions
The revised DfES guidance on the Gifted and Talented Strand of Excellence in Cities (1999) describes four categories of high-ability student:

- Gifted – those with academic ability (defined as ability in one or more subjects in the statutory school curriculum other than art, music, PE and sport)
- Talented – those with ability in art, music, PE, or in any sport or creative art

- All-rounders – students who are good in both academic and 'talent' areas
- Underachievers – students 'who have the potential to achieve, but are not regularly demonstrating high achievement' (DfES 1999)

All of these types of students can be found in FE colleges, although under these definitions we are probably more likely to be working with 'talented' learners where talent includes a wider range of vocational abilities than this definition allows. The limitations of this definition will be discussed later. But it is worth noting here that many underachievers find their way into FE colleges, and go on to be very successful, although this may involve progression other than to higher education (for example, apprenticeships or enterprise).

We discovered very little research or publication in the field of high ability in vocational areas, although there is some work published in the USA and in Germany. Indeed, from the latter country, Rudolf Manstetten laments that '*vocational giftedness* has been a research desideratum' (in Heller 2000).

In the wider literature on gifted and talented education, however, the model of Joseph Renzulli (an American educator concerned to develop 'defensible' programmes of gifted education) has resonance for the FE sector. Renzulli's '3-ring model of giftedness' (1978) was derived from a study of high-performing adults, and identifies three key elements necessary (in varying proportions) for giftedness:

- above-average ability
- creativity
- task commitment (i.e. emotional and dispositional factors such as perseverance and motivation)

Renzulli's emphasis on above-average ability (that is, no less than the top 50 per cent of ability in a given domain) is more inclusive than other definitions that depend on narrower criteria. He also distinguishes between two equally valid modes of giftedness:

- 'school-house' (academic) giftedness, that 'might also be called test-taking or lesson-learning giftedness'

- 'creative–productive' giftedness – the creation of original material in a real-world context, for a real-world audience (Renzulli 2003: 9–10)

These ideas have considerable potential for application in the vocational sector.

So, too, do Robert Sternberg's descriptions of giftedness as 'developing expertise' and, most recently, as 'wisdom, intelligence and creativity, synthesised' (Sternberg 2001, 2003). Both Renzulli's and Sternberg's views of giftedness sit comfortably in the vocational education sector, which encompasses a wider range of human endeavour than simply the academic or artistic. Two other models of giftedness that relate well to vocational education – those of Calvin Taylor and Abraham Tannenbaum – are discussed later in this chapter.

Talent spotting

Research in the traditional school sector has generated checklists that help to recognize students with conventionally understood abilities and talents (Freeman 1998, QCA 2001–2). In our workshop we asked the experienced teachers taking part to create their own checklists for spotting high ability for vocational sectors, especially at the interview stage. Similar key attributes tended to be identified in each workshop, whether the teachers taught business studies, beauty therapy or construction. We have used the collated lists from the workshops (see Table 10) to develop a model which illustrates five facets which contribute to success in vocational education.

Analysis of these lists suggests a multi-faceted model of individual ability where success or achievement is related to the development of each facet.

The facets (see Figure 9) divide into the following five areas:

- cognitive attributes: knowledge, thinking skills (K)
- autonomy (leading to creativity) (A)
- sensori-motor skills (M)
- intrinsic drive (I)
- socio-affective skills (leading to managerial skills) (S)

Table 10: What teachers look for in spotting vocational talent

Ambition	I	Ability to question	A
Drive	I	Enthusiasm	I
Experiences	S	Determination	S
Role models	S	Practical	M
Confidence	S	Originality	A
Flexible skills	S	Self-motivation	I
Leadership skills	S	Independent learning	A
Self-discipline	I	Self-regulation	I
Will to succeed	I	Problem-solving	K
Motivation	I	Research skills	K
Single-mindedness	I	Reliability	S
Spark	I	Teamwork	S
Understanding the signals	S	Challenge	S
Upwards spiral	I	Clear focus	I
Hands–on practical skills	M	Prioritizes	A
Self-esteem	I	Purposeful	S
Commitment	I	Articulate	S
Persistence	S	Breaking rules	S
Creativity	A	Taking risks	S
Self-management	I	Practical talent	M
Organizational skills	S	Application	K
Social skills	S	Problem-solving in context	K
Identifying their own ability	I	Ability to question	A
Focus on making money from their endeavours	I	Discernment/perceptiveness	S
Ability to transfer theory into practice	K	Ability to make strategic alliances	S
Thinks strategically	K	Ability to argue the other side	S
Presents information in a variety of formats and registers	K	Can take advice	S
Ability to interpret a specification	K	Ability to review, reflect and evaluate	K
Analysis	K	Motor skills	M
Action planning	A	Enquiring mind	A

Enthusiasm	I	Love of subject	A
Aware of own learning styles	A	Listens and absorbs information	S
Sees big picture	K	Sensitive to verbal and non-verbal communication	S
Can accept change	S		

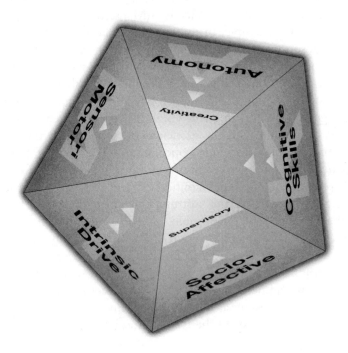

Figure 9: The KAMIS model of vocational talent
(a pentagonal pyramid seen from above)

While the analysis was interesting in itself, its application seems to explain some of the idiosyncrasies that have perplexed teachers for some time. For instance, why is it that many of the 'cleverest' students at school do not seem to achieve particularly well in later life? Why does studying science at higher levels seem so much more difficult than arts subjects? Why do some students who are mediocre at school do really well when they enter the workplace?

In terms of this model, to achieve in arts subjects you need to score high on K, A and I – this would make you academically gifted. To achieve in many of the sciences (for example, chemistry) you need to score highly in K, A, I and M – this would still be referred to as academic giftedness but in fact science students often also have to bring sensori–motor abilities such as lab skills into their studies.

To achieve highly in the vocational world you will need to score highly in the socio–affective (Manstetten 2000) field (S). You may (for example, in motor vehicle, beauty therapy, hair-dressing, sport and recreation) or may not (for example, in leisure and tourism, business studies, or health and social care) need sensori–motor skills, but no one will achieve highly in vocational study without people skills, which develop into supervisory and managerial skills. So in effect vocational talent requires a wider range of abilities than the academic ones on which the com-pulsory school curriculum concentrates. The role of the FE teacher is often to give permission to learn in a different way (see Chapter 6) and to build confidence and self-esteem through engaging learners in the instrumental curriculum which will make them at least employable, and, in cases of multi-faceted high ability as illustrated by the KAMIS model, highly successful.

As we observed earlier, certain areas of human experience are underemphasized and undervalued in the compulsory school curriculum. Some of these, such as the olfactory and gustatory senses, can be essential aspects of certain areas of work (and relate to the M factor of the KAMIS model). In training to be a chef, for example (or a pharmacist, doctor, nurse, or environ-mental health officer), students have to be trained in the use of these underdeveloped senses. Similarly the ability to relate to and care for animals is not valued in the national curriculum (indeed probably for health and safety reasons it is less devel-oped now than in the past). Aptitude in these areas of experi-ence may be innate talents in certain individuals. Some gifted and talented learners may not have been identified as they enter FE, because their particular gifts have not been developed or assessed through the national curriculum. For want of different terminology maybe the DfES definition of talent should be expanded to read 'ability in art, music, PE, or in any sport, creative art, or vocationally essential skill'.

Calvin Taylor and the totem pole

The American educationalist, Calvin Taylor, researching in 1967 into three fields, primary mental ability factors, creativity and world-of-work skills, asserted that 'nearly all children, if evaluated for achievement in several different talent areas, would be gifted in some way' (Maker and Nielson 1995: 283). Taylor's definition of talent is different from the one currently used by the DfES. He uses the terms 'gifted' and 'talented' to refer to relative degrees of ability:

- the 'gifted' are people at the top in any identified area
- the 'talented' are above average, i.e. those whose abilities lie between the average and the top in any area (ibid: 284)

Taylor suggested that teachers should function as talent developers as well as 'dispensers of knowledge'. In essence he proposes a school curriculum that allows individuals to develop world-of-work skills at the same time as subject knowledge; the two should be interrelated. He also suggests that students from less privileged backgrounds often lack opportunities for developing talents such as planning, decision-making and leadership, which are usually acquired in extra-curricular activities (youth clubs, drama and dance performances, Scouts/Guides, charity work).

The world-of-work talents he identified are:

- productive thinking
- foresight
- planning
- communication
- decision-making
- interpersonal skills

(It is worth noting that his theory of multiple talents pre-dates Howard Gardner's multiple intelligences by nearly twenty years. The antecedent of both thinkers is Louis Thurstone, who pioneered a multi-dimensional view of intelligence in 1938 (Cianciolo and Sternberg 2004).)

Taylor stresses the importance of more students being able to excel in at least one talent area (Maker and Nielson 1995). The converse of this is that the more gifted students will benefit from a more rounded and realistic view of ability and of themselves, understanding that they are not best at everything, and that there are areas for them to work on where others in the group are superior.

Taylor developed an approach for profiling the strengths and weaknesses of individual students, which results in 'totem pole' diagrams (see Figures 10 and 11). We decided to share this approach in our workshop, to give participants a technique for analysing the strengths and weaknesses of groups of students.

	Good practical skills	Empathetic listener	Is inquisitive and questioning	Mature emotional intelligence	Is a keen observer	Advocate
Jane						
Alan						
Poppy						
Beatrix						
Tania						
Sophie						

Figure 10: Totem pole for AVCE health and social care students

In this approach:

- list the skills that you consider essential for success in the vocational area you teach (five to eight are suggested)
- record these on a grid as column headings
- put each student's name on an index card (or scrap of paper!) and rank them for each separate skill
- with the top of the table indicating the highest ability, write each student's name in the appropriate 'rank' (relative to the rest of the group) for each of the skills

You can also use symbols rather than students' names, if you prefer. It does not matter which skill you use for the first

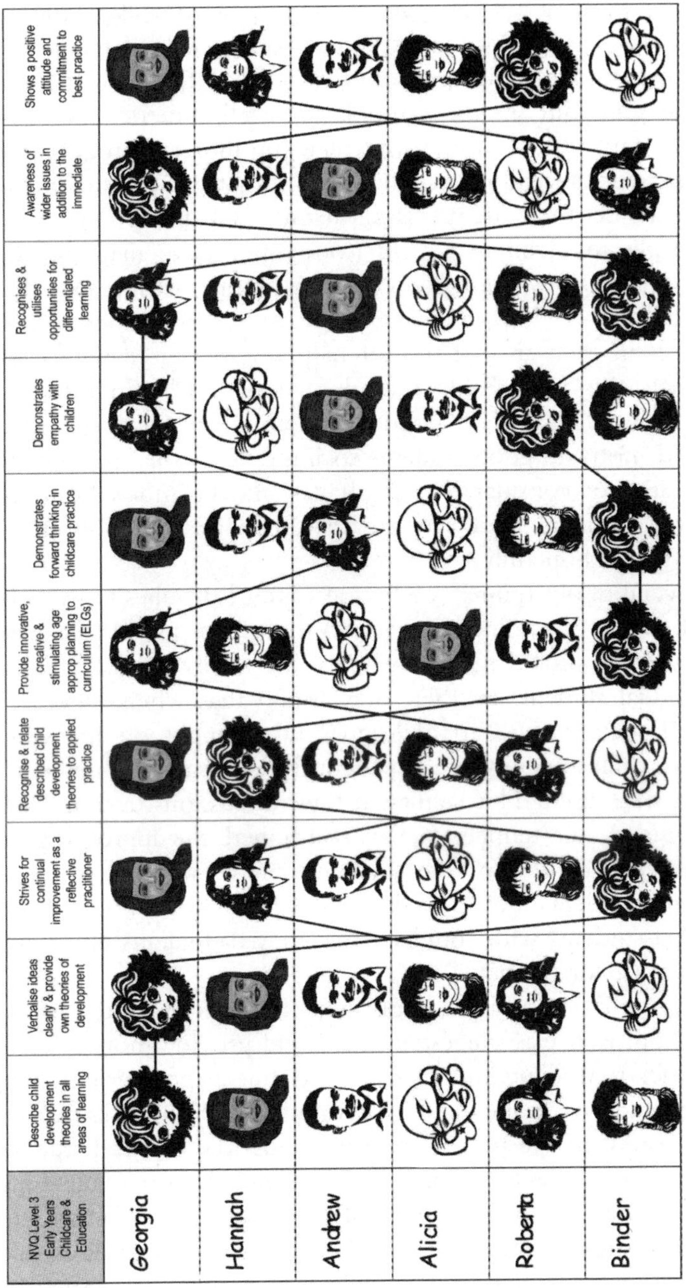

Figure 11: Totem pole for NVQ Level 3 early years childcare and education students

ranking exercise but the symbol you allocate for each student must stay the same for the rest of the exercise. The diagram you end up with looks like a row of totem poles (hence the name). When you join up the symbols for each student what you usually find is that no one student is top in everything.

There are several reasons why you might want to undertake this exercise. It can be revealing first to think about and list the key skills involved in a field (sometimes these map directly against a syllabus, sometimes they are more within your discretion as a teacher), and second, to reflect on your students' abilities in each area. If the totem poles are shared with each student (this is probably best done individually in tutorials, using symbols rather than students' names on the diagrams) it should motivate good students to improve in the areas where they are not considered 'top'. It can also be motivational to weaker students who can see that they are not bottom in everything (hopefully!).

Several of our trainee teachers at Oxford Brookes University tried out this technique and found that it was useful at several levels. It promoted their analysis of the ability profile of each individual student. Further, they found that when they presented their analysis to colleagues who taught on the same course, each student was easily identifiable even though pseudonyms were used. This facilitated their discussions of individual students. As the trainee teachers had hoped, the approach gave them clues as to how to challenge and stretch their most talented students, but they also found it useful to motivate the weaker students who could see that they had talents others did not (as Taylor predicted).

During the Aimhigher workshops a variation on the totem pole approach was suggested that could provide more general feedback to students and teachers, and thus shape course design. For this approach one master sheet is used with the skills needed for mastery in the topic appearing across the top and student names down the side. After each assignment is marked some sort of symbol is recorded that reflects the point of development for each student against the needed skills. A smiley face would indicate achievement; a miserable face or low score suggests 'needs to work in this area'. Some teachers told us they use this as a diagnostic tool for the progress of whole groups. Any skill area where the majority of students had 'miserable faces' would indicate the need for additional teaching or practice.

Designing learning experiences

One of the workshop sessions invited teachers to examine their lesson plans and assignment briefs to check whether more able learners were being extended. This was introduced by an activity – aptly named Make mine a G&T! – in which participants were asked to analyse the learning outcomes for a fictitious course in bartending (see Table 11). The teachers were asked to work in groups to decide the type and complexity of skill needed to achieve the various outcomes, and to rank them according to the degree of higher-level thinking they demanded.

Table 11: Make mine a G&T

Make a gin and tonic
Eject a drunken customer from bar premises
Calculate a 10% service charge
Create an original fruity, creamy or spicy cocktail
Refuse to serve further alcohol without giving offence
Pour a pint of beer
Earn a generous tip
Create a cocktail from a recipe
Recognize the point at which to stop serving a customer alcohol
Create a multi-coloured cocktail from a range of liqueurs in which the order of the layers of colour depends on the specific gravity of each liqueur

© (2004) Westminster Institute of Education, Oxford Brookes University. With thanks to Michele Paule.

The ensuing discussion raised useful issues which led on to a consideration of the one theory that both the PCE and G&T teams were used to teaching, Bloom's taxonomy of educational objectives (Petty 2004, Maker and Nielson 1995). For most qualified FE teachers this would be revision, but our research has shown that teachers can usefully revisit theory learnt in their initial teacher training (Harkin, Clow and Hillier 2003). We asked participants to analyse the lesson plans, schemes of work and assignment briefs they had brought with them according to Bloom's taxonomy in order to ascertain whether their students were given the opportunity to develop higher-level thinking and more complex skills (Kerka 1992). We focused primarily on the cognitive domain: knowledge, comprehension, application, analysis, synthesis, evaluation. Teachers for whom it was relevant were also invited to consider Simpson's taxonomy of psychomotor skills (Simpson 1972, University of Mississippi 2001–2). The thinking behind this exercise was that talents must be developed and for this to happen the more able students need to be given the opportunity to extend their repertoire. If these opportunities were not already present in their planning, the teachers found it fairly easy to include more open-ended activities in their lesson plans or to rewrite assessment criteria for the distinction grade of assignments.

Again we had piloted this activity with trainee teachers, who had found it relatively straightforward to build more challenging activities or assessment tasks into their schemes of work. However, some admitted that they were comfortable using Bloom to extend their A level students but rarely thought about it with students on AVCE, national diploma and NVQ courses, being mostly concerned with motivating the pass borderline students. An issue for reflection?

The learning materials supporting the workshop can be accessed on the Oxford Brookes University website given in the Further reading list at the end of the chapter.

From potential to performance

However carefully each teacher constructs the learning and assessment processes, the talented student's development will depend on a wide range of other individuals both inside and outside the institution. We used Abraham Tannenbaum's metaphor of a starfish (Figure 12) to illustrate the range of

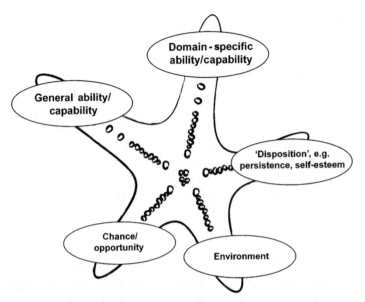

Figure 12 The Starfish diagram (Tannenbaum 1983)
© (2004) Westminster Institute of Education, Oxford Brookes University, after Tannenbaum 1983.

factors and individuals that can support the potential of gifted students (Tannenbaum 1983). According to Tannenbaum, the five 'arms' of the starfish represent:

- general ability (expected in the G&T student)
- specific ability (expected and may also include vocational skills)
- chance/opportunity, e.g. access, experience (may be minimal)
- environmental factors, e.g. learning experiences, expectations (may be limited)
- dispositional factors, e.g. persistence, self-esteem (in the KAMIS model, factor 'I', the intrinsic drive which may be absent on entry to FE college)

Teachers can be supportive in all aspects of development but it is worth remembering others that can provide support for students and compensate for any underprivilege that may exist. Within colleges these include: personal tutors, librarians, learning support staff (G&T students can also have learning disabilities such as dyslexia), technicians, IT support technicians, Connexions staff, college counsellors, peers and student union services.

Access funds may also be useful to purchase protective clothing, books and equipment. Outside college, public librarians, work colleagues, mentors from industry and the community, parents, brothers and sisters, sport and activity leaders or coaches, voluntary or community-work colleagues, and friends can all provide support. Once we suspect that a student has particular gifts and talents they may need direction to tap into compensatory systems that can support their achievement.

University or not?

The government target of 50 per cent of 18–30 year olds in higher education by 2010 may be applicable to many gifted and talented students in further education (DfES 2000b). The widening participation policies, targets and activities of many universities, and the expansion of HE subject areas (especially in the post–1992 universities) to include vocational areas such as leisure and tourism, hospitality, and health and social care, may make higher education increasingly attractive to many more students, including those from 'non-traditional backgrounds'.

However, the current drop-out rate among university students (7.8 per cent overall and over 15 per cent in some universities with high proportions of 'non-traditional' students) indicates starkly that this expansion of numbers is far from painless (HESA 2005). Universities are discovering that they need to be more proactive and flexible in 'levelling the playing field' (for example by introducing programmes to bring literacy and numeracy up to required levels) so that students can access and handle university-level teaching and learning. Even with these efforts, it is to be expected that a relatively high drop-out rate will continue. It may also prove unwise to underestimate the importance of community and family cultures where higher education is not prized, or where a young person's departure from home to attend university is regarded as unacceptable.

In the drive to expand university attendance, it is clearly

sensible to start with the population most able to benefit from and perform highly in higher education – gifted and talented students, some of whom will be on 'vocational pathways' (Howells 2004). Even among this group, however, it is possible that HE's emphasis on exploratory thinking and abstract reasoning, sometimes at the expense of practical application, may alienate some students who nevertheless deserve to be regarded as highly able in their chosen fields. It may be that other routes, such as modern apprenticeships and foundation degrees (combined with employment and located near the parental home) are better suited to the talents, learning preferences and domestic circumstances of talented vocational students.

Conclusion

As we write, an academic–vocational divide still exists in the UK education system, and it remains unclear whether recent changes in the strategy for 14–19 education and training will alleviate or reinforce it. Some professionals involved in gifted and talented education remain nervous about acknowledging vocational excellence. As one colleague remarked about the types of giftedness to be found in Excellence in Cities schools, 'We're not just talking about horse-whisperers'. Such remarks may stem from a concern that any attention paid to vocational ability might dilute or subvert the aspirations of underprivileged young people toward higher education and professional careers. While we certainly wouldn't want to talk only of horse-whisperers, we are equally unwilling not to speak of them at all. Not to recognize, celebrate and nurture high ability in vocational areas would be, we feel, to waste talent, to help entrench hegemonic attitudes about the superiority of purely academic pursuits, and to disenfranchise and reinforce lack of aspiration in a group of gifted and talented young people who deserve parity of esteem.

Further reading

Heller, K. A. (2000) *International Handbook of Giftedness and Talent*, Oxford: Elsevier.

Websites:

A report of a survey by teachers, identifying key characteristics of gifted and talented students in the vocational curriculum. Available at: http://www.redcar-cleveland.gov.uk/Learnin1.nsf/Web+Full+List/ 857B77B33DDC966A80256F1800563DEE?OpenDocument

The workshop materials from Oxford Brookes University (2004) can be accessed at http://www.brookes.ac.uk/schools/education/rescon/ cpdgifted/coordinators_aimhigher.html

Part Three
Working as teachers

9 Work smarter not harder

Trevor Dawn

'Work smarter, not harder' is a phrase that is commonly found in books about management. The basic premise is that the time and effort invested in changing working practices will pay dividends in the long run, even if there is a short-term cost. Often the difficulty is in finding the extra time needed to make the change, irrespective of its potential benefits.

In this chapter, we will look at four facets of the management of teaching and learning where good organization and forward planning can help the teacher feel more relaxed and more in control. The first two are concerned with the practicalities of teaching while the latter two are concerned with a holistic approach to one's subject. They are: juggling one's workload; how to help learners who have missed key sessions; sequencing; and how to prefigure future lessons within the current one.

Juggling one's workload

The likelihood is that you will have several classes to consider at the same time, each with its own scheme of work, and this reinforces the need to 'work smarter'. Many courses are organized in terms or semesters with agreed holiday periods to break up the year. It is in your interests to smooth out the year so as not to have too many obligations that come together at the same time. For example, if you have five classes, each of which you teach for three times a week (4½ hours per class), it is not good planning to have five schemes of work where all the topics last for four weeks, with an assignment at the end of each topic. The marking would be horrendous. If each class has an average of 16 students and each assignment takes about half an hour to mark, you need to find 40 hours from somewhere just to do the marking; or, put it another way, 10 evenings at 4 hours per evening over a concentrated period. It also puts pressure on students if each teacher sets an assignment to be handed in at roughly the same time.

Juggling one's workload is important if you wish to survive as a teacher. It is critical that you stagger the schemes of work and the setting of assignments so that your workload and that of the students is more even. But is there more to this than simply varying the time allocated to topics in different schemes of work? What are the other considerations that can help with workload planning?

1   *Varying the type of assessment.* Not everything needs to be marked by you. You may find that, for one group, a student presentation accompanied by peer marking is valid; for another, self-checking by the learners against a checklist of criteria that can be accessed independently; and, for another, oral feedback in class time by you to the whole class is an acceptable alternative.

2   *Training learners in independent study skills.* You do not have to teach all the time in the more formal sense of the word. You can plan for one or two groups to be engaged in researching a topic, or undertaking a project, if you are at the stage of having to prepare several topics from scratch. We have found that it takes an average of six hours' preparation to produce teaching material of sufficient quality for a 1½ hour class at A2 level if a topic is totally new to the teacher. This does not take into account the time that is needed to think about the approach. Where do these hours come from? They have to be 'found' from somewhere, perhaps by giving less time in the short term to one group of learners on the understanding that the balance will be redressed in the future.

3   *Incorporating key skills into your subject.* You may find that you can use time more efficiently by emphasizing the value of one or more key skills in the way a topic is presented. Here are some examples:
    a) *a collaborative learning project* is one device you could

use to provide a forum for teamwork and problem-solving

b) *a presentation*, which meets the criteria for communication, say, with a requirement to use PowerPoint

c) *a practical session*, with the accent on completing a task which incorporates criteria for one of the levels of the application of number

4 *The strategic use of external sources.* You may find that a guest speaker, or a day conference or visit, or a work-experience placement, or a field trip gives you a break from the detailed preparation of the information-processing kind.

This juggling is legitimate in giving you time and space to manage your whole workload. There are many demands on the teacher's time and the pressures can be debilitating if you do not think in advance of some safety valves. When you have completed all of your schemes of work at the start of term, it is worthwhile looking again at the whole picture to see if you have created some avoidable 'high spots' in respect of assignments and preparation of material which you are teaching for the first time and to see if you can spread the load.

How to help learners who have missed key sessions

Students may be absent for a variety of legitimate reasons. They may be ill, or there may be a problem at home such as a bereavement or a family illness, or there may be adverse weather conditions or they may be attending an interview – the list is quite big.

This is a perennial problem in teaching. Open learning systems have been developed whose selling point is that time, place and pace should not inhibit unduly the progress of the learner. Virtual learning environments or VLEs (Fry *et al.* 2005) have been created for the purpose, among other things, of offsetting difficulties in attendance and accessing information. In their glossary, Fry and her fellow writers define a VLE as 'an electronic tool which facilitates online learning and teaching. It provides an environment in which tutors and students can develop learning content and participate in online interactions of various kinds'. They tend to be more prominent in higher education institutions, with WebCT and Blackboard among the most widely used and a whole educational experience can be encapsulated in these – lecture notes and activities, indicative reading, tutorial support, administrative information and the opportunity for social contact online with fellow learners.

Within the VLE 'family' we also find the Intranet. Many higher education institutions have made a policy decision that all course notes are available on the Intranet, so that no student should be disadvantaged. Each of these solutions is far-reaching and there is insufficient space available here to do them justice (for more detail, see The Essential FE Toolkit book on e-Learning in FE by John Whalley, Theresa Welch and Lee Williamson, Continuum, 2006). In addition, both open learning centres and VLEs should be seen as part of a wider institutional commitment, where certain values and assumptions about learning are embedded in the systems chosen. Some of these responses claim that there are no losses in the learning process by non-attendance, which makes one wonder about the purpose and benefits of conventional teaching.

However, if you work in an institution that does not have extensive provision for open learning or a VLE or the Intranet, or your course is not geared up for it, you will have to work out your own solutions. These will vary from course to course. Some of you have designed a course in such a way that the learning is enhanced by participation, especially where the development of skills is at a premium. Other courses, such as drama, performing arts or sport, place a greater emphasis on collaboration and certain outcomes are not possible if you do not attend and poor attendance can compromise the efforts of other students. There are others such as catering, hairdressing and motor vehicle, where there are clients or customers involved, where it is important that the learner is present to achieve certain outcomes. In addition, you may well have planned your scheme of work to meet a variety of learning styles, with a commitment to a facilitator style. In Chapter 1 and again in Part Four, we have been at pains to point out the strengths of an active, participative approach, which does place a high value on attendance.

Inevitably, there have to be compromises. You may feel that it would be best, in a perfect world, if all students attend 100 per cent of the time. But they don't, and therefore we have to plan to be as helpful as we can. Here are some of the things you can do to help students to catch up what they have missed:

- 'Study buddies'. At the start of the course, you arrange it so that each student pairs up with someone else and undertakes to supply her/him not only with the notes but also with help in going through what happened in class if the 'buddy' has missed a session.
- Devise, or get the students to buy, a course booklet which contains the basic information, so that they can at least read the notes. This is good practice, irrespective of the attendance issue.
- Plan to allocate some of your time for one-to-one sessions such as a tutorial or a review session where the learner has an opportunity to ask you about what you did in the session that they have missed.
- Designate one lesson per half term as a non-teaching lesson with the express purpose of your being available to help those who have missed a session.
- It may be the case that you teach a topic on more than one occasion, either in the same week or later in the year, so you can make your timetable known in advance.

Sequencing

Teaching (and learning) is a sequential activity that takes place over time. In other words, one topic or focus of learning has to come first and another has to be placed last, however long the time allocation. How you conceptualize the allocated time framework is the key to delivering a worthwhile learning experience.

The obvious place to start is with the scheme of work. One can usually find out from the validating body what is expected in terms of the content to be covered and the standard to be achieved. In AS and A2 courses, for example, the range of topics to be covered is specified by the validating body, specimen answers are available, in addition to the comments of the chief examiner, to help gauge the standard, and one can confer with colleagues if one is not sure.

Walklin (1990) has identified a number of factors that need to be considered in designing schemes of work: the student group, their previous experience, prerequisites and age range; the course aims and objectives (outcomes); organizational factors such as location, meeting times, course duration, course content, sequence and so on; methodology; and evaluation. What the scheme of work does is to translate these 'factors' into a working document that converts mere topics into allocated blocks of time, thence into a logical and often progressive sequence and underpinned by learning outcomes that will be assessed.

So, will any old sequence be all right, as long as it is logical? Walklin says, regarding the student group, 'it [the scheme of work] should reflect the learners' needs and take account of learners with learning difficulties, gender, class, religion and race'. This may mean that you think twice before plumping for the most obvious sequence. There are often conflicting claims to be assessed. Here are some questions that you can answer when you start to sketch out your scheme of work:

- Are there fundamental principles that are the basis for understanding the whole course, which need to be established early if the rest of the course is to make sense? Do these come in the form of prerequisites without which further learning would be inhibited?
- Is this a totally new subject to the students and do I have to think about promoting its value in order to motivate them?
- Do I want the first few lessons to exemplify how I like to work?
- If I want to signal to students with different learning styles that the subject is equally relevant, will the sequence of topics help me to do this?
- Can I identify one or more topics that allow me to set

some work early, mark it and give it back, thus creating a one-to-one line of communication with all the class?

How learning is sequenced is important in conveying from the teacher to the learners a sense of security about the whole. They should be able to see how the learning is progressing, to begin to see connections and patterns within topics, leading to deep learning (Marton and Säljö 1976; Entwistle and Ramsden 1983; Gibbs 1992; see also Mark Weyers' book in the Essential FE Toolkit Series on *Teaching the FE Curriculum*, Continuum, 2006). As the course progresses, the teacher can refer back to topics covered earlier with confidence, if the sequence has been carefully thought out. It is good practice if at all possible to choose topics in the early stages of a course that provide a secure foundation for later learning. As the sequence of learning unfolds, you are demonstrating a topic's relevance to modern life, that it is intrinsically interesting. The knowledge, skills and attitudes acquired through engaging with your subject gives status to the learner and transforms them.

How to prefigure future lessons within the current one

As well as being a sequential activity, teaching and learning is also a cumulative one, based on a step by step progress, each step or stage acting as a foundation for the next. The more we know about a topic, provided that the approach has resulted in some deep learning (Gibbs 1992), the more we can make connections with other learning and bring about meaningful interaction. To prefigure is to come across something in one situation and then later to respond to the same thing in another.

Here is an example. When I teach my first lesson to the PGCE post-compulsory class, I hand out a copy of my lesson plan. The actual lesson is on 'Learning Styles' but I give out my lesson plan then, and in subsequent lessons, so that, when 'designing lesson plans' becomes the topic for the day, the students will have become acquainted with much of the rubric implicitly before they are asked to engage with it explicitly. I do the same thing with referencing, writing the references on my handouts and referring to the same handouts later in the course when 'referencing' becomes the lesson topic. I do a 'sorting' lesson quite a few weeks before I introduce the Taba method (1967) in a formal sense.

This approach can be extended to all subjects. We can prefigure later learning by the way in which we model good practice ourselves. Sometimes the sequence is from the specific to the general, as in the lesson plan and the handout examples, where each specific example is underpinned by a general principle, which will be addressed at a later date. You can also prefigure learning from the general to the specific.

Here is an example, again from the PGCE post-compulsory environment. I ask the class to identify one good teacher they have known and assign to her/him up to ten characteristics that exemplified their goodness and the same thing for a bad teacher. The resultant checklist of good teaching characteristics then prefigured many of the session topics that were planned for later in the course.

The way you teach and the way you approach deep learning should have at its core the 'cumulative' phenomenon. There is the danger that teaching and learning will be presented as a series of episodes, all with their own label in your notes and those of the students, but lacking integrative elements. It should become second nature for you to think about the way in which you can subtly engage the learners in knowledge and skills that will be more formally addressed at a later date.

Conclusion

'Work smarter, not harder' is an injunction to change one's behaviour. The behaviour in question is something that has happened in the past upon which now you have had occasion to reflect.

In the first year or perhaps two of teaching, it is natural to prioritize the acquisition and integrity of information. This often means that assembling the 'content' of the lesson has the greatest priority claim on your time and energy and that you have little time to think about other issues.

But as you gain in experience and have had time to reflect,

you will begin to see further possibilities for managing the teaching and learning process that will lead to greater job satisfaction. You will be able to use past experience; you will often be able to locate resources more quickly; you will be able to anticipate problems and plan accordingly; you will be able to cope with the unexpected much better; you will have a sense of proportion when things do not go smoothly.

Above all you will not be too hard on yourself. You have proved that you can manage all the components of teaching and that you have the capacity to improve.

Further reading

Harkin, J., Turner, G. and Dawn, T. (2001) *Teaching Young Adults: a handbook for teachers*, London: Routledge Falmer.

Petty, G. (2004) *Teaching Today: a practical guide*, Cheltenham: Nelson Thorne.

Walklin, L. (1990) *Teaching and Learning in Further and Adult Education*, Cheltenham: Stanley Thorne.

10 Team teaching

Ros Clow

For Maggie, it was her final observed teaching practice. She seemed well-prepared, her lesson plan was clear and seemed appropriate. It was an art AS class in one of the art rooms in an FE college. The lesson was for two hours and included theory and practical – a still-life drawing. As she launched into the first section of her lesson, the dreaded refrain came: 'We did this with Dot last lesson'. My trainee stumbled, gathered herself together, moved on to the next section (which thank goodness was new to them) and went on to complete a successful lesson.

During the debrief Maggie explained that the AS course was taught by two tutors, herself and a part-time tutor who took the group on Thursdays when Maggie was at university doing her PGCE. When I explored the system they had for 'team teaching', it was unsatisfactory. They had no organized way of communicating with each other and they were rarely on campus at the same time. Additionally, I could not think of any text to recommend which might help her.

So, in this chapter, I shall review the different kinds of team teaching which exist in FE, explore their strengths and weaknesses and advise good practice.

Team teaching was an educational fashion in the late 1960s and 1970s. In the USA and in the UK, the usual system of 'one teacher, one class' was experimented with to see if a different approach, using a team of teachers and usually new curriculum materials, gave better educational outcomes (Close *et al.* 1974, Warwick 1972). Results were equivocal and the practice mostly disappeared in both primary and secondary schools. There was one study where team teaching was tried in an FE college. Again, the results were not strong enough to suggest that it should be adopted universally. In all these experiments, groups of students were taught in one large group by one teacher, and then split for follow-up work in which the rest of the team were involved.

Today in FE, team teaching is rarely introduced as possibly educationally more sound. Usually, it is an organizational response to an organizational problem, more often than not caused by underfunding or lack of resources. It can, however, work really well, though there have to be pre-conditions for this to be the case. The pre-conditions are not rocket science! The teaching team have to want to team teach and have to enjoy working collaboratively with each other. Close *et al.* (1974) concluded: 'interpersonal relationships among staff are at least as important as the course work proposed; and unless care is taken ... the scheme can go sadly awry' (p. 80).

Half and half team teaching

The kind of team teaching experienced by Maggie occurs when two different teachers are asked to deliver a course to one group. This is rarely an ideal situation, but can be a solution when one teacher is absent on a regular basis (e.g. when attending a day-release course for their PGCE or Cert. Ed.). One of my very good experiences of team teaching was in the 1980s when I was asked to deliver O level maths in this way. My co-teacher was Harshad, a biology teacher. Neither of us had taught O level maths before. We sat down with the syllabus and identified which topics we felt very comfortable with. Luckily, we were then able to split the syllabus to both our satisfactions, playing to our strengths. There were about four topics that neither of us had studied before; we took two each, so as to share the more difficult preparation (sets and matrices will stay with me forever!). We wrote our own schemes of work, and then checked them with each other so that we could have some idea of what the other had already taught as we introduced each new topic. We met up with each other over coffee from time to time to discuss our own and individual students' progress. This worked well and retention was good. Harshad and I were such a good team that we put on a song and dance act ('We're a Couple of Swells') during the Rag Week Show! This is not compulsory in team teaching!

Together team teaching

Another experience involved teaching general and commu-nication Studies (G&CS) to a large group of carpentry students. They were on day release and only had one slot in their day when they could do G&CS. At this time, only one classroom was available in wood trades, and it had several large square pillars, very convenient for adolescent boys to hide behind. The solution was to ask me to team teach with an hourly paid teacher. It was complete coincidence that the suggested co-teacher was one of my oldest friends. In this case, we planned the scheme of work together. We would both be in the classroom at the same time, but we shared the preparation by each planning and leading on particular topics. This meant that, typically, each of us would take responsibility for two or three lessons at a time. The students benefited, as we were able to pool our resources and ideas, and we could give them more attention when they were working in small groups.

It was in general a very happy teaching experience, except for the one session where I had to teach on my own, as Sue was away. This perhaps shows the wisdom of the original decision always to have two teachers in the classroom, but by this time we had such a good relationship with our students that we did not ask for cover when Sue was invited for an interview for a full-time job. We were in the middle of three planned sessions on 'racism'. The first had gone really well; playing games which explored what it felt like to be outsiders (Rule of the Game and Crossed/Uncrossed – Brandes and Phillips 1979: S18 and Brandes 1982: 10, 11, 88). In my solo session, I asked the class to close their eyes and talked them through a visualization. We had used this before in the course, to demonstrate how prior experience affects how we interpret what we hear, so they complied quite happily. The visualization put them in the position of someone who had been saving up for three years to visit a cousin for a holiday. They are excited as they board the plane, the plane lands; they go through customs and are asked to wait in a small room. Then a customs officer arrives and states that, as they have so much money on them, they are probably not here just for a holiday and they are escorted to the first plane that will take them straight back home. The students were rightfully indignant about such terrible treatment. When asked to guess which airport it had happened at, not one of them said Heathrow, London, which was in fact the truth. At this point, I started to show them the video of the Panorama programme in which I had seen this story. Of course the 'holidaymaker' was a black woman from Guyana. And here it all started to go wrong; within four minutes, the whole group were singing 'We're going Paki bashing' at the tops of their voices! I was so shocked, I stopped the lesson and sent them to lunch. You did not send students out early in wood trades! They were shocked and went to see their course tutor to explain what had happened. I met with Sue and we decided to scrap our third planned lesson, and she would lead next week's lesson on a new topic, the environment. As they came in the next week they were very contrite and the ringleader apologized to me as he walked past to his seat. Maybe we could have revisited 'racism', but neither of us was brave enough. We were both in the classroom together for the rest of the year.

Collaborative team teaching

All my experiences of teacher training in FE have been with collaborative teams. This was the case when I was a trainee, with four or five tutors who delivered sessions regularly and came out to observe us. This is one case where the team element is primarily to provide educational advantage. Trainee teachers look to those delivering the training to them to role-model good practice (Harkin et al. 2001). Thus providing at least three different tutors with different approaches demonstrates that there is not just one way of teaching but that different styles can work just as well: trainees need to find the one they are comfortable with. I had the advantage when working at Swindon College of having a superb boss who was very clear about how to communicate within the team. Each course, whatever time or day it ran, would have three tutors (wherever

possible). One would be a lead tutor and arrange team meetings, about one a term, and also represent the team at course
team meetings. The scheme of work was written as a group,
taking into account strengths and preferences and availability.
This meant there was never any need for cover, as one of us
would always be around. Some sessions had all three tutors
present, especially first sessions or where students were negotiating the future programme, but mostly one tutor led each
session. This was very welcome, as so many courses ran in the
evenings and no one can ever underestimate the opportunity
cost of regularly teaching in the evening. The prime method of
communication was a course file which was held in the office
next to the classroom where the City & Guilds 730 ran. The
file contained the scheme of work and as soon as each of us
completed a session, we filed our lesson plan together with a
copy of all handouts used. Additionally, we wrote on our lesson
plan (in a different colour ink) any useful comments: students
who had struggled, been absent, topics we did not get round to
covering, topics we had covered because the students were
keen to discuss certain issues, things that needed to be repeated,
things the students wanted to talk about next week. If a different tutor was teaching next week, they had to look at this file
before they made the final plan for their lesson. If Maggie had
had this system for her AS art course, she would not have had
the problem which nearly wrecked her final teacher training
observation.

Vocational course teams – macro team teaching?

In the 1980s, BTEC promoted the new idea of a course team.
In effect, any BTEC qualification could move away from
modularization, each unit taught by a different tutor in splendid
isolation. The team would plan schemes of work for the whole
course, avoiding duplication of shared theory or techniques.
For instance, on the BTEC First in Engineering, the students
would only cover Ohm's Law once, not at the beginning of
every unit. This was expected to give teachers more time to
cover other aspects of the units and to some extent to respond

to student criticism. This was revolutionary thinking though it was very hard at the time to convince teachers that this approach might have merits. It is now commonplace to have course teams, with published meeting minutes. However, the growth toward competence-based qualifications has thwarted the desire for true integration that was being espoused before the Council for National Vocational Qualifications introduced NVQs and a pick and mix approach.

This is a kind of macro team-teaching approach, with individual teachers taking responsibility for particular assignments, tests or whole units but the team having overall responsibility for all aspects of the course. In my research into the work roles of FE teachers 100 per cent had attended course team meetings; 78 per cent had led them (Clow 2005).

Key skills team delivery

Before and since the Dearing report (1996) emphasized the importance of key skills, there have been two basic delivery models which require a team-teaching approach and one that does not. In the solo approach, the vocational (or for that matter academic) tutor is so confident in their personal key skills that they can teach and assess within the assessed course work for whichever aspect they are teaching. Frequently, however, the teacher is not confident or competent to assess at least one of the key skills. Typically, someone teaching A level English may not feel competent to assess application of number or possibly IT, and someone teaching motor vehicle studies may not be competent to assess communication.

In either of the latter situations, the college (or school) needs to provide a different teacher to deliver key skills. In effect, they need to set up team teaching. Each college approaches this differently. One model is to have the communications teacher present in all or some of the vocational classes, assisting those who need it, or taking small groups to one side while the vocational teacher works with the rest of the group. In other colleges, a key skills teacher is employed to work on all three hard key skills (AoN, Comms and IT), typically having the whole group for one hour a week and focusing on a different key skill each term.

More commonly, different teachers are employed for each key skill that the vocational tutors cannot cope with and teach a programme appropriate for the main course. In all these team models, there must be team-teaching practice for it to be effective for the students: discussion of syllabus or units; agreement about who will teach what, and agreement on sequencing and structuring assessments. It will work best where the team members like and respect each other. The earlier experiments on team teaching came to similar conclusions: 'interpersonal relationships among staff involved are at least as important as the course work proposed' (Close *et al.* 1974: 80). Probably the biggest problem is incompatible team-mates (Buckley 2000).

There does seem to have been some development of team teaching in post-compulsory education, but not in FE. As a student in HE, I had the best student experience of my life in a research perspectives unit on the EdD. We were a group of 15 education practitioners from all sectors and roles. For this, our first module, we attended on two Fridays and two Saturdays. In nearly every session, whether we had a guest speaker or not, four tutors attended. They came from different research traditions and were able to demonstrate their perspectives in every discussion we had. They were not so much tutors as co-discussants and therefore the quality of our learning was maximized. Absolutely brilliant, but no FE course could ever afford the luxury of a 15:4 student/staff ratio; I doubt many universities could either. Indeed we suspected that there was a lot of goodwill on behalf of the tutors in this particular example. HE provision where students are privy to more than one opinion in any module has to increase student confidence to disagree and so consolidate their own learning. This does exist with larger student groups, where tutors are working in a collaborative team. A recent publication *Team Teaching: What, Why and How* extols the virtues of team teaching in a Jesuit College in the USA (Buckley 2000). Buckley lists pages of advantages for teachers, students and administrators, but the latter term indicates that the setting is very different from FE colleges where usually the teachers are the administrators and, if you are not teaching one group, you are usually teaching another, not preparing for a future session.

When more than one tutor is present, difficulties can arise. Students can find it confusing when two tutors disagree (Buckley 2000: 14; Clow and Mehra 2006). It is important for tutors to agree ground rules for the way they behave when present with a group of students. In the City and Guilds 730 example mentioned above, we had a rule that whoever was leading any section of the session would be the only one who spoke. The others would remain quiet unless asked to contribute. It is always hard for teachers to remain quiet. But what do you do in this situation when the leading tutor is saying something which you think might not be quite right, or worse still, you know is completely wrong? I had the latter situation when the leading tutor (a new member of the team) was teaching the difference between open and closed questions. He became completely muddled and transposed the definitions. Did I embarrass him in front of the group or wait and repair the damage next week when I was teaching the group on my own? Well known for my cowardly tendencies, I chose the latter route, and additionally had a quiet word with the tutor the next time I saw him on his own. I suppose if our ground rule had been that we always invited colleagues to add anything at the end of the session we had led, we would not have had this problem. Although this is an example of a case in which team teaching went wrong, it was still a better outcome than if he had been unobserved in his mistake.

However, if you are the one that makes the mistake, you might prefer that no other colleague was there to see it! One evening, I was teaching on the 730 and my part of the evening was to cover role-play as a teaching method. It was not my usual topic and I had not prepared properly. I borrowed a prepared acetate off my boss, Marilyn, who was our expert in that area. In the latter part of the evening, the students were gamely copying the headings from the acetate while I suggested definitions, using the time-honoured reveal technique. As I revealed about the seventh heading I realized to my horror that I had no idea what it meant. I used bluff! Said something quickly and moved on to give a full definition of the next heading. I thought I had got away with it! The students were tired and wanted to go home. I could look it up for next week.

Then my team colleague perked up and said he did not quite understand what I had meant and would I like to expand! Later in the car park he said that as soon as he saw the expression on my face he knew he should have kept quiet!

Team teaching going wrong

Team teaching does not always work. I have collected examples where team teaching became difficult or non-existent.

The first is to do with basic differences with respect to the underlying philosophy of the course. In one example, two teachers had totally differing approaches to teaching A levels: one lectured using well-prepared notes but allowing little student discussion, the other used lots of activities and student interaction. When timetabled to teach on the half and half model of team teaching, this proved to be a stressful experience for both the teachers and the students, who preferred one approach to the other. Similarly, I was involved in a team where one team member believed that, on a competence-based course, the students should be given all the competences in the first session, they should read them and then request the underpinning knowledge which would decide the programme. The other two teachers did not agree with this approach but went along with it, as he was the leader of this course team. When he left at Christmas, we wrote a scheme of work that we thought they needed and were so relieved to do so. Right or wrong, we did not believe that students can really know what they need to know until the basics have been covered.

Another team-teaching experience that did not work was when a college combined groups because there were not enough rooms available. Teachers were told at the last minute that both groups would be together and they would be team teaching all 40 students at the same time. Where the two teachers were friends, this was a great success, using the collaborative model where they took turns with one preparing and leading, but the other always there to help with discipline and group-work. In two other examples at the same college, it did not run so smoothly. One teacher turned up to each class, but did not prepare any lessons. In each class 'he sat hunched over the computer with his back to the class'. He refused to teach alternate classes, perhaps because he did not like being observed. In a second example, an hourly paid teacher turned up to teach as timetabled. When he discovered that he was expected to team teach he 'stormed out' and was never seen again! Buckley (2000) suggests that 'some teachers are rigid personality types' or 'do not want to risk humiliation and discouragement at the failures that may occur' (p. 13).

The inspector calls

No matter how good the system is in team teaching, it is only as strong as the weakest link. On a 730 course I was leading, we were expecting a visit from HMI. I had all the timetable sorted out so that she would see our very strongest staff in action. But she was ill and postponed her visit. A few weeks later, she announced new dates for her visit. She would not see our best in action, but we were a strong team, so I was not too concerned. The week before the visit, the students were fretting about the resources they were making, so I suggested they all brought a resource in the following week. I duly wrote it up in the course file – please put half an hour aside for students to look at each other's resources. The two colleagues who were to teach in front of the inspector decided a visit to the local pub would be better preparation than reading the boring old course file. The lesson progressed according to plan (their plan). They were performing very well when a student spoke up: 'When are we going to show each other these resources we've dragged in?' The inspector was not impressed. In retrospect, I knew I should have flagged up the change by internal memo or phone call. We all learn from experience.

And watching colleagues teach during team teaching can be the best learning experiences of all, and a useful technique for developing new teachers.

Learning support assistants

Many FE teachers now find that there may be one or two learning support assistants (LSAs) in the class with them. This is another kind of team teaching. In this model, the teacher is the professional in charge and has responsibility for the class, their learning and health and safety. The LSAs will have a variety of roles: working with an individual student with behavioural problems; a general help; a support for the physical needs of a student who uses a wheelchair; a sign language interpreter for a deaf student; a note-taker; help for a student whose first language is not English ... As a general rule the teacher should write the lesson plan giving clear indication of what the LSA will be doing at each stage of the lesson. This will include when to help and when to hold back from helping. The LSA should be given a copy of the lesson plan before the lesson. Often the LSA will be able to help cooperatively in the planning process, but the teacher should never lose sight of the fact that they are the professional and must take responsibility for all aspects of the lesson. This is particularly the case when the teacher is new and the LSA is part of the establishment. The teacher must take charge.

I have noticed that when good LSAs are promoted into the role of lecturer, they often have problems 'bossing' their LSA about, and this can be quite difficult in the area of safety. It is a key part of the professional role of the teacher that they have responsibility for health and safety.

Conclusion

Team teaching can be very effective and stimulating for students and teachers, for everyone in the classroom. For the positive effects to be achieved, there are some basic rules:

- the team members need to know about it in advance
- ideally, the team members should enjoy working together
- the team needs to meet to plan the scheme of work
- communication needs to continue through meetings, phone calls/emails and a central course file
- the team needs to agree rules for when they are in the classroom together
- the team should play to its strengths

- new preparation should be shared between the team members
- it is essential that in advance everyone is clear about what they should be doing

Further reading

Buckley, F. J. (2000) *Team Teaching: What, Why and How*, London: Sage.

There is little of relevance written about team teaching so if you want to base a CPD module on it, it would probably help to reflect in depth on the experiences you encounter. Research evidence shows that reflection is deepened when a framework is used to provide a structure for reflections and questions that will challenge our thinking. These articles suggest frameworks to support reflection and to help practitioners self-assess their reflection.

Bain, J. D., Ballantyne, R., Packer, J. and Mills, C. (1999) 'Using journal writing to enhance student teachers' reflectivity during field experience placements', *Teachers and Teaching: theory and practice* 5 (1): 51–73.

Brookfield, S. (1995) *Becoming a critically reflective teacher*, San Francisco: Jossey-Bass.

Hamlin, K. D. (2004) 'Beginning the journey: supporting reflection in early field experience', *Reflective Practice* 5 (2): 167–79.

Johns C. (1995) 'Framing learning through reflection within Carper's fundamental ways of knowing in nursing', *Journal of Advanced Nursing* 22: 226–34.

Kreber, C. (2004) 'An analysis of two models of reflection and their implications for educational development', *International Journal for Academic Development* 9 (1): 29–49.

Part Four
Putting it into practice

11 Teaching strategies

Trevor Dawn

Introduction

The choice of teaching strategy is very personal and is affected by a variety of factors, among which are: one's personality and state of confidence, one's training, the extent of one's experience, the nature of the students you teach, the climate of the institution and the support of one's colleagues and so on. The same applies to the ideas expressed here. They may or may not suit you for the same sort of reasons. We hope you will look at the ideas, not with any expectation that they will directly meet your needs or that one or two can be 'taken off the shelf' and used immediately – that would be a bonus – but that they might trigger thoughts that will result in a new idea from yourself. Give a person a fish and you feed them for a day; teach them to fish and you feed them for life.

In Chapter 1, we looked at the importance of beginnings to topics or lessons, the nature of the teacher-centred and student-centred balance in any lesson and the ways in which a facilitative approach can overcome apathy, hostility and loss of confidence in learners. In Chapter 4 we explored the many values of using role-play in teaching. In this chapter, we will look at teaching from a number of practical perspectives:

1. anticipating learner difficulty or resistance
2. finding common ground – activities that start with things that the learner knows, as a basis for new learning
3. facilitating through choice or opinion
4. creating a forum for discussion
5. intrigue and curiosity
6. devising role briefs

First of all, though, a few words about 'mind-sets'.

Improving one's mind-set

Knowing that it pays in the long run to think through your scheme of work and to plan your lessons does not of itself guarantee that the learners will be impressed by your endeavours. For many reasons, learners can be hard to excite, especially if they have been socialized in their previous education or in other classes into a more reactive and passive compliance with receiving information as given by the teacher (Harkin *et al.* 2001). A culture of acquiring 'good' notes and having the learning heavily directed can be hard to change, even with students who are committed. A culture of non-work or apathy can be even harder to handle.

This is where the mind-set comes in. The reaction of your students or your contemporaries when you were a student can be turned to your advantage. It may force you to ask yourself why anyone should be interested in any particular subject matter. Just because you are interested in something or the syllabus dictates that it should be included, doesn't automatically mean that others will be switched on. It is true that new learning can be rewarding by dint of it being made challenging, but for some learners the challenge can seem too great. Harkin and his colleagues make the point about the confirmation–challenge continuum (Harkin *et al.* 2001), asserting that judgement is needed to get the balance right for each lesson.

You may need to anticipate potential rejection, or indifference or the fact that some of the concepts may at first acquaintance be too difficult for some of your learners – the issue of inclusion referred to in Chapter 3 – but feel confident that the way you present them will have the right balance of challenge and conformation. You may need to see whether you can find some common ground between a topic as *you* see it and the topic as the students may perceive it. Is there something in their lives that is tangential to the subject that you can use to prepare the learners for the new ideas? Sometimes you will present the learning in the form of a choice or opinion, thus prefiguring concepts that will come in later; at other times you

will devise prompts or structures to provide a forum for discussion that allow the learner to engage with a topic where
their experience may be indirect or limited. Finally, there are
times when it is necessary to use intrigue and curiosity to
enthuse your charges.

Seeing teaching as a 'last resort' and not the first option, is the
key mind-set to gaining and sustaining learner interest.

Practical examples

Anticipating learner difficulty or resistance

There are times when we know from experience that a particular topic will be difficult for some students. It could be
because we are asking too much at one time of a particular
group of learners or there might be an unwillingness even to
engage with something if it looks difficult. We may fear also
rejection of a particular topic because the subject matter might
be uncomfortable for some learners. In all such instances, we
need to find a way of interesting students almost without their
realizing it.

a) Possible unwillingness to engage – English A level
Yeats's poem, 'Sailing to Byzantium', is one such case. The
teacher recognized that the poem was not straightforward and
that he could anticipate some reluctance to engage with perhaps
the language or the style or the sentiments. So he decided to
present the poem in a different way from the normal approach
of reading the whole poem with the class. Before you see the
whole poem, perhaps you would like to see what the teacher
showed the students and the task he set.

Some of the phrases in the poem were cut up, put on to cards
in an envelope as in Table 12 below and the students were
asked in pairs to sort them into two columns (which need not
be equal), one where the emphasis is on youth and what it feels
like to be young and the other about old age or metaphors
associated with being older. If the students were not sure of the
category, or where they could make a case either way, the
item(s) were to be placed in the middle.

Table 12: Exercise based on 'Sailing to Byzantium'

the young in one another's arms	gather me into the artifice of eternity	for every tatter in its mortal dress
once out of nature I shall never take my form from any natural thing	caught in the sensual music of delight	an aged man is but a paltry thing
monuments of unageing intellect	consume my heart away	that is no country for old men
all summer long		

Here is the poem in full, with the permission of Poetry X.com:

Sailing to Byzantium by W. B. Yeats

I

That is no country for old men. The young
In one another's arms, birds in the trees
— Those dying generations — at their song,
The salmon-falls, the mackerel-crowded seas,
Fish, flesh, or fowl, commend all summer long
Whatever is begotten, born, and dies,
Caught in that sensual music all neglect
Monuments of unageing intellect.

II

An aged man is but a paltry thing,
A tattered coat upon a stick, unless
Soul clap its hands and sing, and louder sing
For every tatter in its mortal dress,
Nor is there singing school but studying
Monuments of its own magnificence;
And therefore I have sailed the seas and come
To the holy city of Byzantium.

III

O sages standing in God's holy fire
As in the gold mosaic of a wall,

Come from the holy fire, perne in gyre,
And be the singing-master of my soul.
Consume my heart away; sick with desire
And fastened to a dying animal
It knows not what it is; and gather me
Into the artifice of eternity.

IV

Once out of nature I shall never take
My bodily form from any natural thing,
But such a form as Grecian goldsmiths make
Of hammered gold and gold enamelling
To keep a drowsy Emperor awake;
Or set upon a golden bough to sing
To lords and ladies of Byzantium
Of what is past, or passing, or to come.

In the feedback on the sorting activity, some of the themes such as youth and age, disillusionment, reflections on the past and its relationship to the future, possible 'monuments' the poet might leave (in comparison with other monuments) and why he might feel that way were discussed. The class then compared 'Sailing' with earlier poems by Yeats and reasons for the change in language and style were explored.

The lesson went well for a number of reasons: the novel approach bore in mind the value of the Yerkes–Dodson curve; the first task was made simple and accessible in line with planning beyond the traditional triangle to reach the accommodator style learners; because the accent was not so much on getting it right but on opening up the class to a discussion on the themes and ideas of the poem.

b) Asking too much at one time of a group of learners – the information system of the Automobile Association (AA)
A class of AVCE computer studies students were given a case study about the information system of the AA and the following questions were asked:

1   What is the purpose of the AA's information system?
2   Describe the uses to which it might be put?

3   Make a list of the factors which might influence its effectiveness?

Prior to the three questions, the case study contained a lot of information, some of which was about the nature of the business: services to members, finance and insurance, retail and travel, its own driving school and publishing. Other information was about open information systems, about annual expenditure on IT and about key performance indicators. It was written in continuous prose and the teacher was concerned that the task would be too abstract in that form for the students to do it justice.

So the first activity was introduced as a practical task before the students attempted the three questions. The teacher designed a simple sheet as in Table 13, where the nature of the business was laid out like a board in a game and the students would place various types of customer requests for information, in the form of cards (Table 14), on the most appropriate section on the board. If a case could be made out for more than one place, that item should be noted somewhere for further discussion when the 'answers' to the game were discussed.

Table 13: The nature of the AA's business

services to members		travel
insurance and finance		AA driving school
retail		publishing

The teacher and the class went through the answers, agreeing alternative or duplicate locations for each enquiry. The students now had more of an idea about the sort of business that the AA was involved in and more advanced tasks could be introduced. The students then could either design a database or a website, transforming the information into a practical format. The next stage was for the students to brainstorm the various ways customers could contact the AA, after which they could then answer the original three questions.

Table 14: Customer requests to the AA

Buying a CD-ROM to learn German	Someone has lost their AA credit card
Reporting a breakdown	Buying a car torch
A quote for house insurance	Enquiry about a personal loan
Booking driving lessons	Renewing motor insurance
Request for an inspection of a prospective car purchase	Buying the AA guide to camping in France
Buying a child's car seat	Booking a car ferry to Ireland
Special offer to schools on introductory driving lessons	Job advert for a qualified driving instructor
Enquiry about the 'best' route	Buying a travel guide to Germany
Request for legal aid	Reminder to renew AA membership
Someone phones with a 'home start' request	

c) Rejection of a particular topic because the subject matter might be uncomfortable for some learners

A topic such as 'aggression' is potentially uncomfortable for most learners and perhaps traumatic for a few. In such cases, it is important to find an objective and non-emotive beginning to the lesson. I have found that line drawings or freehand sketches of particular poses, accompanied by the question 'which of these poses is aggressive?', generates a lot of sensible discussion on the topic (with reasons accepted for and against). Pairs or threes work well. Lots of useful vocabulary emerges which both helps define the term and helps introduce notions of body language, non-verbal signals and social context which will all feature later in the lesson.

d) When students think they know it already (but do they?)

Teaching students to use Harvard referencing accurately is a necessary part of academic life but more difficult than one might imagine, especially when many in the class think that they are already competent in this regard. In line with the general principle of 'teaching as a last resort' we have devised an active approach to make referencing more interesting.

STAGE 1

We organize the class in small groups (threes or fours) and supply each group with a sheet of Harvard references and ask them to devise between five and eight rules that they have found. In the debrief they come up with such standards as surname of the author first, comma before the initials, which are in capitals followed by full stops, followed by the date of publication in brackets with no further punctuation followed by the title of the book or publication and so on. They tell us the rules.

STAGE 2

We then give out books, articles and periodicals on certain themes and ask the groups to write on flip-chart a short set of references (about six to eight). We deliberately introduce some with joint or multiple authorship, some by the same author, and stipulate that they include some from journals and government publications. In the debrief we extend their range of usage so that they can cope with the non-standard examples and discuss the reasoning behind the system.

Points of interest about these approaches

By anticipating that there might be some learner difficulty or resistance the teacher can disarm this by making the learning 'task' focused. The tasks are arranged in bite-sized stages so that the learners gain in confidence and can see for themselves that they are making progress. The tasks are self-referencing, by which we mean that the 'answers' are obvious and can be tested by argument. This invests the learning with relevance and leads to greater ownership.

Finding common ground – activities that start with things that the learner knows as a basis for new learning
There are lots of simple ideas that are based on the same philosophy as that of the preacher in Chapter 1, i.e. how to find an opening to a topic that the audience will respond to which will lead them into its more erudite aspects later.

a) Three things
I asked an AS class (the subject will be revealed later when you have thought about it), working in pairs or threes, to write down at least three things they know about the following people:

Tony Blair
Cherie Blair
Dawn French
Alex Ferguson
Liz Hurley
Chris Evans
X (one of their teachers, with permission of course – even yourself)
Richard Branson
Peggy Mitchell (NOT Barbara Windsor but the *EastEnders* character)
Kelly Holmes

You need to be careful about gender balance and racial balance. You will also need to think about the topicality of the people you choose.

When the class had had time to do the task, I then took answers from all the pairs/threes and wrote them against each name on the overhead transparency. There were all sorts of snippets of information from newspapers and magazines and hearsay. When I had recorded all the answers, I asked what they all had in common, including X, and it transpired, as planned, that we know people by their occupation, since most, if not all the pairs/threes had mentioned occupation.

Points of interest about the approach

I could then reveal that the topic for the day was about work and identity (sociology) and went into more orthodox sociological material. It was fun and inclusive and generated all sorts of interesting ancillary points relating to gender stereotyping, the influence of the media, public taste and morality, attitudes to celebrities and so on that would be useful later in the lesson. It was quite revealing to me as to who knew what!

b) Alison's jar

An accounts teacher (AA) carried the same principle into her lesson on establishing the costs of a product.

She produced a jar of stewed apples and asked the class (small groups) to identify the costs, additional to the raw materials, that would contribute to the final price. All sorts of things were mentioned, including the costs of the jars, the labelling, the cooking and processing costs, the wages of the workers, the costs of distribution to the shops and so on. Because there was a visible object, the teacher could ask probing questions and establish the differences in costs.

Points of interest about the approach

It is important for some learners to be able to have a concrete basis for accounts principles. The jars of apples are physical, tactile and visual, giving a level of prompts to some students that an abstract task ('I want you to think about what goes in to a jar of apples') would not do so well.

c) Wealth

This exercise (see Table 15) was developed to teach a business studies lesson early in the course to a class for whom the 'business' module was not the main part of their course. The idea was to use examples of business activity in real life that they would recognize and to do it in a fun way.

The matching exercise is then followed by three questions (I tend to put them on the same sheet).

Table 15: Match the appropriate pairs

1.	A prison inmate	A.	Natural resources
2.	A premier league team	B.	Crack cocaine
3.	A celebrity	C.	Profit
4.	A charity	D.	Cash in hand
5.	Someone lost in the desert	E.	Number of children
6.	At a car boot sale	F.	Tobacco
7.	In some African tribes	G.	Water
8.	A petty criminal	H.	Jewellery
9.	Vodafone	I.	Size of squad
10.	A developing country	J.	Number of sponsors

QUESTION 1
How would you define 'wealth' as a result of this exercise?
(You should aim to identify at least *five* different characteristics.)

QUESTION 2
Which of the above are the most important for wealth creation in an advanced developed country?

QUESTION 3
What other 'ingredients' do you think are important in the development of an advanced developed country?

Debriefing the wealth exercise

THE MATCHING TASK
When the students have completed the matching task, their answers should be compared and suggestions discussed. There may well be conflicting claims, for example is the best match for the prison inmate tobacco or crack cocaine; the petty criminal crack cocaine or jewellery? Some lightness of touch works well here, by allowing differences of opinion to stand. Exactness is not the point of the exercise, though some students will push for it.

DEBRIEFING QUESTION 1

Lots of answers will emerge: wealth as status (jewellery); wealth as surplus (Vodafone and profit, car boot sale and cash in hand); something in demand (tobacco and the prison, water in the desert); reserves and assets (the premier league team and size of squad); natural resources; the ability to attract financial backers (charity and the number of sponsors).

DEBRIEFING QUESTION 2

You might expect natural resources, profit and water to figure highly here. You may want to explore with the class what you and they understand by the term 'advanced developed country' prior to accepting answers.

DEBRIEFING QUESTION 3

You will get lots of interesting answers here: national health and social security, education, law and order, political stability, the infrastructure (transport, banking, communications, including telephone and television networks, emergency services). You might also get answers about culture, or traditions or lifestyles.

Points of interest about the approach

You will have noticed that the matching exercise contained very few 'conventional' business examples, such as profit and natural resources. Many of the examples, such as the car boot sale, the prison inmate, the premier league team and so on, were chosen partly because of their immediacy through popular culture and partly because of their lack of conventionality, the idea being to demystify the subject and make it less precious.

All three examples were consistent with utilizing the upward direction of the Yerkes–Dodson curve, the use of a different starting point on the Kolb cycle, avoiding an automatic default to the teacher-led opening and with the focus on facilitation rather than transmission.

Facilitating through choice or opinion

Sometimes it is important to establish a fundamental basis for theory, perhaps in an either/or proposition such as legal or illegal, mandatory or discretionary, or perhaps by asking for opinions. The objective in both cases is to explore the wider parameters of a subject in an open and simple manner, working from the specific to the general. Here we include five examples. You will find other examples in Harkin *et al.* (2001). The prompts are visual and factual.

a) Advertising

You will have collected about ten or twelve adverts from newspapers or magazines in the month before the lesson, thus ensuring that the adverts are current. The adverts should be of two types: those that contain facts and hard information about the product or service, giving the consumer reasons for buying, and those that are trying to create atmosphere or suggest a mood. If you are lucky, you will find one or two that satisfy both criteria.

You pass the adverts round the class, who are sitting in groups of three, and ask them for their views (reasons why or atmosphere or both) and in the feedback you can record the class consensus on a chart like the one in Table 16. I would cover up the explanations at the bottom until the consensus is finished.

Table 16: Advertising exercise

Advert	'reason why'	'atmosphere'
	The principle is based on the fact that: The consumer is *rational* and the market is *expanding* (the battle ground is over '*market penetration*')	The principle is based on the fact that: The consumer type can be *profiled* and the market is *saturated* (the battle ground is over '*market share*')

You can then ask supplementary questions about the messages and selling points of particular adverts, leading on to the more theoretical issues such as the law, the voluntary codes and the psychology of advertising. The idea here is that all of the more theoretical aspects of the topic are prefigured in the first exercise – a classic example of moving from the specific to the general.

b) Free press
You can use a similar idea in a media studies lesson on the freedom of the press. Choose a variety of cuttings from the national daily press and put to the students this simple question: 'should this article have been published – yes or no?'

Your choice of articles, with maximum visual impact, will to some extent determine the range of answers, but the key principles of the public interest and press controls should emerge. You should be able to draw out from the examples the key points that you need to establish so that the students can answer academic questions on the topic. Once more, starting with the specific and proceeding to the general gives the teacher a basis for inclusion and differentiation.

c) Preparing for a video
One of the best ways of using a video is to devise an exercise that prefigures or rehearses some of the major themes that will crop up later. We saw overtones of this in the section on anticipating difficulty, only this time it isn't the worry about how the class will react that is the driving force for the strategy, but the need to heighten their awareness.

The video was about Uluru (Ayers Rock) in Australia, but before they watched it, I wanted the students to think about the way ancient, traditional and modern civilizations interact with each other. So I devised three different pen portraits of the three civilizations and asked the students to say which was which and why.

Try it yourself.

EXAMPLE A
- Freedom from arrest without being brought to court within 24 hours
- One person–one vote
- Government by the consent of the governed
- Open access for refugees
- Banks and businesses can stay open 365 days a year and 24 hours a day
- No censorship
- Free movement of labour
- Pluralist society, i.e. no official or established religion but they all coexist

EXAMPLE B
- All strangers must be given hospitality
- No alcohol allowed
- Everyone should pray five times a day
- 10 per cent of all personal wealth to be given for the benefit of the poor
- Women should not show bare flesh in public
- Corporal punishment is legal
- Monotheist, i.e. a state religion with belief in one god (but tolerant of other religions), with authority derived from a key book
- No interest to be charged on loans

EXAMPLE C
- People should live in harmony with nature and the land
- No animal to be killed unless for food or clothing
- Laws decided by elders in council and reinforced by an oral tradition
- All property held in common by the whole community
- No money
- Certain sites and natural phenomena are sacred
- Pantheist, i.e. the belief in a number of gods

Points of interest about the approach
Presenting learning in the form of a choice or opinion is dependent on providing a framework for the choice. The key is

to find simple propositions that can be easily understood so that the learners can engage in processing their thoughts in a safe environment.

All three examples were consistent with utilizing the upward direction of the Yerkes–Dodson curve, the use of a different starting point on the Kolb cycle, avoiding an automatic default to the teacher-led opening and with the focus on facilitation rather than transmission.

Creating a forum for discussion

Discussion is ranked highly in the Bethel research of 1964 (see Chapter 1), because it fosters deep learning. It is unwise, however, to base one's lesson on an open discussion in case the students are unable to participate or benefit, for whatever reason. You are more likely to get good reactions if you provide visual or verbal prompts and a framework for processing ideas.

a) Democracy and protest

Judging by the statistics of those who vote in elections in the United Kingdom, young people have the reputation of being uninterested in politics. If this is so, how do you get them to discuss politics, rationally and sensibly? One way of doing this is to appeal to their anarchic and rebellious side. You can try the following exercise (see Table 17), either in small groups or with the whole class.

Table 17: Graded levels of protest

Low level	Medium level	High level
Labels or stickers	Protest march	Kidnap

THE TASK

'Using the grid provided, see how many different forms of protest you can think of to put in each column. I have not supplied definitions of the three levels, but the examples will give you some sort of clue as to what you might wish to include.'

You can imagine the sorts of answers you might get: letters to one's MP, letters to the press, strikes, riots, work to rule, hunger strikes, bombs, petitions, boycotts, chain to railings, mass resignations, blockades, go slow, suicide bombs, tactical voting, heckling, withdrawal of subscription, resignation, murals, graffiti, sit in.

You can then ask questions about the relative effectiveness of each. I managed to video the blockade of the petrol refineries in the autumn of 2000 and used that as an example of a medium to high level of protest that has had no long-term impact on either the price of petrol or the political process. The value of the Yerkes–Dodson curve can be seen in both the three levels of protest and the use of the video and this exercise sets up the rest of the lesson, which can proceed along lines that analyse and consolidate the ideas that the students have generated. The law is one of the main avenues of development here, such as trade union legislation, the laws safeguarding personal freedoms, the proposed legislation on fighting terrorism, but one might also include the General Strike. Teachers of A level law have told me that they have used this idea to great effect in their lessons.

b) Beliefs and values

It can be equally difficult to get young people, or adults for that matter, to discuss politics, values and beliefs. One way of doing this is ask them to talk to their partner about something they would not do as a matter of principle and for their partner to see if they can overturn their resolve (Harkin et al. 2001). I was concerned that answers to a question in the previous year's examination paper – 'in what ways might a serious comparison be made between soccer and religion' – that I had set for a mock exam paper had not been answered well by many students.

Here is another approach. Again, it is based on a mixture of the Bethel principle 1964 (see Chapter 1) that 50 per cent of information is retained through discussion and the use of prompts.

Table 18: Cards for 'the real concerns of religion'

To pray for the safety of those engaged in dangerous occupations such as fishing or mining	To solemnize oaths of allegiance (such as in Parliament, the armed forces, etc.), or as a witness or a juror in court
To bring us comfort when we are anxious or worried	As a way of making sense of life and death
As the basis for the way of life for a whole society (sometimes called a 'theocracy')	As a way of acknowledging my spirituality and the existence of my soul
In giving thanks for a 'good' harvest	As an expression of our insignificance
To celebrate the birth of my child	As the basis of the moral code by which I try to live my life
As a place for the public valediction or tribute for the life of someone who has just died	To sanctify my commitment to a lifelong relationship with one man or one woman
For the initiation of the Head of State (e.g. as in a corronation)	To pay homage to the creator of life and the universe
To explain those things which cannot be explained by reason and/or scientific proof alone	Voluntarily belonging to an organized religion and attending worship

Make a selection of cards (see Table 18), laminate them, put them into envelopes and distribute to pairs with the instruction to choose the 4 cards which for them most strongly represent the real *concerns* of religion. If they have a humanist or an atheist stance, you can ask them to choose up to 4 cards that might be reworded to express things they believe in. Of the 4 cards, each student should be prepared to speak for about 30 seconds why one particular card has resonance for them. This would also be practice for the key skills requirement of giving a presentation.

This activity is a prime example of the benefits of providing prompts. It is easier to persuade most adolescents to talk when they have had chance to rehearse their arguments and to consider some alternatives than to be asked to 'supply' arguments from their head.

c) Business fundamentals

This is a simple activity if you want to introduce your class to the fundamentals of the business world.

Table 19: Cards for the 'fundamentals of business'

Demand	Producers	Retail	Brand(s)
Markets	Consumer(s)	Wholesale	Free choice word

Devise a number of cards (Table 19); ask the class in pairs to arrange them to make one or two sentences, saying that they can add small words like 'and' or 'in' or 'with', etc., for fluency. Try it yourself.

In the feedback phase, you ask each pair to tell the whole class their sentence and you write them up: how many depends on time and the type of students. Some will start with the consumer, some with the producer and some with the market, thus highlighting the three drivers of business. You can then develop the lesson by getting the students to examine situations where one of these drivers predominates – car manufacturers, shopping malls, Internet shopping, insurance, Mars bars, jewellery and so on – leading to an analysis, perhaps using statistics of the Christmas shopping trends in the last ten years and whether there are now changes in business fundamentals.

Points of interest about the approach

All three examples have prompts at their core. Prompts help to establish parameters and to reduce anxiety by supporting the learner in the early stages. Sometimes, as in the protest example, the prompts will be minimal, more like examples really. They are simply used to get things going. At other times, such as the beliefs example, you are asking students to open up about themselves and they may not have the experience to put their ideas into words, hence the use of more detailed prompt cards. In changing the dynamic of learning, you are facilitating discussion.

All three examples were consistent with utilizing the upward direction of the Yerkes–Dodson curve, the use of a different starting point on the Kolb cycle, avoiding an automatic default to the teacher-led opening, with the focus on facilitation rather than transmission.

e) Empathy

A poem can sometimes be used to encourage empathy in situations where it is important to see something from another person's point of view. We have used Charlotte Ansell's poem 'Manchild' to persuade PGCE students to see situations.

MANCHILD

The poem 'Manchild' gives some indication of the 'baggage' that some young people carry.

Manchild
8.45, another day in hell
as the bell signals the end of registration,
he comes in late again
slouching down the hall
when out of nowhere he is lifted by the ear,
the stench of bad breath.

'what have we here?
I suppose your alarm clock broke again?
or perhaps you dropped your homework in the rain?
Well boy? I'm waiting, what was it this time?'

(you know teachers always do such a nice line in sarcasm)
the boy mutters under his breath
'go fuck yourself'
but the teacher hasn't heard,
has other fish to fry and besides
– he can't really be bothered.

'You know what? Get out of my sight.
I don't even want to have to look at you.

Don't let me hear any more from you today –
if you know what's good for you you'll stay out of my way,
because so help me I'll come down on you so fast
you won't know what's hit you,
you think anyone will believe your word against mine?
You're nothing sunshine, that's just it – you're pathetic!'

The words stick, and the words sink in
somewhere deep inside of him, believes them.
'Well go on then, on your way!'

So he gets himself to class,
opens the door, waiting to be asked:
'What time d'you call this?
You decided to grace us with your presence eh?
9B feels honoured I'm sure.
Don't backchat me boy,
don't even start. You're a disgrace, you're an excuse,
I've got kids in here who want to learn,
kids worth ten of you.'

The words stick, and the words sink in,
no one has asked him 'how you doing today?
Everything ok at home?'
Of course they don't.

No, she turns the page,
teaching him the only lesson
he's ever learned in this place;
to behave
is to be overlooked,
getting attention
equals:
you're in trouble and you're no good.

So already at five to ten the morning has angered him,
he is up and running through the corridors,
setting light to the bins, kicking at the doors,
swearing at the teachers who shout at him to stop,
and he's gone – trying to run
from every fucking thing.

Because
at home
his mum is drowning every night,
the house just like a building site,
with cans and fag ends littering the floor,
the eviction notice came through days before,
she can't cope anymore,
with his dad never there, when he is
knocking them both around and calling him
a 'worthless little shit' saying 'you ain't a man son'

The words stick and the words sink in,
as his dad goes 'come on then'
seeing the fury in his eyes
trying to choke back tears of rage
because he's seen too much,
seen him touch her with no trace of love, call her slut
seen him slam her against the wall too many times
seen the blood trace lines
down her cheeks where no tears fall
her eyes blind with alcohol,
trying to defend against it all,
he gets himself to school just to get away
but what's the point
because they just exclude him anyway,
think he's trouble,
doesn't know how to behave,
no discipline, no respect in him,
the way he is, is how he'll stay,
is how he's always been
beyond help already – not yet fifteen.

He feels so lost but he carries on,
thinking he's got to try and save his mum,
feels he should protect her,
because in some mad way he feels responsible
thinks if he weren't always messing up
and getting letters home
she might stop drinking,
if he could stop his dad from trying to kill her,

she might stop sinking,
he's carrying all this, all the time and more,
shot through to his core with helplessness and endless
    frustration
and despair and yeah what relevance
are SATs and GCSEs and records of achievement when he
    can't see a future?

but I want to tell him,
if it weren't so alien to him
you are a precious thing
you are a bright, bright star
you are incredible just to survive
somehow managing to stay alive
you are a child with so much potential
if only your pain could be heard and soothed
if only you were given the chance to prove yourself
if only the love you need so badly
were available
to you.

Ros uses this poem with full-time and part-time students on the PGCE and Cert. Ed. courses to encourage empathy and to address practical matters such as how to challenge a student when, say, he/she is persistently late or uncooperative.

Points of interest about the approach
The reward for the student is being noticed and this negative reinforcement of behaviour needs to be replaced by positive ones related to work and progress. The poem makes one stop and think about the underlying issues and offers the opportunity to discuss the pros and cons of the teacher challenging lateness head on. Using this approach deflects trainee teacher emotion into the poem and not the classroom experience itself.

Intrigue or curiosity

a) Creative use of texting in key skills

Sometimes you can present learning experiences in a way that surprises the learners. Imagine what the reaction would be if, having been consistent in banning mobile phones in class, one day you allow them. There are several variations: working in pairs, A writes a text message and B transcribes it as a report in formal English (and vice versa); you phone 'customer services' and the students take down the message in text and then transcribe it as a memo to their boss.

b) Descartes

You may need a little ingenuity when introducing philosophical ideas to some students. Take the Descartian proposition *'cogito ergo sum'*, which was based on the notion of uncertainty. The key idea is the principle of 'uncertainty'. One way of introducing this to the students is through perception, i.e. how can one believe one's senses. All new data have to pass through one or more senses before we can process them.

So, before we even mention Descartes, I need to tackle the issue of 'uncertainty' via perception. There are many examples of visual perception one can borrow such as the young woman/old woman picture or the two heads/Greek vase picture, or pictures that purport to show one boy standing on another's head whereas, from a different camera angle, they are merely in different parts of the field. I have also brought in masks and conducted part of the lesson with us all in disguise. I have shown pictures of myself as a young man of 21 and asked the students what they see, and, when they guess it is a photograph of me, what they now see.

There are lots of supplementary questions you can use, as in Table 20.

Then I can introduce Descartes and some more standard ways of examining his ideas.

c) The beginnings of modern art

One way of approaching this was to present the students with four photographs of paintings, two by one artist and two by another. The first task was to identify the correct pairings.

Table 20: Things which can affect and change our perception of reality

Memory
Our age
Environment, upbringing, experience
Magic and illusion
Images and idealized forms
Representations such as pictures
Make-up (lipstick, mascara, blusher, coloured contact lenses, etc.)
Plastic surgery – facials, nose jobs
Wigs, hair colouring, image
Makeovers

When this was done, I asked the groups to say, for each pair, which painting they thought was the earlier painting and which the later, and why. The artists chosen were Picasso and Cézanne and the paintings chosen in each case were from 1900 and 1906 respectively.

In saying which came earlier or later, the students were able to see that one was more representational and the other more abstract and we also discussed why the change had taken place. As one might expect, the discussions were a mixture of the objective and the subjective. A list of further discussion points was used, as in Table 21.

Points of interest about the approach
Intrigue and curiosity bring us back to the preacher in Chapter 1. All learners respond to something that is different. This does not mean that every lesson needs to have a novel twist or novelty will lose its potency. But there should be sufficient injections of new ideas, in line with the principles of the Yerkes–Dodson curve, to reactivate the arousal of the students.

All three examples were consistent with utilizing the upward direction of the Yerkes–Dodson curve, the use of a different starting point on the Kolb cycle, avoiding an automatic default

Table 21: Issues in modern art

What is the function of prizes (such as the 'Turner')?
The purchasing policies of public galleries such as Tate Modern
How to encourage innovative artists – Monet was despised in his day and Van Gogh only sold one painting in his lifetime
How do you know what is 'good' art? What is wrong with 'I know what I like'?
Are there any objective criteria for evaluating the greatness of a particular work?
Does it matter that it is the real thing; isn't a copy just as good?
Should galleries be subsidized? Or should there even be free admission?
How should art be taught in school?
Does art make the world a better place and, if so, why? Please give examples

to the teacher-led opening and with the focus on facilitation rather than transmission.

Devising role briefs

In Chapter 4, we explored the use of role-play for a variety of purposes. Below is an example of the briefing material that would be given to each of the four characters in the unemployment scenario.

Example brief

Each character brief would be printed on a different page. The 'actors' would each be given their brief and their brief only. They will need about 5 minutes to read the brief; you need to be available to answer any queries. Then the teacher invites them back into the classroom and the role-play begins. Stop the role-play when you judge it has either run out of steam or it has provided good stimulation for the discussion to follow. In the role-play below it will probably work best if the initial interaction is between Graham and Lynda, with each child making their own entrance and so developing the scenario bit by bit.

GRAHAM

You are in your early 40s, have been quite happily married to Lynda for nearly 20 years, and have two teenage children. Ian is 17 and going to the local FE college to do some sort of computer qualification and Claire is still at school. You think she is doing OK.

You couldn't wait to get away from school. It was a real pain. You were always in trouble, couldn't be bothered to do any homework and anyway you knew you would get a job at Motorworks factory; they were desperate for men to work the production line. You did well there, becoming a supervisor after five years. Then the bombshell struck. Motorworks decided to 'relocate', that was the posh word they used. What it meant was that you and all your mates would lose their jobs. That happened three years ago and you've been on the dole ever since. The Jobcentre has tried to get you to do courses, but they're all to do with computers and you see no reason why you should learn about them; you've managed OK so far in your life without them. Also, if the truth be told, you were never very good at reading and writing, so you think you'd look a fool when the computer seems to know more about spelling than you do.

Claire brought you a form to fill in to apply for a job at the local garage. Anything like that and you just get into a panic, so you pretended you weren't interested – anyway the job would probably involve lots more form filling and you can do without that.

Lynda gave up work in the Wages Office when she had Ian and you were proud that you could support them and she could stay at home. She always had your tea ready when you got back, whether you had done overtime or not.

You now realize that, during the day, she has always been doing something at the Community Centre, that's where she is now. It keeps her happy and it gives you a bit of time to watch sport on the telly. She'll cook the tea when she gets back; she has always been a good housewife and knows her place. After that, you'll nip down the local for a swift half – or two. The dole doesn't stretch to as many as you'd like.

LYNDA

You are nearly 40 and have been married to Graham for 20 years. He has been a good husband and always provided – well at least until the Motorworks factory closed down three years ago. You have two teenage children. Ian is 17 and is doing really well on the business studies course at the local college. He is applying to go to university next year. You are very proud of him, but money is going to be even tighter when he goes off. You think there are grants and things, but no one has told you how to get hold of them. There's no way Graham would get off his backside and fill in any forms.

Claire is 15 and still at school. She wants to go to the college as well. She would like to do beauty therapy, but she knows there are very few jobs around here if she gets the qualification.

Ever since they were little you have been active at the Community Centre. First, it was Playgroup, then you made tea for the old dears in the Silver Threads Club. Then you started organizing Whist Drives for them. Now you are on the committee and seem to be organizing nearly everything that goes on in the daytime. In the evenings you need to be home to cook Graham's tea and, when they were younger of course, for the kids. Graham still likes to go down the local even if there isn't enough money for it now.

And then this – today! You had been worrying about when Mr Atkinson retired. Would the next Assistant Manager be as good? And today they have offered you the job! It's full-time which will mean some evenings, but the money is good, nearly as much as when Graham was working. You will have to tell him as soon as you get home. What on earth will be his reaction?

IAN

You are 17 and currently going to FE college to do the BTEC national diploma in business studies. The course is quite good, the teachers are great but it would all be a lot easier if you had a computer at home, and Internet access would make it even better. There's no chance of that. Mum has never worked since she had you, and Dad was made redundant three years ago. He doesn't seem to be even trying to get a job, and he gives up on all the courses he is supposed to do. He says he hates computers; anyone would think they were a new invention. You are the only one in your class who has to go into college to use their computers for your assignments – well p'raps not the only one, but it feels like that.

College wants you to apply to university. You'd love to go, it would be a ticket out of this dump. There's not even any part-time jobs for students around here. But how would they afford it? There are fees to pay and accommodation, and all students have to have their own laptop!

You're on your way home now. You're a bit worried about Mum. She confided in you that she had to go and see the manager of the Community Centre this morning.

Surely, after all she's done for them, they wouldn't ask her to step down from the Committee? She loves it there, she is the life and soul of the place, loved by all ages and she does such a good job for them.

CLAIRE

You are 15 and in Year 11 at school. You can leave at the end of this year and you probably will. You could stay on, but what would be the point? You doubt that Mum and Dad will be able to afford to let Ian, your brother, go to uni, let alone you as well. You have told Mum that you want to go to college to do beauty therapy; that sounds quite interesting, and, once qualified, you could travel by working on cruise ships – and get away from this place!

The worst thing is that all your GCSE coursework is due in the next two months, and you don't have a computer at home to do it on. Since Dad was made redundant there has been no money for anything extra. He doesn't even seem to be trying to get a job. There was a job going at the local garage as an administrator and you got the forms for him, but he didn't even fill them in. Mind you there's always enough money for his Sky television for his football and to go down the pub nearly every day.

You have homework to do tonight; you're supposed to research the budget ready for class tomorrow. All the others just went onto the Internet and printed off a few bits. You'll have to go down the library and read through last week's newspapers and take notes. It will take so long!

And you're worried about Mum. She had to go and see the manager at the Community Centre this morning. You hope it was nothing bad. She really likes all the voluntary work she does there. You suppose she did have a proper job once, but you've no idea what it was. Dad doesn't seem to think that women should work, they should just stay at home and get the tea ready. Dear God! Voices are raised as you reach the door.

Points of interest about the approach
The debrief is classic Kolb. The performed role-play is the concrete experience; reflection is promoted by asking the students to think on their own what might happen next or who is in the right here; the teacher facilitates a whole-group discussion to build wider understandings (abstract conceptualization); and then a new basis for learning would have been created which encourages active experimentation. The role-play can act as a marker in the intellectual development of the learners to which reference can be made throughout the course.

Conclusion

When training teachers, we introduce them to the maxim 'Teach as a last resort'. We want to encourage the notion that the teacher does not have to lead on every topic. You will often get better responsiveness by setting up an experience for the learners to process ideas than by teaching in the traditional sense. Using the ideas of the learners as the basis for deeper understanding is fundamental to both inclusion and differentiation.

The art of good teaching is to create ownership of the learning in the learners. You are only a partial and transient factor in their learning and you have but a short time with them. You need to be clear about the best use of that time and that relationship so that the students are best equipped to develop their learning independently when you are not there, through reading, the Internet, practice and reflection, which are the more substantial and the more lasting elements of their education.

Further reading

Harkin, J., Turner, G. and Dawn, T. (2001) *Teaching Young Adults: a handbook for teachers*, London: Routledge Falmer.

Jensen, J. P. (1988) *Super Teaching: Master Strategies for Building Student Success*, San Diego, CA: Turning Point for Teachers.

Petty, G. (2004) *Teaching Today: a practical guide*, Cheltenham: Nelson Thorne.

Conclusion

Ros Clow and Trevor Dawn

This book is about survival but it is also about laying the foundation for successful teaching throughout your career, which comes in stages.

1: The first two years or so part-time or full-time

Characteristics
At times bewilderment, as lots of things are new and strange; at times exhaustion, as so many things are needed simultaneously and there are only 24 hours in the day; all your teaching notes and materials have to be built up from scratch, which encroaches into your social and family time; you may feel anxiety as things do not go to plan, or you make mistakes; but you also experience levels of pleasure and satisfaction unknown in previous life, training as well as working.

What we have tried to do here is give you
- practical tips for lesson design
- clues about how to focus on the learner
- a foundation for professional practice in key areas

2: You have survived two years

Characteristics
Things seem less strange; you have learned to be better at managing your workload; you can cope with the pressure and you stop taking every setback personally; you know a little more about what works for you in the classroom; you can think

beyond the short term and see the whole year in perspective; you feel more like a teacher.

What we have tried to do here is
- blend theory, some of which may be new to you, with practice
- use this in harness with reflective practice
- give you conscious competence
- extend your range and repertoire
- encourage you to become more creative within a secure foundation

3: Increased responsibility (this varies from three years upwards)

Characteristics
You are likely to be fully trained and qualified; you will have leadership of a subject or a substantive aspect of the curriculum; you are now an experienced teacher to whom other 'rookies' at Stage 1 look for guidance and support.

What we have tried to do here is
- present you with ideas that you can develop in your own professional practice, and explore in depth and in breadth as part of your continuing professional development (CPD)
- suggest ways of continuing to explore your own teaching approaches while acknowledging that your changing role will lead you to other CPD possibilities such as leadership or quality assurance

Final thoughts

This book has been a learning opportunity for us. It has made us think about what we value in teaching and what has sustained us throughout our careers. We have had the opportunity to reread articles and books that we have consciously and unconsciously used for years and to remind ourselves of formative influences. We have also been excited by new ideas and how they have shaped our present (and future) professional lives.

It has made us remember why we are teachers and we can count on two hands the number of lessons that were 'perfect'. This book is not about the impossible but about raising your overall job satisfaction.

Bibliography

Ambady N. (2004) *First impressions*, available at http://enews.tufts.edu/stories/021704/Ambady.htm

Auden, W. H. (1966) 'Prologue: The Birth of Architecture', *About the House*, New York: Random House.

Bain, J. D., Ballantyne, R., Packer, J. and Mills, C. (1999) 'Using journal writing to enhance student teachers' reflectivity during field experience placements', *Teachers and Teaching: theory and practice* 5 (1): 51–73.

Baumler, G. (1992) 'Eine kritische Revision des "Yerkes–Dodson Gesetzes" von 1908', in Gundlach, H. (ed.) *Psychologische Forschung und Methode – Das Versprechen des Experiments. Festschrift für Werner Traxel*, Passau: Passavia Universitätsverlag, pp. 39–50.

Berne, E. (1966) *Games People Play: the Psychology of Human Relationships*, London: Penguin.

Biggs, J. (1996) 'Assessing learning quality: reconciling institutional, staff and educational demands', *Assessment and Evaluation in Higher Education* 21 (1): 5–15 in Livingston *et al.* (2004).

Biggs, J. (2003) *Teaching for Quality Learning at University* (2nd edn), London: McGraw-Hill Education/Open University Press.

Blair, T. (2001) Speech to the Confederation of British Industry, 5 November, available at http://www.pm.gov.uk/output/Page1642.asp (accessed from the World Wide Web 11 May 2006).

Blakemore, S.-J. and Frith, U. (2005) *The learning brain: lessons for education*, Oxford: Blackwell.

Bloom, B. S. (1956) *Taxonomy of Educational Objectives*, Book 1: *Cognitive Domain*, London: Longman.

Board of Education (1948) *Handbook of Suggestions for Teachers*, London: HMSO.

Brandes, D. (1982). *Gamesters' Handbook Two*, London: Hutchinson.

Brandes, D. and Phillips, H. (1979) *Gamesters' Handbook*, London: Hutchinson.

Broadhurst, P. L. (1959) 'The interaction of task difficulty and motivation: the Yerkes–Dodson law revived', *Acta Psychologica* 16: 321–38.

Brookfield, S. (1995) *Becoming a critically reflective teacher*, San Francisco: Jossey-Bass.

Buckley, F. J. (2000) *Team Teaching: What, Why and How*, London: Sage.

Burton, D. (1988) 'Do anxious swimmers swim slower? Reexamining the elusive anxiety–performance relationship', *Journal of Sport Psychology* 10: 45–61.

Butler (1996) *Sport Psychology in Action*, Oxford: Butterworth-Heinemann.

Buzan, T. (1989) *Use your head*, London: BBC Books.

Buzan, T. and Buzan, B. (1995) *The Mindmap book*, London: BBC Books.

Cairns, R. B. and Cairns, B. D. (1994) *Lifelines and Risks: Pathways of Youth in our Time*, Hemel Hempstead: Harvester Wheatsheaf.

Callaghan, J. (1976) Speech at Ruskin College, Oxford, 18 October.

Cianciolo, A. and Sternberg, R. (2004) *Intelligence: a brief history*, London: Blackwell.

Close, J. J., Rudd, W. G. A. and Plimmer, F. (1974) *Team teaching experiments*, Windsor: NFER.

Clow, R. (2001) 'Further education teachers' constructions of professionalism', *Journal of Vocational Education and Training* 53 (3): 407–19.

—(2005) 'Just teachers: the work carried out by full-time further education teachers', *Research in Post-Compulsory Education* 10 (1): 63–81.

Clow, R. and Mehra, S. (2006) 'The evaluation of vocational training in three regions', *British Dental Journal*.

Coffield, F., Moseley, D., Hall, E. and Ecclestone, K. (2005) *Learning styles and pedagogy in post-16 learning: a critical and systematic review*, London: The Learning and Skills Research Centre (LSRC).

Crowther, Sir G. (1959) *15–18: A Report to the Central Advisory Council for Education (England)*, London: HMSO.

Curtis, S. J. (1966) *An Introductory History of English Education since 1800*, London: University Tutorial Press.

Daloz, L. A. (1986) *Effective Teaching and Mentoring: Realizing the Transformational Power of Adult Learning Experiences*, San Francisco: Jossey-Bass.

De Bono, E. (1978) *Teaching Thinking*, Harmondsworth: Penguin.

Dearing, R. (1996) *Review of qualifications for 16–19 year-olds*, London: SCAA.

—(1997) *Higher Education in the Learning Society, Report of the National Committee of Inquiry into Higher Education*, London: HMSO.

Department for Education and Skills (DfES) (1999) 'The identification of

the gifted and talented cohort', available at http://www.standards.
dfes.gov.uk/giftedandtalented/guidanceandtraining/roleofcoordinators/
identificationofgt/ (retrieved from the World Wide Web on 26
September 2005).

—(2000a) 'Radical changes will prepare higher education for the 21st
century – Blunkett', Press Notice 2000/0064, 15 February, available at
http://www.dfes.gov.uk/speeches/search_detail.cfm?ID=28 (retrieved
from the World Wide Web 11 May 2006).

—(2000b) 'Blunkett: New drive to widen access to higher education',
Press Notice 2000/0200, 10 May, available at http://www.dfes.gov.
uk/speeches/search_detail.cfm?ID=28 (retrieved from the World
Wide Web 11 May 2006).

—(2004) *14–18 Curriculum and Qualifications Reform. Final Report of the
working group on 14–19 reform* (Chairman Mike Tomlinson), Annesley:
HMSO.

—(2005) *14–19: Education and Skills*, Annesley: HMSO.

—(2005) *Realising the potential. A review of the future role of further education
colleges* (Chairman Andrew Foster), Annesley: HMSO.

—(2006) *Youth Cohort Study: Activities and Experiences of 16 Year Olds:
England and Wales 2006*, ref. SFR21/2006, Annesley: HMSO.

Dickson, A. (2002) *A woman in your own right*, London: Quartet.

Edexcel (2000) *BTEC Higher Nationals in Electrical/Electronic Engineering*,
Guidance and Units Issue, 1 March.

Education Act 1944, London: HMSO.

Education Act 1987, London: HMSO.

Education Act 1996, London: HMSO.

Egan, G. (2002) *The Skilled Helper: a problem-management and opportunity
development approach to helping* (7th edn), Pacific Grove, CA: Brooks/
Cole.

Eggen, P. D. and Kauchak, D. P. (1988) *Strategies for Teachers: Information
Processing Models in the Classroom*, Englewood Cliffs, NJ: Prentice Hall.

Eggen, P. D., Kauchak, D. P. and Harder, R. J. (1979) *Strategies for Teachers:
Teaching Content and Thinking Skills*, Englewood Cliffs, NJ: Prentice Hall.

Entwistle, N. (1987) *Understanding Classroom Learning*, London: Hodder
& Stoughton.

Entwistle, N. and Ramsden, P. (1983) *Understanding Student Learning*,
London: Croom Helm.

Freeman, J. (1998) *Educating the Very Able: current international research*,
London: Ofsted.

French, J. R. P. and Raven, B. H. (1958) 'The bases of social power', in
Cartwright, D. (ed.) *Studies in Social Power*, Ann Arbor, MI: Institute
of Social Research, University of Michigan Press.

Fry, H., Ketteridge, S. and Marshall, S. (2005) *A Handbook for Teaching and Learning in Higher Education: Enhancing academic practice*, London: Routledge Falmer.

Fryer, R. H. (1997) *Learning for the Twenty-first Century: First Report of the National Advisory Group for Continuing Education and Lifelong Learning*, London: HMSO.

Gardner, H. (1993) *Frames of Mind: The Theory of Multiple Intelligences*, London: Fontana Press.

Gibbs, G. (1992) *Improving the Quality of Student Learning*, Bristol: Technical and Educational Services.

Ginnis, P. (2002) *The Teacher's Toolkit: raise classroom achievement with strategies for every learner*, Carmarthen: Crown House.

Goleman, D. (1996) *Emotional Intelligence: why it can matter more than IQ & working with emotional intelligence*, London: Bloomsbury.

Green, M. (2001) *Successful tutoring: good practice for managers and tutors*, London: Learning and Skills Development Agency.

Green Paper (2002) *Extending Opportunities and Raising Standards*, Annesley: HMSO.

Hamlin, K. D. (2004) 'Beginning the journey: supporting reflection in early field experiences', *Reflective Practice* 5 (2): 167–79.

Hankey, J. (2006) *Evaluation of DfES-funded research into using ILPs with trainee teachers* (awaiting publication on Web).

Hardy, L., Jones, G. and Gould, D. (1996) *Understanding Psychological Preparation for Sport: Theory and Practice of Elite Performers*, Chichester: Wiley.

Harkin, J., Clow, R. and Hillier, Y. (2003) *Recollected in Tranquillity? FE teachers' perceptions of their initial teacher training*, London: Learning and Skills Development Agency: 47.

Harkin, J., Turner, G. and Dawn, T. (2001) *Teaching Young Adults: a handbook for teachers*, London: Routledge Falmer.

Hart, N. (1996) 'The role of the tutor in a college of further education: a comparison of skills used by personal tutors and by student counsellors when working with students in distress', *British Journal of Guidance and Counselling* 24 (1): 83–96.

Hay, J. (1992) *Transactional Analysis for Trainers*, London: McGraw-Hill.

Hayes, A. (2006) *Teaching Adults in FE*, London: Continuum.

Hebb, D. O. (1955) 'Drives and the CNS (conceptual nervous system)' *Psychological Review* 62: 243–54.

Heller, K. A. (2000) *International Handbook of Giftedness and Talent*, Oxford: Elsevier.

Henshaw, G. (1973) *Teaching Counselling*, Manchester: Manchester Polytechnic.

Heron, J. (1975) *A Six Category Intervention Analysis: Human Potential Research Project*, Guildford: University of Surrey.

Higher Education Statistics Agency (HESA) (2005) *Non-continuation following year of entry: full-time first degree entrants 2002/03*, available at http://www.hesa.ac.uk/pi/0304/t3a_0304.xls (retrieved from the World Wide Web 12 May 2006).

Hirst, P. H. (1974) *Knowledge and the Curriculum*, London: Routledge & Kegan Paul.

Hirst, P. H. and Peters, R. S. (1970) *The Logic of Education*, London: Routledge & Kegan Paul.

Hogg, M. A. and Vaughan, G. M. (2005) *Social Psychology* (4th edn), London: Pearson Prentice Hall.

Horrocks, J. E. (1976) *The Psychology of Adolescence* (4th edn), Boston, MA: Houghton Mifflin.

Howells, K. (2004) 'Widening Participation in Higher Education: developing vocational pathways', speech of 9 December, available at http://www.dfes.gov.uk/speeches/speech.cfm?SpeechID=174 (retrieved from the World Wide Web 12 May 2006).

Huscinski, A. and Buchanan, D. (1997) *Organisational Behaviour: an introductory text*, London: Prentice Hall.

Jensen, J. P. (1988) *Super Teaching: Master Strategies for Building Student Success*, San Diego, CA: Turning Point for Teachers.

Johns C. (1995) 'Framing learning through reflection within Carper's fundamental ways of knowing in nursing', *Journal of Advanced Nursing* 22: 226–34.

Joines, I. and Stewart, V. (1987) *TA: A New Introduction to Transactional Analysis*, Nottingham and Chapel Hill, NC: Lifespace.

Kennedy, H., QC (1997) *Learning Works: Widening Participation in Further Education*, Coventry: Further Education Funding Council.

Kerka, S. (1992) 'Higher order thinking skills in Vocational Education', *ERIC Digest* 127, Report EDO-CE-92–127, Columbus, OH: ERIC Publications.

Kolb, D. A. (1984) *Experiential Learning: Experience as the Source of Learning and Development*, London: Prentice-Hall.

—(2000) *Facilitator's Guide to Learning*, Boston: Hay/McBer.

Kreber, C. (2004) 'An analysis of two models of reflection and their implications for educational development', *International Journal for Academic Development* 9 (1): 29–49.

Kroger, J. (2004) *Identity in Adolescence: the balance between self and other*, London: Routledge

Learning Pyramid (nearest attribution 1964) National Training Laboratory (NTL), Institute for Applied Behavioral Science, 300 N. Lee

Street, Suite 300, Alexandria, VA 22314. 1-800-777-5227; also located through NTL at Bethel, Maine, USA (1964).

Lejk, M. and Wyvill, M. (2002) Peer assessment of contributions to a group project: student attitudes to holistic and category-based approaches', *Assessment and Evaluation in Higher Education* 27(6): 569-77.

Lejk, M., Wyvill, M. and Farrow, S. (1996) Survey of methods of deriving individual grades from group assessments', *Assessment and Evaluation in Higher Education* 21(3): 267-80.

Livingston, K., Soden, R. and Kirkwood, M. (2004) *Post-16 Pedagogy and thinking skills: an evaluation*, London: Learning & Skills Research Centre.

Loftus, E., and Ketcham, K. (1991) *Witness for the defense*, New York: St Martin's Press.

Mackay, I. (1995) *Asking Questions*, London: Chartered Institute of Personnel and Development.

Maker, C. J. and Nielson, A. B. (1995). *Teaching Models in Education of the Gifted*, Austin, TX: Pro-ed.

Manstetten, R. (2000) 'Promotion of the Gifted in Vocational Training' in Heller, K.A. *International Handbook of Giftedness and Talent*, Oxford: Elsevier: 439–46.

Martindale, C. (1991) *Cognitive psychology: A neural-network approach*, Pacific Grove, CA: Brooks/Cole.

Martinez, P. and Munday, F. (1998) *9,000 voices: Student Persistence and Drop-out in Further Education*, London: FEDA.

Marton, F. and Säljö, R. (1976) 'On Qualitative Differences in Learning; 1. Outcomes and Process', *British Journal of Educational Psychology* 46: 4–11.

Maslow, A. (1943) 'A theory of human motivation', *The Psychological Review* 50(4): 370–96.

McCarthy, B. (1990) 'Using the 4MAT System to bring learning styles to schools'. *Educational Leadership*, 48(2), 31–7.

McCullers, J. (1978) 'Issues in learning and motivation', In Lepper, M.R. and Greene, D. (eds.), *The hidden costs of reward* (pp. 5–18). Hillsdale, NJ: Erlbaum.

McLelland, D. (1961) *The Achieving Society,* Princeton, NJ: Van Nostrand.

McManus, M. (1989) *Troublesome Behaviour in the Classroom*, London: Routledge.

Mehrabian, A. (1972) *Nonverbal Communication*, Chicago, IL: Aldine-Atherton.

Minton, D. (1991) *Teaching Skills in Further and Adult Education*, London: City & Guilds/MacMillan.

Montgomery, D. (1989) *Managing Behaviour Problems*, London: Hodder & Stoughton.

Moseley, D., Baumfield, V., Elliott, J., Gregson, H., Higgins, S., Lin, M. and Robson, S. (2003) *Thinking Skills frameworks for Post 16 Learners: an evaluation*, London: Learning & Skills Research Centre.

Moser, Sir C. (Chairman) (1998) *A Fresh Start – improving literacy and numeracy* ('Skills for Life'), London: Basic Skills Unit.

Napper, R. and Newton, T. (2000) *Tactics: transactional analysis concepts for all trainers, teachers and tutors, plus insight into collaborative learning strategies*, Ipswich: TA resources.

Nelson-Jones, R. (2004) *Practical Counselling and Helping Skills* (4th edn) London: Sage.

Novak, J. D. and D. B. Gowin (1984) *Learning How to Learn*, Cambridge: Cambridge University Press.

O'Connor, J. and Seymour, J. (2002) *Introducing NLP: Psychological Skills for Understanding and Influencing People*, London: Element.

Ogunleye, James (2006) *Guide to Teaching 14–19*, London: Continuum.

Oxford Brookes University (2004) 'From Potential to Performance' workshop materials. Available at: http://www.brookes.ac.uk/schools. education.rescon.cpdgifted/coordinators_aimhigher.html (retrieved from the World Wide Web 11 May 2006).

Park, B. (1986) 'A method for studying the development of impressions of real people', *Journal of Personality and Social Psychology* 51, 907–17 in Hogg, M. A. and Vaughan, G. M. (2005) *Social Psychology*, 4th edition, London: Pearson Prentice Hall.

Pask, G. (1976). 'Styles and strategies of learning', *British Journal of Educational Psychology* 46: 128–48.

Peters, R. S. (1966) *Ethics and Education*, London: George Allen & Unwin.

Peters, R. S. (ed.) (1967) *The Concept of Education*, London: Routledge & Kegan Paul.

Petty, G. (2004) *Teaching Today: a practical guide*, Cheltenham: Nelson Thorne.

Piaget, J. and Inhelder, B. (1966) *The Psychology of the Child*, London: Routledge & Kegan Paul.

Priory Group (2005) *Adolescent angst* www.prioryhealthcare.com/adolescentangst

QCA (2001–2) 'Identifying gifted and talented learners: Characteristics to look for' available on: http://www.nc.uk.net/gt/general/01_characterstics.htm (retrieved from the World Wide Web on 26 September 2005).

Race, P. (2001) *A Briefing on Self, Peer and Group Assessment*, York: Learning and Teaching Support Network (LTSN).

—(2005) *Making Learning Happen: a guide for post-compulsory education*, London: Sage.

Ramsden, P. (2003) *Learning to Teach in Higher Education*, London: Routledge Falmer.

Renzulli, J. (1978) What makes giftedness? Re-examining a definition' *Phi Delta Kappa* 60: 180–4.

—(2003) 'What makes giftedness and how can we develop high levels of talent in young people?' *Gifted and Talented* 7:2 (December: 8–18.

Report of a survey by teachers, identifying key characteristics of gifted and talented students in the vocational curriculum, available at http://www.redcar-cleveland.gov.uk/Learnin1.nsf/Web+Full+List/857B77B33DDC966A80256F1800563DEE?OpenDocument

Rogers, C. and Freiberg, H. J. (1993) *Freedom to Learn* (3rd edn.), New York: Merrill.

Rust, C. (2001) *A Briefing on Assessment of Large Groups*. York: Learning and Teaching Support Network.

Salzberger-Wittenberg, I., Henry, G. and Osborne, E. (1983) *The Emotional Experience of Learning and Teaching,* London: Routledge.

Simpson, E. (1972) 'The classification of educational objectives in the psychomotor domain', *The Psychomotor Domain*, Washington DC: Gryphon.

Stenhouse, L. (1975) *An Introduction to Curriculum Research and Development*, London: Heinemann.

Sternberg, R. (2001) 'Giftedness as developing expertise: a theory of the interface between high abilities and achieved excellence', *High Ability Studies* 12:2 (December) 159–79.

—(2003) 'WICS as a model of giftedness', *High Ability Studies* 14:2 (December: 109–37.

Taba, H. (1966) *Teaching Strategies and Cognitive Functioning in Elementary Schools*, Research Project 2004, Washington DC: US Office of Education.

—(1967) *Teacher's Handbook in Elementary School Studies*, Reading, MA: Addison-Wesley.

Taba, H., Durkin, M. C., Fraenkel, J. R., and NcNaughton, A. H. (1971). *A teacher's handbook to elementary social studies: An inductive approach* (2nd edn). Reading, MA: Addison-Wesley.

Tannenbaum, A. (1983) *Gifted Children*, New York: Macmillan.

Thorndike, E. L. (1924) 'Mental discipline in high school studies', *Journal of Educational Psychology*, 15, 1–22.

Tomlinson, J. (Chairman) (1996) *Inclusive Learning: Principles and recommendations; a summary of the Findings of the Learning Difficulties and/or Disabilities Committee*, Coventry: Further Education Funding Council.

Tuckman, B. W. (1965) 'Developmental Sequence in Small Groups', *Psychology Bulletin* 63, (6): 384–99.

University of Mississippi (2001–2) *Bloom's Taxonomy: Psychomotor Domain*, modification of works by Simpson, Gronlund, and others, available at: http://www.olemiss.edu/depts/educ_school2/docs/stai_manual/manual10.htm (retrieved from the World Wide Web on 11 May 2006).

van Ments, M. (1999) *The Effective Use of Role-Play* (revised edn; originally published 1983), London: Kogan Page.

Walklin, L. (1990) *Teaching and Learning in Further and Adult Education*, Cheltenham : Stanley Thorne.

Wallace, S. (2007) *Getting the Buggers Motivated in FE*, London: Continuum.

Wardle, D. (1970) *English Popular Education, 1780–1975*, Cambridge: Cambridge University Press.

Warwick, D. (1971) *Team Teaching*, London: University of London.

Watson, J.B. (1931) *Behaviourism*, London: Cassell.

Weyers, M. (2006) *Curriculum Development in FE: Teaching the FE Curriculum*, London: Continuum.

Whalley, J., Welch, T. and Williamson, L. (2006) *e-Learning in FE*, London: Continuum.

White, J. (1998) *Do Howard Gardner's multiple intelligences add up?* London: Institute of Education, University of London.

Whitehead, A. N. (1967) *The Aims of Education and Other Essays*, New York: Free Press (first published by Macmillan in 1929) in Ramsden, P. (2003) *Learning to Teach in Higher Education*, London: Routledge Falmer.

Yeats's poem, 'Sailing to Byzantium' (published 1927, found at http://poetry.poetryx.com/poems/1575/).

Yerkes, R. M. and Dodson J. D. (1908) 'The relation of strength of stimulus to rapidity of habit-formation', first published in *Journal of Comparative Neurology and Psychology* 18: 459–82.

Yerkes-Dodson curve htttp://psychclassics.yorku.ca/Yerkes/Law/

Yerkes-Dodson curve and athletics/sport http://www.athleticinsight.com/Vol1Iss2/Cognitive_Behavioral_Anxiety.htm (accessed 26 June 2006).

Index

(Most significant locations in Bold)

academic 22, **50–2, 59–63**, 88, 100, 105, 108, 113, 118, 131, 140, 163–5, 168, 177, 195, 201, 211, 218
academic–vocational divide 50, 177
accounts 37, **214**
active listening **115**
 minimal encouragers 115
 not interrupting 115
 repetition 115
 paraphrasing 115
 summarizing 115
adolescence 145, **92–8**, 100–2, 106, 145
adult education 50
advertising 217–18
Ansell, C. 227
antenatal teaching 33, 79
apathy 7, 12, 144, 205–6
arousal **13–16**, 229
assertive 40, **157–8**
assertiveness 1, **70–2**, 76, 85
assessment 14, 16, 22, 38, **43–4**, 60, 63, 83, 87, 174, 182, 196
 baseline assessment 57
 in role play 83
attending (listening skill) 113, **115**
assimilation and accommodation 16
attitudes (also see values) 84, 96, 98, 119, **121–2**, 125, 144–5, 177, 187
 balanced **121–2**
authoritative interventions **118–19**
authority 98, 142–3, 146, **149–56**, 219

balance (attitude) 121
beginnings 7, **9–12**, 24, 205
Berne, E. 147–8

Bethel, Maine 1964 **24–5,** 220–1
Blakemore, S-J. **94–5**, 132, **134**
Bloom, B.S. **58**–60, 161, 173–4
body language 40, 80, 115, 211
boundaries 103–4, **127**
brain (left & right) **132–3**
 in adolescents **94–5**
BTEC 84, 131, 194, 232
Business Studies 53, 165, 168, 214, 232
Buzan, T. **132–3**

cards 26, 38, 45–7, 66, 207, 210, 222–4
Callaghan J 53
Citizenship 107
closing (lessons) **27–30**, 62
Clow, R. 70, 107, 129, 161, 174, 195, 197
Coffield, F. 21, 23, 130
college code 151, 157
communication 113, 116, 124, 135–6, 137, 158, 167, 169, 183, 187, 195,
 skills **71–3**, 84, 87
 studies 1, 53, 195
competence 52, 56, 131, 198, 237
competence based 83, 195, 198
confirmation–challenge continuum 206
Construction 1, 2, 82, 165
counselling 83, 111, **118–21**, **127–8**
Crowther Report 50
cultures 102, **113–14**, 124, 176, 206, 216
 sub cultures **103–4**
Curriculum 12, 21, **51–2**, 107, 132, 135, 163, 168–9, 178, 187, 237

Daloz, L.A. 121
Dawn, T. (Harkin et al) 20–1, 23, 26,
    29, 76, 99, 158, 174, 193, 206,
    217, 221
Dearing Report 1997 59, 195
De Bono, E. 33, 60
debriefing (role play) 77, **79–80**, 85–6
deep learning 63, **187–8**, 220
Delphi Technique 39
democracy 154, 220
de-motivated 19, 26, 42, 132
Descartes, R. 228–9
differentiation 50, **55–6, 59–60**, 129,
    162, 218, 234
discipline (managing behaviour) **142,
    144, 152, 159, 198**
disruptive behaviour **143–5**, 157
Down's syndrome 80
dyslexia 57, 127, 175
dyslexic 38

Egan, G. 112
Eggen, P.D. 25
emotional intelligence 25, 138
Engineering 37, 71, 81–4, 131, 194
examinations 29, 50, **63–6**, 92
    mock examinations **66–8**, 221
experience (learning cycle) 18, **20–4**,
    27, 74, 80, 91, 99, 131, 139–40,
    168, 173, 186, 188, 192, 197,
    207, 228, 234

facilitating 121, 205, 216, 224
facilitation **24**, 30, 61, 122, 216, 220,
    224, 230
facilitative interventions **119–21**
Family and Community studies 78
FENTO (Further Education National
    Training Organisation) 130
field trip 183
Foster, A. 54
Frith, U. **94–5**, 132, **134**
Fry, H. 183
Fryer, R.H. 52
fun 1, 11, 44, **91–2**, 149, 214
Further Education (FE) 1–4, 50, 70,
    85, 107, 129, 176, 191, 193

Gardner, H. **134–5**, 169
gender 33, 103–4, 162, 186, 213–14

general to specific or vice versa 21, 25,
    217–18
General Studies 37, 81
General & Communication Studies 1,
    84, 192
Gifted and Talented 34, **161-4, 168–9**,
    175–8
global economy 51
GNVQ (General National Vocational
    Qualification) 35
Goleman, D. 138–9
Green, M. 109–10
groups 27, 30, **31–49**, 59, 66–7, 73,
    83, 92, 145, 155, 173, 182, 192,
    195, 212, 214, 217, 220, 229
    discussion in 30, 33, 41
    based assessment **44–8**
    small groups **31–49**, 59, 92, 195,
        212, 214, 220
    guess what's in the teacher's head 43

hairdressers 73–4, 168, 184
Harkin, J. **20–1**, 23, 26, 29, 76, 99,
    158, 174, 193, 206, 217, 221
Harvard **211–12**
Hay, J. **147–8**
Hayes, A. 92, 99
Health Economics 80
Henshaw, G. 122
Heron, J. **118**
Higher Education (HE) 48, 50–2, 54,
    59, 63, 93, 104, 107–8, 162–4,
    176–7, 184, 196
Hirst, P. **53**
holist – serialist **138**
Horrocks, J.E.100–1

inclusion 50, **55–7**, 59, 62, 129, 162,
    206, 218, 234
Individual Learning Plan (ILP) **108,
    110–11**, 113, 116,
Information Technology (IT) 53, 134,
    195
initial assessment 57
in loco parentis 98
interest (initiating & sustaining) **7–12**,
    15, **17–20**, 30, 61–2, 207
international competitiveness 51
interventions **118–19**
    authoritative 119

confronting 119
informative 119
prescriptive 118
facilitative 119
catalytic 119
cathartic 119
supportive 119
interview skills 84, 87
intranet 44, 110, 184

Jensen, E.P. 28, 138
Joines, I. 147–8

Kauchak, D.P. 25–6
Kennedy, H. 52
Key Skills 45, 52, 87, 103, 118, 144,
    182, **195–6**, 200, 222, 228
Key Stage 4, 12, 52
Kolb, D. **18–19**, 22, 60, 130–2, 216,
    220, 224, 229, 234
Kroger, J. 97

language 136, 151, 200, 209
    body language 40, 80, 115, 211
    of teenagers **102–4**
Law 32, 82, 216, 218, 219, 221
Learning:
    difficulties 186
    outcomes 16, 28, 56, 173, 186
    process 27, 131–2, 140, 148, 150,
        184, 189
    pyramid 24
    theories of 22, 130
learning styles **18–19**, **21–3**, 28,
    59–60, 105, 130, 140, 166, 184,
    186–7
    learning styles research **21–3**
Learning and Skills Sector 39, 130, 161
Learning Support Assistant 33, 175,
    199–200
Learning & Skills Research Centre
    (LSRC) **21–2**, 39, 57, 63
Leaning & Teaching Support Network
    48
lesson planning **14–16,** 18, 152
listening skills 39, 81, **111–18**, 123–4,
    130, 140,
Livingston, K. 63

market 217, 223

Martinez, P. **129**, 140
matching/mismatching 137
mentoring 105, 121, 138, 163, 176
mind maps 20, **133–4,** 141
Minton, D. 63
mock examinations 66, 221
moot 82
mobile phone 101, 129, 146, 228
motivating 48, 61, 87, 91, 174, 186
motivation 14–15, 101, 134, 164, 172
Motor Vehicle 1, 84, 168, 184, 195
Multiple Intelligence (MI) **134–5**, 169
Munday, F. 129, 140

National Childbirth Trust (NCT) 1,
    80
Neuro-Linguistic Programming (NLP)
    135
    rapport 137
non-verbal communication 167, 113,
    211
    eye contact 35, **113–15**
    facial expression 114
    head movement 114
    orientation 114
    posture 114
    proximity 114
notes – teacher 41, 105, 188, 198, 236
notes – learner 20, 29, **43–4**, 47,
    61–2, 133, **184–5**, 206
note-taker 200
Nuffield 96

objectives 58, 64, 112, 174, 186
    Setting in role play 74, 77
Ogunleye, J. 92
Open Learning **183–4**

parachute discussion 39
Pask, G. 138
performing arts 184
performance **13–17**, 19, 83, 100, 119,
    134, 139, 169, 174, 210
personally meaningful learning **20–1**
Peters, R.S. **53–4**, 153
Piaget, J. 16
planning 209
poem 207–9, 224–7
post compulsory 3, 12, 14, 17, **50–3**,
    55, 62–3, 145, 161–2, 187

power-point 17, 43, 61, 183
power 82, 87, **98–9**, **149–54**
    coercive 149–50
    expert 149, 154
    legitimate 149, 151
    negotiated 149, 154
    referent /charismatic 149, 152
    reward 149, 150
preparation **64–5**, **182–3**, **191–2**, 201
    role play **76–7**, 82–3
presentation 9, 28, 44, 46, 85, 133–4,
    155, 182–3, 222
Priory Group 94, 96, 98, 100, 106
profile **36–7**, 172
professional judgement 34, 37, 130
prompts 25, 27, 33, 44, 76, **157–8**,
    207, 214, 217, 220, **222–4**
protest 220, 221, 223
psychodynamic 128

questioning 43, 84, 111, 130, 137, 140
quiz **46–8**

rainbow groups 38
Ramsden, P. **20–1**, 59, 187
raps 44, 135
records of achievement 57
reflective practice 88, 105, 154, 201,
    237
reward 15, **149–50**, 154, 157, 159,
    206, 227
role models 79, 143, 152, 166, 193
role play 1, **70–88**, 230, 234
    in assessment 83
role names **76–7**, 79, **81–2**, 86
Rust, C. 45

Salzberger –Wittenberg, I. 128
scheme of work 2, 14, 16, 74, 104,
    107, 138, 152, 174, **181–6,**
    191–2, 194, 198, 200, 206
serialist–holist **138**
sexual intercourse 95, 103
skilled helper 112, 125
SMART 112
social and life skills 1, 70, 73
specific to general (and vice versa) 21,
    25, 188, **217–18**
Sperry, R. 132
sport 13, 37, 163, 168, 176, 184

Stenhouse, L. 48
Stewart, V.147–8, 160
storming 40
support 33, 56–7, 99, 108, 111, 121,
    127–9, 135, 140, 142, 159–60,
    175–6, 184, 199–200, 223
surface learning 20–1

Taylor, C. **168–9**
transactional analysis (TA) 147, 160–2
Taba, H. 21, 25–6, 58–60, 69, 188
task sheet 33
taxonomy / taxonomies 26, 56–9, 62,
    69, 118, 161, 173–4
team teaching **190–201**
technology 53, **101–2**
teenagers 9, 35, 73, 86, **97–8**, 102, 104
telephone skills 79, 87
textonym 103
Tomlinson, J. 52
Tomlinson report 2005 **50–1**, 63
traditional triangle **17–20, 22–3,** 59,
    105, 209
training needs analysis (TNA) 85
Tuckman, B. 40, 49
tutorials **107–41**
    academic 108
    disciplinary 108, 113
    group 107
    listening skills in **111–17**, 123, 130,
        136, 140
physical arrangements 110
    questioning skills in 111, 137, 140
    structuring 112
    whole class 107
tutorial pitfalls **122–8**
    being judgemental 124
    gruesome twosome 124–5
    lack of trust 125
    over clarification 122
    promising confidentiality 126–7
    story telling 123
    time 125
    tolerating silence 124

Van Ments, M. 3, 70, **74–9**, 85, 87,
values 50, **52–3**, **59–60**, 63, 68, **98–9**,
    101, 124, 184, 205, 221
values and attitudes 121, 125
    acceptance 122

congruence 122
empathic understanding 122
VAK 130, 135
    visual 23, 27, **135–6**, 158, 214,
        217–18, 220
    auditory **135–7**
    kinaesthetic **134–7**
virtual learning environment (VLE)
    183–4

Walklin, L. 58, 63, 186, 189
Wallace, J. 184
Wallace, S. 158

Wardle, D. 51
warm-ups **76–7**
WebCT 184
Welch, T.184
Williamson, L. 184
White, J.135
Whitehead, A.N. 59
work-based skills 84
working with others (WWO) **45–6**

Yerkes Dodson Curve **12–14**, 16,
        19–20, 23, 25, 59, 62, 209, 216,
        220–1, 224, 229